Saving Words

Saving Words

20 Redemptive Words Worth Rescuing

EDITED BY

Joseph S. Pagano
and Amy E. Richter

FOREWORD BY

Bishop Michael B. Curry

CASCADE *Books* · Eugene, Oregon

SAVING WORDS
20 Redemptive Words Worth Rescuing

Copyright © 2021 Wipf and Stock Publishers. All rights reserved. Except for brief quotations in critical publications or reviews, no part of this book may be reproduced in any manner without prior written permission from the publisher. Write: Permissions, Wipf and Stock Publishers, 199 W. 8th Ave., Suite 3, Eugene, OR 97401.

Cascade Books
An Imprint of Wipf and Stock Publishers
199 W. 8th Ave., Suite 3
Eugene, OR 97401

www.wipfandstock.com

PAPERBACK ISBN: 978-1-7252-6222-5
HARDCOVER ISBN: 978-1-7252-6220-1
EBOOK ISBN: 978-1-7252-6221-8

Cataloguing-in-Publication data:

Names: Pagano, Joseph S. [editor]. | Richter, Amy E. [editor] | Curry, Michael B. [foreword writer]
Title: Saving words : 20 redemptive words worth rescuing / edited by Joseph S. Pagano and Amy E. Richter ; with a foreword by Bishop Michael B. Curry.
Description: Eugene, OR: Cascade Books, 2021.
Identifiers: ISBN 978-1-7252-6222-5 (paperback) | ISBN 978-1-7252-6220-1 (hardcover) | ISBN 978-1-7252-6221-8 (ebook)
Subjects: LCSH: Language and languages—Religious aspects | Spirituality | Theology | Communication—Religious aspects
Classification: BR118 P34 2021 (print) | BR118 (ebook)

Permissions

Unless otherwise noted, all Scripture quotations are from New Revised Standard Version Bible, copyright © 1989 National Council of Churches of Christ in the United States of America. Used by permission. All rights reserved worldwide.

Scripture quotations marked (ESV) are from the ESV® Bible (The Holy Bible, English Standard Version®), copyright © 2001 by Crossway, a publishing ministry of Good News Publishers. Used by permission. All rights reserved.

Scripture marked (NKJV) is taken from the New King James Version®. Copyright © 1982 by Thomas Nelson. Used by permission. All rights reserved.

Scripture quotations marked (NIV) are taken from the Holy Bible, New International Version®, NIV®. Copyright © 1973, 1978, 1984, 2011 by Biblica, Inc.® Used by permission of Zondervan. All rights reserved worldwide. www.zondervan.com. The "NIV" and "New International Version" are trademarks registered in the United States Patent and Trademark Office by Biblica, Inc.®

Dedication

This book is dedicated to the theology faculty at the School of Religion, Philosophy and Classics at the University of KwaZulu-Natal in Pietermaritzburg, South Africa, especially Gerald West, Rico Settler, Charlene van der Walt, and Sithembiso S. Zwane.

Contents

Contributors

Anthony Bash teaches New Testament at Durham University. He is also vice-master of Hatfield College, Durham University. Anthony is the author of *Forgiveness and Christian Ethics* (2007), *Just Forgiveness* (2011), *Forgiveness: A Theology* (2015), and *Remorse: A Christian Perspective* (2020).

Laurie M. Brock is an Episcopal priest serving in Lexington, Kentucky and attorney. She is the author of *Horses Speak of God: How Horses Can Teach Us to Listen and Be Transformed* (2018) as well as the co-author of *Where God Hides Holiness* (2012). Her essays have been included in several books about gender and spirituality, and she is a frequent contributor to online devotional sites. She is an avid equestrian and is currently working on her third book.

Brian Cole is the fifth bishop of the Episcopal Diocese of East Tennessee. Prior to being elected bishop, Cole served in parishes in Lexington, Kentucky and Asheville, North Carolina. He has served as an adjunct instructor at Wake Forest University Divinity School and has led numerous retreats on the writings of Thomas Merton. Brian and his wife, Susan Parker Weatherford, make their home in Knoxville, Tennessee.

The Most Reverend Michael B. Curry is the presiding bishop and primate of The Episcopal Church. Elected in 2015, he is the first African-American to lead the denomination. He was previously bishop of the Episcopal Diocese of North Carolina. A noted advocate for human rights and author of several books, including *Love is the Way: Holding on to Hope in Troubling Times* (2020) and *The Power of Love* (2018), Bishop Curry is recognized as one of the most popular preachers in the English language. He and his wife, Sharon Curry, have two daughters, Rachel and Elizabeth.

John Gibaut, a priest in the Anglican Church of Canada, is president, provost and vice-chancellor of Thorneloe University. Before moving to Thornloe, he served as director of unity, faith and order at the Anglican Communion Office in London, UK, and previously as the director of the Faith and Order Commission, World Council of Churches, Geneva, Switzerland.

Malcolm Guite is a poet and priest, working as chaplain of Girton College, Cambridge. He lectures widely in England and North America on theology and literature. His books include *Sounding the Seasons: Seventy Sonnets for the Christian Year* (2012), *The Singing Bowl: Collected Poems* (2013), *Parable and Paradox* (2016), *Mariner: A Voyage with Samuel Taylor Coleridge* (2017), and *After Prayer* (2019).

Robert S. Heaney is professor of theology and mission and director of the Center for Anglican Communion Studies, Virginia Theological Seminary, USA. Widely published, his most recent work includes *Post-Colonial Theology: Finding God and Each Other Amidst the Hate* (2019) and with William L. Sachs, *The Promise of Anglicanism* (2019).

Wesley Hill is associate professor of biblical studies at Trinity School for Ministry in Ambridge, Pennsylvania and a priest associate at Trinity Episcopal Cathedral, Pittsburgh. His PhD in New Testament studies is from Durham University in the UK. He is the author of *Washed and Waiting: Reflections on Christian Faithfulness and Homosexuality* (2nd ed. 2016), *Paul and the Trinity: Persons, Relations, and the Pauline Letters* (2015), *Spiritual Friendship: Finding Love in the Church as a Celibate Gay Christian* (2015), and *The Lord's Prayer: A Guide to Praying to Our Father* (2019). A contributing editor for *Comment* magazine, he writes regularly for *Christianity Today*, *The Living Church*, and other publications.

Katie Karnehm-Esh, a 2002 alum of Indiana Wesleyan University, returned to the Midwest to teach composition and creative writing courses in 2008 after completing her PhD in creative writing at the University of St. Andrews, Scotland. She mentors student editors of Indiana Wesleyan University's literary magazine *Caesura*, co-leads a May term travel writing class in Ireland, and teaches community yoga classes, all of which inspire her research and writing. Her essays and poetry have been published in *Fourth Genre*, *The Cresset*, *The Other Journal*, *Topology*, *Barren Magazine*, *Whale Road Review*, and *Windhover*.

John Kiess is associate professor of theology and director of the Office of Peace and Justice at Loyola University Maryland. He pursues research at the intersection of religion, conflict, and peace. He is the author of *Hannah Arendt and Theology* (2016) and numerous articles and chapters that have appeared in *Modern Theology*, *The Journal of Moral Theology*, *The Christian Century*, and various edited collections. He lives in Baltimore, MD with his wife and three boys.

Ian S. Markham is the dean and president of Virginia Theological Seminary and professor of theology and ethics. He has degrees from the King's College London, the University of Cambridge, and the University of Exeter. He is the author of many books, including *Liturgical Life Principles* (2009) and *Understanding Christian Doctrine* (2007). He is a priest associate at St. Paul's Episcopal Church in Old Town Alexandria, VA. He is married to Lesley and has one son, Luke.

John Milbank is a British theologian, philosopher, and political theorist. He was educated at the universities of Oxford, Cambridge, and Birmingham and has taught at the universities of Lancaster, Cambridge, Virginia, and Nottingham. Currently he is emeritus professor of religion, politics, and ethics (Nottingham), president of the Centre of Theology and Philosophy, and visiting professor at the Edith Stein Institute of Philosophy, Granada. He is the author of several books, including *Theology and Social Theory* (2nd ed. 2006), *Being Reconciled* (2003), *Beyond Secular Order* (2014), and most recently (with Adrian Pabst) *The Politics of Virtue* (2016).

Duane Alexander Miller is researcher and lecturer in Muslim-Christian relations of The Christian Institute of Islamic Studies. His doctoral research was on the contextual theologies proposed by Christian converts from Islam—what do they claim to know about God, and what attracted them to the Christian faith? His thesis was published in 2016 as *Living among the Breakage: Contextual Theology-Making and ex-Muslim Christians* (2016). He contributed an essay to *Common Prayer: Reflections on Episcopal Worship.*

Joseph Pagano is an Episcopal priest and author of *The Origins and Development of the Triadic Structure of Faith in H. Richard Niebuhr.* Along with Amy Richter, he is coauthor of *Love in Flesh and Bone* (2014) and *A Man, A Woman, A Word of Love* (2012), and coeditor of *Common*

Prayer: Reflections on Episcopal Worship (2019). He currently serves in the Anglican Parish of Pasadena and Cormack in Newfoundland, Canada. He is a faculty member in theology at Queen's College in St. John's, Newfoundland.

Amy Peterson is a writer, teacher, and postulant for ordination in The Episcopal Church. Her work has appeared in *Image, Christianity Today, Books and Culture, River Teeth, The Millions, The Other Journal, The Cresset, Christian Century,* and elsewhere. She is the author of *Where Goodness Still Grows* (2020) and *Dangerous Territory: My Misguided Quest to Save the World.* She lives with her husband and two kids in Durham, North Carolina.

Amy E. Richter is an Episcopal priest and author of *Enoch and the Gospel of Matthew* (2012) and *Antimony* (2019). Along with Joseph S. Pagano, she is co-author of *Love in Flesh and Bone* (2014) and *A Man, A Woman, A Word of Love* (2012), and coeditor of *Common Prayer: Reflections on Episcopal Worship* (2019). She currently resides in Newfoundland, Canada, where she serves as a parish priest and on the theology faculty of Queen's College.

Catherine Ricketts's writing about the arts, grief, and spirituality has appeared in *Image, Paste Magazine, Measure,* and *Relief,* and online at The Millions. She studied writing at the University of Pennsylvania and holds an MFA in creative nonfiction from Seattle Pacific University. By day she works at the Philadelphia Museum of Art, where she manages performance programs.

Stephen Spencer is director for theological education at the Anglican Communion Office in London, facilitating networking and online resource development for seminaries, colleges, and courses across the Anglican Communion. He has worked as a parish priest in England and Zimbabwe and has been a tutor, director of studies, and vice principal in theological education in England, most recently with St. Hild College, Mirfield. He is author of the SCM study guides on Christian Mission, Anglicanism and Church History, and of books on William Temple. His most recent book is *Growing and Flourishing: The Ecology of Church Growth* (2019).

Ragan Sutterfield is an Episcopal priest serving a parish in his native Arkansas. Ragan is the author of *Wendell Berry and the Given Life* (2017), *This is My Body* (2015), *Cultivating Reality* (2013), and the small collection of essays *Farming as a Spiritual Discipline* (2012). Ragan is now at work on a book exploring humus and humility, soil science and Christian spirituality. More about his work can be found at ragansutterfield.com.

Jane Williams is McDonald professor of Christian theology at St. Mellitus College, which is an Anglican seminary. St. Mellitus College helped to establish "context-based" training for ordained ministry. Jane was born and brought up in South India, where her parents were CMS missionaries.

Jesse Zink is principal of Montreal Diocesan Theological College and canon theologian of the Diocese of Montreal. He is author of several books about mission and the world church, including *Backpacking through the Anglican Communion: A Search for Unity*.

Foreword

FOR ANYONE WHO HAS ever opened up a Bible, it is clear that WORDS are important. Right there at the beginning, we read, "God said, 'Let there be light'; and there was light." A word was spoken, and something happened. Throughout the Hebrew Scriptures and the New Testament, we witness the power of words to heal and to hurt, to build up and to bring down. And at the start of the Gospel According to John, we find an extraordinary statement of faith that the divine Word, which had been present at creation itself, "was with God, and was God." More than this, the passage goes on to proclaim that this Word "became flesh and lived among us."

As we look at Jesus of Nazareth and listen to the words he shared—"Blessed are the poor in spirit," "Your sins are forgiven," "Of course I want to, be clean," "Neither do I condemn you," "Today you will be with me in paradise"—the consistent message again and again was *love*. God loves us. We should love God, ourselves, and one another. Even when Jesus spoke words that were harsh, underlying those words was love. Tough love, perhaps, but love nonetheless, expressed in ways appropriate to each different context.

In certain cases, Jesus took words that had been hijacked by others and, like stones, were thrown at him, in order to entice or challenge or trip him up. Each time he somehow said or did the unexpected thing in response, and in doing so, breathed new life into tired, misused utterances. And in answer to his own words of promise, the Spirit came in power, and reversing the curse of Babel, filled the words proclaimed by those initial followers of Jesus with loving, liberating, life-giving meaning for the benefit of all who would listen, then and now.

Words are important. Words can indeed break down and hurt, but by God's grace and our choices they can also build up and heal. Words can save. And so we need to save, and give new life, to such words. That's what this book is about. It is, as the editors put it, a search and rescue project in which we can reclaim and renew those spiritual words and expressions that have been neglected in some cases or usurped in other cases.

As you read through the essays that follow, I pray you will find yourself invigorated, as if discovering a treasure trove that for whatever reason had been buried, with precious gems inside ready to be brought forth anew. Like those spirituals once sung by slaves that were given new life a century later, there are treasures just waiting to be reclaimed, words ready to be saved that, in turn, will help save us.

—The Most Rev. Michael B. Curry
Presiding Bishop of The Episcopal Church and
author of *Love is the Way: Holding on to Hope in Troubling Times*

Acknowledgments

THIS PROJECT WAS CONCEIVED and developed while we were Visiting Academics at the School of Religion, Philosophy and Classics at the University of KwaZulu-Natal in Pietermaritzburg, South Africa. Versions of our chapters were presented at the Theological Café, a forum for sharing ongoing research with faculty, students, and staff. We are grateful for the hospitality we experienced and for the School's providing time and space for research and reflection. Thanks especially to Gerald West, Rico Settler, Charlene van der Walt, and Sithembiso S. Zwane for collegial conversations and encouragement.

We would also like to thank the Global Missions Office of The Episcopal Church with whom we served while we were in South Africa. Thanks especially to David Copley, Chuck Robertson, Elizabeth Boe, and Yanick Fourcand. It was a privilege to serve with them.

Thanks also to our editor Robin Parry for his expert guidance and enthusiasm for this project.

Introduction

LANGUAGE HAS TAKEN A drubbing. The same words are claimed as true and false. We abandon words because they've been bullhorned by the wrong side. We substitute a vague term already familiar rather than invite a hearer or reader to decelerate and become acquainted with a word that's so far a stranger. We worry that specificity means exclusion, so we jettison seasoned signposts and offer shapeless suggestions that can be taken or not.

The leveling of late modern culture has left shards of words underfoot. We need not picture this as a post-apocalyptic ruin in which rootless individuals hunt and gather fragments of broken traditions in order to express their feelings or impose their wills. The idle talk and distracted curiosity of mass culture tramples authentic and humane traditions effectively enough.

A way-marker from the *camino* or the exquisite cornice on the abandoned building stir feelings of yearning and melancholy. Is there a path to follow? What was the whole place like? Take a snap. Type "#Makes you wonder!" Click, post, send. Now what?

Meanwhile, the earth burns, racism destroys, viruses mutate. We are in trouble, and it makes a difference whether someone offers us a life ring or a circle that could turn out to be a Froot Loop or a sewer cover as easily as a buoy.

The task in this book is to find some of the words and phrases of our religious life that still have a pulse and try to revive them, those things that still have a trace of breath and give them mouth-to-mouth resuscitation, those embers still burning, feed them twigs, and blow on them until they spark to life.

We asked people we admire in The Episcopal Church and the Anglican Communion to write about words they worry are falling into disuse or misuse, words that are crucial to our practice of the Christian life and participation in God's redemption. Authors were free to write on words of their own choosing. The only thing we asked was that they write personal essays. We didn't want dictionary articles that end up being general summaries of the literature. That would have defeated the whole purpose. We wanted sharp, particular essays that show as well as tell the ways saving words shape Christian lives and sensibilities. We wanted essays that only the authors could write in their distinctive voices, their storied lives, their own experiences of joy and suffering and redemption.

The project here is not to offer grand theories of Christian principles or explanations of everything that end up explaining nothing. The authors of these essays, all deeply rooted in our Episcopal and Anglican traditions, are more like workers on a mission to search and rescue, to find those places and people and words that still resonate and tend to them until they can speak again and tell us what they know. Their message may prevent the next shipwreck or point beyond the horizon to wonders we can't yet fathom.

These rescue workers, however, can revive lost words only by allowing them to grow in their own lives. Humility in a backyard. Lament during drought in South Africa. The impassible God in a girl's boarding school in India. Fatherhood in Philadelphia. Sacrifice while fostering a child in Indiana. Marching for peace in Baltimore with a seven-year old. These words aren't preserved in mason jars or pinned like moth wings under glass. They thrive and give life, shimmer and sparkle in Christian lives poured out in love and service.

These essays will not "Conquer all mysteries by rule and line / Empty the haunted air," as Keats warned philosophy might "clip an Angel's wing." But they may, by naming particular mysteries, claiming specific graces, and pointing to experiences with some precision, keep us tethered to the One who spoke the creation into being.

I

Adiaphora

WESLEY HILL

I WAS TWENTY-TWO BEFORE I had my first taste of beer. Well, cider, not beer, technically. Which was an important distinction to me at the time.

A few weeks earlier, I had graduated from college and moved to Minneapolis. My plan was to work there as a pastoral apprentice for two years, while enrolled in an unaccredited seminary program at a Baptist church whose pastor was an outspoken teetotaler. I had been raised Baptist, and teetotalism was so taken for granted as to be unremarkable. Now here I was with two other apprentices who had scoped out a trendy bar in Uptown where they wanted to take me. The autumn air was deliciously crisp when we stepped out of the car and walked the few blocks to our destination early in the evening on a weeknight. Entering, noting the slim crowd, and congratulating ourselves for having avoided weekend revelry, we descended a flight of stairs to the basement, where the bare brick walls were lit by retro chic neon signage and the tables were long and high, with swiveling iron stools and a slick concrete floor that you could drop peanut shells on (a touch that, I remarked a bit giddily to my friends, added a flair of the transgressive to my first time).

I remember looking over the menu of microbrews, as lost as if I were trying to pronounce cuisines in a language I didn't know to a waiter who didn't speak English. My heart beating fast, I asked my friend Mac what I should order. I made a joke of my naivete, but I didn't need to. My friends—also graduates of an evangelical college—had only had a little more tasting experience than I had, though it seemed to have led to a slight uptick in their quotient of worldly wisdom. Mac suggested I order a cider. I had to ask him if it contained alcohol and, if so, to give me a preview of what to expect. Would it make me sputter? I wondered.

Prior to that excursion to the bar, I had thought about whether my conscience would permit me to go, and I had turned to the Bible for help. To those who weren't raised fundamentalist, it's hard to convey just how profoundly *interpretive* the Christian culture of my childhood and young adulthood was—and how much that culture continued to shape my way of being after I'd left home. Writing about his Pentecostal upbringing, the professor and critic Michael Warner might have been describing my Baptist one: "Where I come from, people lose sleep over the meanings of certain Greek and Hebrew words. . . . Being a literary critic is nice, I have to say, but for lip-whitening, vein-popping thrills it doesn't compete. Not even in the headier regions of Theory can we approximate that saturation of life by argument."[1] From before I knew what alcohol was, I knew these verses from the Old Testament book of Proverbs: "Who has woe? Who has sorrow? Who has contentions? Who has complaints? Who has wounds without cause? Who has redness of eyes? Those who linger long at the wine, those who go in search of mixed wine. Do not look on the wine when it is red, when it sparkles in the cup, when it swirls around smoothly; at the last it bites like a serpent, and stings like a viper."[2] And I knew that, were I ever to give beer or wine a taste, I'd need to have an exegesis of these verses ready to wield, if for no one's sake but my own.

I don't remember if we talked that night about how to justify the frosty steins we gripped with a happy sense of youth and mild rebellion, but we probably did. Someone would have brought up the fact that Jesus made world-class vintage for an already-tipsy wedding party. Someone else would have countered that Baptists have always said that the wine of the first-century was non-alcoholic, or at least minimally alcoholic, with such a tiny percentage that no one could be expected to have gotten drunk from what our Lord served them. Probably none of us thought to point out that non-alcoholic wine wouldn't have been safe in a culture without refrigeration, but there's no question someone *would* have pointed out the apostle Paul's injunction to his protégé Timothy to "use a little wine for your stomach's sake and your frequent infirmities."[3] That had to

1. Warner, "Tongues Untied," 216–17.
2. Proverbs 23:29–32 NKJV.
3. 1 Timothy 5:23 NKJV.

be factored in alongside whatever we wanted to say about Jesus's earthly ministry. And so the hermeneutical game—or, likelier, battle—would be afoot. And the conclusion would have been clear enough from our empty mugs: we had "Christian freedom"; Jesus had declared all foods (and beverages) "clean"; our imbibing was, if not exactly virtuous, at least not a moral infraction. We were in a realm not of black and white but of shades of gray.

It was only later that I learned to associate the word *adiaphora* with moments like this. A transliteration from Greek, *adiaphora* is usually glossed in English, with pleasantly archaic word order, as "things indifferent." The Hellenistic school of philosophy known as Stoicism deployed the term in discussions of the moral life. Epictetus (ca. 50–135 CE), for instance, distinguished *adiaphora* from right and wrong action: "Now the virtues and everything that shares in them are good, while vices are evil, and what falls in between these, namely, wealth, health, life, death, pleasures, pain, are *adiaphora*"—"things indifferent."[4] *Adiaphora* names a whole set of realities that can't be classified as good or bad but instead are neutral, capable of being used, perhaps, for good or ill but not praiseworthy or contemptible in themselves.

Despite its later Christian pedigree, the word *adiaphora* doesn't show up in the New Testament, though, arguably, the concept does. According to the Finnish biblical scholar Heikki Räisänen, in the fourteenth chapter of Romans, "Paul's topic is an *adiaphoran*."[5] That penultimate chapter of Paul's argument in his greatest letter addresses the matter of a dispute in the Roman church over what Christians could or should eat in light of their allegiance to their new Lord: "Some believe in eating anything, while the weak [in faith] eat only vegetables."[6] Paul's stance on the issue is non-partisan: "Let all be fully convinced in their own minds." His verdict seems to boil down to this: no one should use the disagreement over what to eat as an excuse to pass judgment on a fellow believer. Rather, says Paul, each Christian "must please our neighbor for the good purpose of building up the neighbor."[7] Paul's counsel rests on his prior theological conviction that "everything is indeed clean"—ritually pure, that is—and

4. Epictetus, *Discourses, Books 1–2*, LCL 131:2, 19, 13.
5. Räisänen, *Paul and the* Law, 247.
6. Romans 14:2 NRSV.
7. Romans 14:5; 15:2 NRSV.

therefore no one in the Christian church should imagine that keeping kosher or observing the complex purity code of the law of Moses, despite God's having mandated it originally for the Jews, is a matter of Christian virtue or vice; it is a choice that believers may make for reasons of conscience, Paul seems to think, but not one that should be imposed on any believer unwilling to make it.[8]

It would be several centuries after Paul that not only the matter but also the word *adiaphora* would move to center stage in the Christian church, in the aftermath of the death of the Reformer Martin Luther in 1546. In the months following Luther's demise, Protestant Christians faced a compounded grief. The Emperor Charles V conquered the princes who had sheltered the Protestants in their territories and had supported them in preaching and worshiping according to Luther's reforms. Emboldened by his victory, the emperor imposed a decree that required Protestants to revert to traditional Catholic beliefs and practices. Luther's right-hand man Philip Melanchthon proposed a compromise with the emperor: Protestants would acknowledge Charles's claim, but they would keep their allegiance to the doctrines of "grace alone" and "faith alone" while agreeing to restore various Catholic ceremonies deemed by Melanchthon to be *adiaphora*: "matters of indifference that may be observed without injury to the divine scriptures," as he wrote in the infamous "Leipzig Interim." The "true believers" in Luther's theology—as they styled themselves—were aghast at how much Melanchthon was willing to concede. In their eyes, Melanchthon had given away the store. "By proposing that much of Catholicism lay in the realm of the 'indifferent' or inconsequential (that is, adiaphora)," says Carlos Eire in his book *Reformations*, Melanchthon and his followers "painted themselves into a corner, for many Lutherans saw their theological flexibility as a betrayal of Luther."[9] For the next three decades, controversy over *adiaphora* would rage until the Formula of Concord of 1577 drew a line in the sand: If any ruler were to *require* the practice of what Melanchthon's ilk judged to be *adiaphora*, then it would be the duty of Christian consciences to refuse them. "Disagreement in fasting"—a matter of indifference—"does not destroy agreement in the faith," the Formula said, quoting a Melanchthonian slogan; and yet, if certain forms of fasting were to be imposed,

---

8. Romans 14:20 NRSV.
9. Eire, *Reformations*, 566.

then those impositions would have to be refused so as not to dilute the primacy of Reformation faith in the gospel.

This Lutheran dispute may have given the word *adiaphora* its fame and staying power in Christian controversy, but it was hardly the only example of intra-Christian disagreement that seemed to many of its participants to concern matters of secondary or tertiary importance. During the English Reformation, the Archbishop of Canterbury Thomas Cranmer famously clashed with the Scottish reformer John Knox on whether kneeling to receive Communion was properly an "indifferent thing" (Cranmer's view) or a matter of worshiping creaturely realities (that is, the bread and wine of Communion) and thus always and everywhere wrong (Knox's position). The matter was consequential, since it would require spelling out in the new Book of Common Prayer that would shape the entire nation's corporate worship. Ultimately, as with Melanchthon's effort, a compromise was reached. Kneeling would be permitted so long as Cranmer would write a new guideline to be included in the Prayer Book—a rubric, the "Black Rubric," as this one came to be called for the color of its ink—that made clear its theological import: The bread and the wine, being (still) creatures of God's good earth, "may not be adored, for that were Idolatry to be abhorred of all faithful Christians." Kneeling could be classed as an *adiaphoran* only if it were hedged with a theological warning against construing it as worship.

With punctuated regularity, disputes over *adiaphora* have continued to crop up in Christian churches in subsequent centuries. Sometimes these disputes have turned violent. The "Black Rubric" compromise among the Anglicans, to stick with that example, didn't prevent the later Puritans from tearing the altar rails out from church sanctuaries and setting them ablaze. Clergy sometimes were jailed "when they would neither recant, nor refrain from enacting, their preferences in candlesticks," writes Alan Jacobs of the nineteenth century's Anglo-Catholic movement. "And that," says Jacobs, with delicious understatement, "is a remarkable thing."[10] Where people have landed on the status of *adiaphora* has sometimes, in the rancorous community we call the Christian church, meant the difference between life and death.

I no longer worry about whether consuming alcohol is a "thing indifferent" that Christians are free to do or not do in good conscience, and

10. Jacobs, *The Book of Common Prayer*, 137.

the only pang of guilt I now feel when I nurse a cider or another adult beverage is inflicted more by modern medical knowledge, not religion. And yet the matter of *adiaphora* haunts me as much as it ever did when I was still a Baptist.

A few years ago, when I was living in the UK to attend graduate school, I got confirmed in the Church of England, and, more recently, back in the US, I was ordained a priest in The Episcopal Church. As even very casual observers of contemporary religion are likely to know, the Anglican family of churches—a "Communion," we call ourselves, with noteworthy spiritual and theological ambition—has been riven by disagreement over sexual ethics. The branch of the Anglican family to which I belong, at a recent meeting of its General Convention, voted to make same-sex marriage rites available in every one of its dioceses, to ensure that Christian couples in each of its parishes who wish to take marriage vows can do so. "All sacraments for all people" is the rallying cry that seems to have carried the day. A minority of us in The Episcopal Church—though I'm gay, I'd number myself among them—agree with the majority of the wider Anglican Communion that such a position isn't sufficiently warranted by the scriptures we profess as our authority, and thus we find ourselves in the awkward, doubt-inducing, often agonizing place of having to navigate a disagreement about a matter that seems, to most of us, not of secondary but of fundamental importance to our identities and our flourishing (or not). How do we manage to do it?

One answer is that we appeal to *adiaphora* as a kind of pressure-release valve. If we can't agree about human sexuality—what it's for and how it should be ordered in Christian lives—then we might at least be able to view our disagreement as an in-house division, one that, while not about a peripheral matter, may perhaps be understood as not quite so fatal to our common life as we thought. I've had several public dialogues with other gay Christians about these matters, virtually all of which have wended their way eventually to the passage from Paul's letter to the Romans that I mentioned earlier, the one in which Paul offered this definitive exhortation: "Welcome one another, therefore, just as Christ has welcomed you, for the glory of God."[11] Both of us on stage, by the end of a lengthy airing of our differences, are usually eager to land somewhere like that, with an affirmation of our shared faith in the gospel, with a determination not to see each other as enemies whose opposing views

11. Romans 15:7 NRSV.

undermine any possibility of shared faith. My friend Justin Lee, author of the book *Torn: Rescuing the Gospel from the Gays-vs.-Christians Debate*, has pointed out that Paul sometimes makes a categorical ruling when it comes to moral matters, brooking no dissent. But at other times, in settings where the behavior in question isn't viewed uniformly, Paul seems to counsel an "agree to disagree" approach, along with a healthy dose of charity: "[W]hen there was serious disagreement within the Body of Christ, Paul encouraged people to follow their consciences and allow other believers to do likewise."[12] Then Justin says: "I believe the situation we're facing today [with regard to gay Christians] is the latter type."

Whether or not this is a good and right way to play the *adiaphora* card, it doesn't always help. Conservatives have left—or been pushed out of, as some of them would say—more progressive Anglican churches, forming their own denominations and families of churches in response. And progressives have sometimes signaled that celebrating gay relationships isn't a "thing indifferent" for them; it's a *mandate* of the gospel of Jesus, which is said to affirm all genuine human love, regardless of how it's expressed. In both cases, it seems that stronger medicine than *adiaphora* is needed if we're going to continue worshiping together instead of walking apart.

I have at times worried about how the basket of *adiaphora*—into which I'm quick to want to put most disagreements with my fellow Christians, so that I don't have to contemplate relational ruptures and recriminations—has stretched to accommodate much of what our Christian forebears would regard as disagreements about matters of primary importance. Perhaps more of us need to find the courage of our convictions and say, in the heat of debate, "This is a conviction I can't see as negotiable. I can't pretend I think it's okay that we aren't of one mind about it." Doesn't *adiaphora* have its limits? If stretched too far, will it break?

But then, what are the alternatives? If I am to go on serving and bearing witness alongside other Christian believers who disagree with me about what I take to be fundamental, is there another way to relate to them if I don't opt to lump our disagreement under the heading "thing indifferent"?

Not long ago, after another round of praying a string of imprecatory psalms at Morning Prayer, the psalms in which the poets rain down curses on their enemies, I found myself so uncomfortable with the sentiments

12. Lee, *Torn*, 247.

expressed that I started googling for theological help. One of the articles I came across was by a Mennonite pastor, Melissa Florer-Bixler. Titled provocatively "The Forgotten Christian Discipline of Loving Your Enemies," the essay contains this startling insight: "Rightly having enemies is an unsung discipline of the Christian life. More often than not we abandon the task before we get started; we wrongly assume we should not have enemies. But the expectation of the gospel of Jesus Christ is that we *will* have enemies. We know this because Jesus gives us a command to love our enemies. And in order to love your enemies, you first have to know who they are."[13] It may be, Florer-Bixler suggests, that sometimes you do have to let first-order disagreements be just that, without seeking to demote them to differences over *adiaphora*. Sometimes you really do need to view other people as *in the wrong*. Theologian Stanley Hauerwas, in one of his memorable quips, has said that most of us "do not go to church because we are seeking a safe haven from our enemies; rather, we go to church to be assured we have no enemies."[14] But what if we behaved as if we had real enemies? Hauerwas goes on to ask. Enemies who are not outside but with us inside the church. Enemies who are, at times, ourselves.

A couple of springs ago I had dinner on a charming Texas backyard patio with a fellow Episcopalian named Steven, an ordinand like me, and his husband, who had prepared the salmon and niçoise salad we enjoyed. Other friends were present, and as we sat around a gas fire, sipped wine, and listened to the crickets chitter late into the evening, the talk roved from politics to art to parenting to real estate to God (our lapsed Christian friend who was there was interested in hearing about our efforts to live with integrity as people of Christian faith). It was an evening to remember, filled with what looked for all the world like the rarest and most precious form of camaraderie, of an exchange of gifts, of life in communion.

Is my friend Steven, someone with whom I differ on sexual ethics, my theological enemy? Perhaps so—or at least, perhaps partially so, at least in one limited arena. Or is he simply someone with whom I differ about a "thing indifferent," a matter of some importance, clearly, but not one that should hinder our Christian fellowship? Our ability to eat

13. Florer-Bixler, "The Forgotten Christian Discipline of Loving Your Enemies," para. 10.

14. Stanley Hauerwas, "No Enemy, No Christianity," 208.

together, to feast and be happy in each other's company, surely suggests as much, however many qualifiers I might want to add.

Our dinner on the patio together came as the climax of a weekend of dialogue about the prospect of "communion across difference" in our church. Our conversation was deeply personal—and, at times, if not heated, then at least spirited—for both of us. I am choosing a life of celibacy out of an effort to be faithful to what I believe scripture teaches about marriage, and Steven described his marriage to his husband as part of his discipleship, a means through which they together are able to bless and enrich their church community. Our two lives attest to two incommensurable convictions regarding the nature of human sexuality. If those convictions aren't *adiaphora*, perhaps we may at least see each other's as grave wrongs that we are capable of enduring, of bearing with, as we seek to love like the One who loved even the ones who betrayed him. If *adiaphora* doesn't and can't always offer a way out of our ecclesial divisions, perhaps we may agree that the goal of its invocation—our ability to belong together, despite our differences—is one that is always worth striving for.

Bibliography

Eire, Carlos. *Reformations: The Early Modern World, 1450–1650*. New Haven: Yale University Press, 2018.

Epictetus. *Discourses, Books 1–2*. Translated by W. A. Oldfather. Loeb Classical Library 131. Cambridge, MA: Harvard University Press, 1925.

Florer-Bixler, Melissa. "The Forgotten Christian Discipline of Loving Your Enemies." *Sojourners* (September/October 2019). https://sojo.net/magazine/septemberoctober-2019/forgotten-christian-discipline-loving-your-enemies-ICE-immigration.

Hauerwas, Stanley. "No Enemy, No Christianity: Preaching between 'Worlds.'" In *Sanctify Them in the Truth: Holiness Exemplified*, 2nd ed., 204–14. London: Bloomsbury/T. & T. Clark, 2016.

Jacobs, Alan. *The Book of Common Prayer: A Biography*. Lives of Great Religious Books. Princeton, NJ: Princeton University Press, 2013.

Lee, Justin. *Torn: Rescuing the Gospel from the Gays-vs.-Christians Debate*. New York: Jericho, 2012.

Räisänen, Heikki. *Paul and the Law*. Philadelphia: Fortress, 1986.

Warner, Michael. "Tongues Untied: Memoirs of a Pentecostal Boyhood." In *Curiouser: On the Queerness of Children*, edited by Steven Bruhm and Natasha Hurley, 215–24. Minneapolis: University of Minnesota Press, 2004.

2

The Birds of the Air

BRIAN COLE

I MET MARK AND Greg my first semester of seminary. We were all students at the Baptist Seminary in Louisville, Kentucky. I was a new college graduate, not yet twenty-two years old, while Mark and Greg were in their thirties, both having worked for a decade between college and seminary studies.

We met in New Testament Greek class. We all sat near the front and bonded over a shared academic earnestness and dry sense of humor.

So, I was excited when they invited me to go bird watching with them. I had never done any real bird watching before then, but I knew how to recognize cardinals, robins, and blue jays. How difficult could this be?

Turns out, it can be difficult.

For starters, there's the equipment. You do not simply go out and see what you can see with your own two eyes. Binoculars are necessary. In the case of Mark and Greg, the binoculars were quite pricey. They let me borrow an older pair.

Also, I discovered you need a bird book, both to help identify what you see and to record when and where you see the bird. In doing so, you create your bird list.

Before we went, they also told me it would be helpful to listen to cassette tapes of bird calls. So, before you saw the bird, you could hear it.

This was going to be more than cardinals, robins, and blue jays.

The Saturday morning arrived for our bird excursion. At least, I looked like a bird watcher, with binoculars and bird book, khaki shorts and good walking shoes.

I soon discovered that bird watching can last a long time, if you go with serious "birders." Mark and Greg were serious. And this long amount of time includes a great deal of not seeing birds. Actually, the bird watching time is the briefest part of the day. Finally, when you see a bird, you often barely see the bird, whose full view is blocked by branch and leaf, shade and cloud.

That day, with my two friends, I discovered I was not a bird watcher. I was a friend of bird watchers. I more enjoyed watching Mark and Greg watch birds. It was a joy to see these birders in their element. If seminary is a time to discern call, I knew that day that bird watching was not mine.

Having grown up Southern Baptist, the Bible was the book that shaped my life, both in church and culture. As a Southern Baptist, there were many, many opportunities to attend church services, where the primary act was the preaching. Most of the preaching I heard before attending seminary focused exclusively on the letters of St. Paul.

So, the Gospels were, in many ways, new to me in seminary. Along with Greek and a New Testament survey class, I took a class on the Gospel of St. Matthew.

Shortly after my first bird watching trip, our professor in the Matthew class devoted a few lectures to the Sermon on the Mount.

"*Look at the birds of the air*; they neither sow nor reap nor gather into barns, and yet your Heavenly Father feeds them. Are you not of more value than they?" (Matt 6:26 NRSV)

Turns out Jesus was a birder.

The professor that day led us in a great discussion on the power of this passage, with Jesus's everyday reminder about anxiety and worry and the call to trust that our God does not abandon us in the everyday. Look and consider the birds of the air who find provision in God's world. While we worry about so many things we cannot control, the birds delight in being birds. God delights in them. If God provides for them, will not God sustain us, too?

While I was moved by the teaching, I felt the same as when I had gone bird watching. To look at, or consider, a bird, you have to go where the birds are. Since I was no birder, could Jesus provide me with an indoor illustration regarding anxiety and worry and trust?

About this time, I was introduced to the writings of Thomas Merton and the practice of Centering Prayer. Outdoor bird watching problem solved. I could let go of anxiety and worry and trust in God's care for me without leaving my room. If Mark and Greg and the first hearers of Jesus's Sermon on the Mount wanted to look at birds, I was fine with that. Meanwhile, I would practice Centering Prayer, praying in silence, meditating on the Jesus Prayer. It would be my interior life that took flight.

For several years, I was at ease with the outdoor/indoor divide on how Christians could manage anxiety and worry. Even in my own marriage, this worked. My wife, Susan, is a lover of birds and delights in their beauty and presence in the now. She also feeds them daily, which is another reason the birds do not have to worry. Being a bird in our backyard comes with a meal every morning and refreshed water in the birdbath three times a week.

In Jesus's invitation to look at the birds, he is calling his disciples to see what is all around them in the everyday. As long as there are birds to see, then Jesus's teaching on anxiety and worry can speak to us, both birder and non-birder.

However, in 2019, a study published first in the journal *Science* and soon picked up by numerous news services told of a startling discovery. In the last fifty years, beginning in 1970, there were three billion fewer birds in North America. We all, if we were looking, were seeing a loss of more than one in four birds in our part of the world.

The researchers believed the deep decline in bird population was as a result of numerous factors. Loss of habitat, climate change, insect decline, outdoor cats, glass skyscrapers, and pesticide use were the most frequently mentioned causes that had contributed to such bird population decline. While too many of us were not looking at the birds, they were disappearing from our world.

Presiding Bishop Michael Curry reminds us that The Episcopal Church is one branch of the global Jesus Movement. As people who are followers of the Jesus Movement, the words of Jesus shape and form our identity and our way of seeing the world anew. From ancient biblical teachings, we continue to find sacred wisdom for living in the here and now of the twenty-first century. We continue to be a people given over to anxiety and worry. If anything, we are a people who find more things about which to be anxious and worry over. The bird population in North America may be in decline, but anxiety and worry are all around.

So, if we ever needed a word from Jesus on how to live beyond anxiety and worry, now would be that time. Jesus tells us to look at the birds. Looking and seeing birds now in North America requires more work on our part for they are fewer in number. The fact that there are fewer birds to see, therefore, can become another reason to be anxious and to worry.

Do you see the problem? In our current age, have we taken a word of comfort from Jesus and changed its very meaning? "Look at the birds, if you can . . . ." Instead of being a people shaped by a wisdom teaching from Jesus, we have become a people able to reshape and diminish the very world that Jesus came to love and save and restore.

In North America, we are an anxious and worried people who tend to respond by finding things to consume in order to tamp down the anxiety and worry. If I possess enough, I will be satisfied, ignoring that the God of Creation remains the God who sustains and gives real life.

Consumption driven by anxiety and worry, however, is never able to come to a place of enough, of resolution. Consumption driven by fear requires more consumption. We do not trust the God we say we believe in and follow. We trust that becoming full-time consumers in order to overcome anxiety and worry will bring us peace. From the Sermon on the Mount, Jesus was already teaching us to avoid that false and life-denying way.

That false way has us now living in a world where our consumption overwhelms the birds of the air. The everyday living examples that the Creator provides for the least of these who do not consider tomorrow, but live in this moment, sustained by God, are now imperiled. These birds are imperiled because of our consumption, driven by anxiety and worry. We have not followed Jesus's teaching on the birds. Instead, we are on the brink of making it a "false" teaching, by doing the very opposite and failing to live as stewards of a healed and restored creation.

If we were to forget Jesus's teaching on the birds of the air by losing the very birds of the air that the teaching invites us to see, how much poorer we would be while striving for enough and more. What can a living and active scripture say to us, if we cannot restrain ourselves from misshaping God's world?

Enter COVID-19.

Like so many people around the globe and particularly in North America, the year 2020 for me, in March, went from being a time of many important plans ahead to nothing being planned at all. My first years as an Episcopal bishop were measured in countless miles traveled by car across the diocese and numerous airline flights across the globe. Suddenly, with the arrival of COVID-19 and calls to shelter at home, I was now overseeing the diocese from my home study. Those first few weeks of sheltering at home gave me a great deal of time to walk, both by myself, with my wife, and with my dog. These were not simply daily walks. They were twice a day walks or three times a day, even. In order to manage my own anxiety and worry about the pandemic, I decided I would walk in and around our neighborhood each day.

It was while I was walking, walking with the hope that I could stay ahead of my anxiety and worry, that I first heard them. The birds. The birds of the air. Upon hearing them, I also began to see them. I did not need binoculars or a bird book. I did not begin to make a list of what I saw. I simply kept walking and hearing and seeing.

"Look at the birds of the air . . . ."

As a non-birder, as a Centering Prayer, Thomas Merton devotee kind of Episcopalian, I have often taught others the important lesson that we are not in control of our own lives. I have taught that idea to numerous groups on prayer and contemplation and holy silence. We are not in control, I have told them, and so allow yourselves to surrender to God's grace and mercy and delight in you. I have taught that belief for years. And I have even said I believed it.

But in this season of a global plague, this time when all our calendars and our plans mean so little, I have been forced to see that I struggle with believing and trusting in God's sustaining presence. I really did think I was in control of my life. I had plans, for this month and the next and this year and the next.

This plague has taught all of us that we are not in control of our lives. While I thought that to be a good and holy thing while teaching on contemplation in safe and sacred church spaces, I am aware that not being in control is a frightening and anxious knowing. So, what do I do with my fear and my anxiety?

I go walking into God's world.

And I hear and see them, the birds of the air. While I know their numbers are in deep decline, in the spring of 2020, while we were sheltering in home, while we were not driving our cars or flying in planes, the birds of the air seemed to be everywhere. Each morning when I walked, the bird songs seemed louder than normal, though I had to admit I did not know the normal volume of bird song in my neighborhood before now.

I have not been alone in looking and seeing birds in this strange and terrible year of 2020. Many news outlets, according to *Audubon* magazine, have devoted coverage to the benefits of birding now and how bird watching can ease anxiety and depression.

Jesus's teaching to look at the birds in order to trust that God will sustain us might find a renewed depth of meaning now. This renewed meaning is coming in the very age when birds are also in decline. Despite our neglect or intentional harm to the world where birds live and thrive, they are still with us. They sing their songs, which an anxious and depressed people may overhear. The very birds that we have neglected end up easing a portion of the collective pain and anxiety of this plague season.

I am still not a birder.

I have come to realize, however, that the birds are not there simply for the birders. The birds exist in our world because God created them and delights in them. There are many things that God has created and delighted in that we have failed to see or neglected or even destroyed. Still, God loves us, with all our anxiety and worry.

While I am not a birder, I will confess now that I am becoming a student to the birds in my neighborhood who are teaching me ancient wisdom from Jesus. I am looking and hearing.

In this time, I am not in control. Neither are the birds. Still, the birds of the air flap, glide, and hover; perch, hop, and flit; trill, chirp, and sing an avian confidence in the God who is looking at us and sustaining us now. If we hope for a redeemed future, the birds may show us how we get there.

3

Catholic

JESSE ZINK

WHEN I WAS IN college in the early 2000s, one of the hottest political issues on campus could be summed up in a single word: globalization. In 1999, protests at the annual meeting of the World Trade Organization turned violent and became known as "The Battle for Seattle." Naomi Klein's *No Logo* was an important reference text for people concerned about the growing power of multinational corporations—the "McDonaldization" of eating habits or the "Disneyfication" of the culture industry. The fear was that corporations were gaining so much power that they would be able to override local offerings with a single global cuisine or culture.

There were also concerns about the real human impacts of globalization. I remember in early 2000 when the people of Cochabamba, Bolivia rose up in protest against a sharp increase in the price of water in their city. Under pressure from the World Bank, the Bolivian government had privatized municipal water service. Seeking a profit and money to invest in refurbishing the water system the private company that now controlled the water system started turning off the taps of people who couldn't pay. The protest was, many said, an indication of the way that globalizing a set of economic norms imposed real human costs—depriving people without means of water—and failed to account for local realities.

About a year later, leaders from across North and South America came together in Quebec City for a so-called Summit for the Americas. Their goal was to make progress on a free-trade agreement spanning the two continents. It was the major political event on the calendar that spring and attracted immense news attention. A friend and I attended a weekend teach-in at our university where we learned about the difference between free trade and what was called "fair trade." We also sat together on the floor and learned the techniques of non-violent civil disobedience and what to do if we were arrested. In the end, we never went to Quebec City but I remember the energy around the event and the attention it commanded.

In the twenty years since, the discourse and activity surrounding globalization has shifted and changed. Anti-globalization protests like the Battle for Seattle no longer happen. But awareness of our global interconnectivity has only grown. I need not look far to see this. I am writing this chapter on a computer designed in California, manufactured in China with parts and materials from around the world, and sold to me in Montreal. I refreshed my memory about the date of the Cochabamba protests with some Internet research made possible by routers, modems, and other equipment that are similarly designed in one part of the world, manufactured in another, operated in a third, and which bring information to me regardless of where I sit on the globe.

The truth is I've been a beneficiary of our interconnected world. Since graduating from college, I've taken advantage of the ease of international travel to visit countries around the world and learn about different cultures, contexts, and churches. That travel has shaped my outlook on the world and my vocational path. My horizons have been expanded and I think in new ways about what is considered "normal" and about how different societies approach the challenges we all face. Today, I live in a city that is one of the most multicultural in all of Canada. My neighbors are from the Ivory Coast, Algeria, and Guinea, as well as Canada. The theological college I run and the university where I teach have students from across the globe. I use modern communication tools that mean I can be in touch with someone across the world almost as easily I can with someone down the hall from my office. The clothes I wear, the food I eat (pineapple in Montreal in April?), and the technology I rely on all show evidence of the global influences that shape my life.

But increased global interconnectivity hasn't been equally good for everyone. People at the Battle for Seattle and the Summit for the Americas spotted this with their concerns about fair trade. That rhetoric has now been joined by opposition from different points on the political spectrum. New Populist politicians have risen to prominence expressing concern about the loss of state sovereignty, the economic impacts of trade agreements, and the vanishing manufacturing industry in their countries. I lived in England during the Brexit referendum of 2016 and the debate in that campaign followed these lines. Opponents of membership in the European Union were protesting the way in which they thought EU membership disadvantaged the United Kingdom. They combined concern with rising rates of immigration with more nebulous appeals to concepts like sovereignty and the desire to "take back control."

The COVID-19 pandemic has again demonstrated the fact of global interconnectivity: a virus that originated in central China quickly spread across the world, piggy-backing on the global travel networks we take for granted. Global trade linkages have made it possible to outsource the production of some medical equipment to the lowest cost producer regardless of their location. But the fragility of these supply chains and the shortage of personal protective equipment during the early stages of the pandemic made some leaders realize this may not always be desirable.

At the heart of globalization is a tension between the local and the universal. Indeed, I find the most helpful definition of globalization to be precisely in those terms: globalization is the bringing together of a local particularity and a universalizing norm. The universalizing norm of common Internet and email standards, for instance, brings together my local situation with that of others around the world. By the same token, the universalizing norm of common economic expectations for countries came together with the local particularity of water service in Cochambamba in a way that left many Bolivians upset. The universalizing norm of the free movement of people in the European Union sat uncomfortably with the sense of uncontrolled change that many people felt in communities across England. The universalizing norm of low-cost production and integrated supply chains is now rubbing against the desire for local control and assurance about the supply of essential medical equipment. As countries have become more closely tied to one another through international trade, the integration of global supply routes and chains of production has become increasingly important. But part of the opposition to globalization has been rooted in the way in which these universalizing forces sit uneasily with the shuttered factories in local communities across the world.

As I've experienced it, for much of the last twenty years the answer that the world provides to this tension between universalizing norm and local particularity has been, basically, this: get over it. Think of yourself as a consumer first and enjoy the cheap clothes, good food, and fancy technology at low cost. Don't you understand that this system is the most efficient—and therefore best—way to structure our society? There is little meaningful engagement with those who cannot find their way. Globalization is the way it needs to be. But Brexit, the presidency of Donald Trump, and the rise of similar populist leaders reaffirms what I learned in college: not everyone is on board the globalization express.

It seems likely that the COVID-19 pandemic will undo some of the forces of global integration. Travel will be curtailed, governments may look to bring more essential services home, and borders may rise higher between countries. But the technology of our world is such that universalizing forces and local contexts will continue to be brought together—and the results may not always be pretty. If economic globalization is not the answer, we still need to find a way to have these encounters between global and local. I find that answer in a word with deep roots in the Christian tradition: *catholic*.

Catholic can be a misleading word. My father grew up in a Lutheran church that recited the Apostles' Creed on Sundays. But they made one change in their recitation. Rather than affirm the line, "I believe in the Holy Ghost, the holy catholic church," they said they believed in "the holy Christian church." For a church that was constituted through its break with Roman Catholicism, the historic affirmation was a step too far. The congregation was mixing up what you might call big-C Catholic—the name of a church—and little-c catholic. It's that latter word that is of interest to me here.

Etymologically, catholic means something like "universal." Its Greek root words mean literally "in respect of the whole," so when we say that catholic means universal we are also saying something like "related to wholeness." Wholeness itself is a word with deep roots in the Judeo-Christian tradition. The Hebrew word *shalom* runs throughout the Old Testament and is often translated as peace. But a more accurate translation might be "wholeness" in reference to the full, complete, and whole relationships that God creates for God's people. Catholic stands in this tradition and reminds us of how God acts to create wholeness for God's people.

Catholic is such an important word that Christians have made it one of the four fundamental affirmations of the church: in the Nicene Creed we say that the church is one, holy, catholic, and apostolic. Historically, the affirmation that the church is catholic has been interpreted in a couple of different fashions. Most simply, the catholic church is a universal church in the sense that it is present around the world. That's something I've learned and re-learned as I've taken advantage of the travel links of our globalized world to visit far-off places and always find Christians at the end of the journey.

But even on the day of Pentecost, the "birthday of the church" when the followers of Jesus were in Jerusalem, the church was catholic. The catholicity of the church is not simply about its extent but about the comprehensiveness of its teaching and the salvation it offers. The fourth-century theologian Cyril of Jerusalem famously wrote:

> [The church] is called catholic then because it extends over all the world, from one end of the earth to the other; and because it teaches universally and completely one and all the doctrines which ought to come to men's knowledge, concerning things both visible and invisible, heavenly and earthly; and because it brings into subjection to godliness the whole race of mankind, governors and governed, learned and unlearned; and because it universally treats and heals the whole class of sins, which are committed by soul or body, and possesses in itself every form of virtue which is named, both in deeds and words, and in every kind of spiritual gifts.[1]

In his affirmation of the catholicity of the church, Cyril is making a double argument. First, that the church proclaims the fullness of the gospel. Second, that the gospel is for all types of people. Cyril writes about the governors and governed, learned and unlearned, but I hear in this echoes of the famous passage in Revelation when a whole host of people "from every nation, from all tribes and peoples and languages" are praising the lamb on the throne (Rev 7:9). The catholicity of the church means that the church is for all types and conditions of people everywhere, and it embodies for those people the fullness of Christ's good news. To affirm that the church is catholic is to affirm both that the gospel teaches people all they need to know and is all for all people.

These historic teachings about the catholicity of the church are important. But in a globalized world, catholic takes on new salience and

---

1. Cyril of Jerusalem, *Catechetical Lecture 18*, para. 23.

significance. To understand why, it's important to see the parallels be-tween the dynamics of globalization and the dynamics at the heart of the Christian gospel. Whether it is water protests in Cochabamba or the EU referendum in England, globalization is about a tension between the local and universal. So too is the Christian gospel. On the one hand, Jesus Christ is the incarnate Son of God whose good news is for all people everywhere. That's why he tells his followers to take his good news to the ends of the earth and why the church has, in the centuries since, spread across the world. The Christian gospel is a universalizing force. But the foundation of the Christian gospel is a set of events—birth, life, death, resurrection—that took place at a particular and unique moment in a particular and unique place: Palestine under Roman occupation two thousand years ago. In the interplay between those unique events and their universalizing impetus is found the gospel of Christ.

There are countless examples of this. In one instructive example, a group of Christian missionaries in Papua New Guinea faced a dilemma: the people among whom they were working had no knowledge of sheep. The animal simply didn't exist in their culture. But Christ is, the Bible tells us, the lamb of God. The universal message about Christ as the sacrifice of God for the world was entangled in a very particular wrapping, that is, by reference to an animal that was commonplace in first-century Pal-estine but not present in this part of New Guinea. What was well known, indeed central to the Papuan culture, was the pig, an animal with reli-gious, economic, and social uses. Did Papuans need to learn about lambs before they could learn about Christ? The answer that some early Bible translators in Papua New Guinea gave was no. In some versions of the New Testament, Christ became "the pig of God who takes away the sins of the world."[2] The first-century Jewish people who first heard the gospel would have found pigs unclean, and the translation sounds odd to those used to thinking of Jesus as a lamb, but in this context the translation seemed to work. The universal claims of the Bible needed to be mediated through the specific knowledge of a particular place.

There are many other examples of the way in which the tension be-tween the particular and the universal crops up in the life of the church. The Bible is suffused with agrarian imagery and metaphors—seeds, planting, mustard bushes. But how do hunter-gatherer societies under-stand this? Feminist theologians have asked how the particular fact of

2. The story is told in Farhadian, *Christian Worship Worldwide*, 14.

Jesus's maleness influences their understanding of the universal message of salvation: can a male Messiah save women? Peter, Paul, and other early Christian missionaries encountered a similar difficulty. The first Christians were Jewish and thought nothing of following the Jewish dietary laws and practicing male circumcision. It was a particular practice that made sense to them. But the universalizing force of the gospel brought them into contact with people who wanted to follow Jesus but weren't Jewish: did they have to follow the dietary laws and be circumcised? The New Testament tells us that it wasn't an easy question to answer, but the answer, ultimately, was no. It was possible to follow the universalizing impetus of the Christian gospel but leave behind local particularities of its expression.

The way globalization resolves this tension between global and local is, more or less, to have the former steamroll the latter. A single set of global norms is, in an ideal globalized world, meant to structure all interaction. But the answer the church provides is, at its best, somewhat more nuanced. To affirm the catholicity of Christianity is to affirm the value of *both* the global and universal on the one hand *and* the local and particular on the other. Rather than prize an undifferentiated uniformity, the catholic church embraces a glorious, often messy, unity. Rowan Williams, the former archbishop of Canterbury, described it this way:

> The catholic is the opposite of the globalized, because the catholic is about wholeness, about the wholeness of the person, the wholeness of local culture and language. Therefore it's not simply opening the same fast-food shop in every village on the globe, and it's not like the global economy, in which people are drawn into somebody's story and somebody's interests which in fact makes others poor and excluded. The catholic is the opposite of the globalised because the catholic is about everyone's welfare, everyone's growth and justice.[3]

The way in which the gospel is expressed in one context may be different from the way it is expressed in another context. But there is a universal tie that binds them together.

In my theological imagination, I associate catholic with wholeness, unity, and the church. These words in turn bring me to another phrase: body of Christ. Central to the New Testament understanding of the Christian community is the idea that in order to fully follow Christ,

---

3. Williams, "One Holy Catholic and Apostolic Church."

we need other Christians. We need to give gifts to the community and receive from others. When I think about the church in this light, I am reminded that the catholicity of the church isn't simply an interesting feature of Christian life to affirm in the creed. It is, rather, essential to my own ability to follow in the way of Jesus. I've been reminded of this countless times when I've taken advantage of our global interconnectedness to meet Christians from other contexts. When I've worshipped with indigenous Christians in northern Canada, I've learned about how their faith is tied to their relationship with the land—and wondered how I am called to relate to God's creation in my urban environment. When I've worked with South Sudanese Christians who are leading the way to building a peaceful country, I've learned about how Christians are called to be active in the public and political spheres where they find themselves—and wondered how I am called to do the same in my own context and work to support my sisters and brothers in Christ in South Sudan. The tensions and challenges posed by a catholic church are not always easily resolved or answered. The Anglican Communion has in the recent past found itself stuck with how to resolve the tension between a universal claim to "bonds of affection" between Anglican churches and the stark differences in how Anglicans respond to LGBT people in their communities. Seeking the unity of a catholic church rather than the uniformity of a globalized world is not easy.

No matter what happens in a post-pandemic world, globalization is not going away. The technologies we have created will continue to bring local contexts across the world into contact with universalizing forces. Experience shows us that, particularly in economic realms, the logic of globalization is to direct us towards uniformity. As the political turmoil of recent years has demonstrated, few people are satisfied with this logic. It is in this context that I see an opportunity for the church to affirm its catholicity in new ways. Christians who affirm the catholicity of their church have an opportunity to show the world how the tension between local and global, particular and universal can be not only managed but turned into a place of flourishing. God calls all people to wholeness and Christ's church is meant to embody this by offering the wholeness of the gospel to all people. When we remember this, we can truly affirm that we are a catholic church, good news to a globalized world.

Bibliography

Cyril of Jerusalem, *Catechetical Lecture 18*, paragraph 23. https://www.newadvent.org/ fathers/310118.htm.

Farhadian, Charles E. *Christian Worship Worldwide: Expanding Horizons, Deepening Practices.* Grand Rapids: Eerdmans, 2007.

Williams, Rowan. "One Holy Catholic and Apostolic Church: Archbishop's Address to the Third Global South to South Encounter Ain al Sukhna, Egypt." 28 October 2005.   http://aoc2013.brix.fatbeehive.com/articles.php/1675/one-holy-catholic-and-apostolic-church.

4

Communion: My Life with a Word

John Gibaut

The Gift of Communion

EARLY ON A WINTRY Sunday morning in late February 1970, my father woke me, bundled me up—no breakfast—and took me to church. It was the 8:30 said service of Holy Communion, with very few people around. At that service, I walked to the altar rail with my father and received Holy Communion for first time. It was as close as I had ever come to what I would later describe as a mystical experience. As I held the host, and then the chalice in my hands, with the odd feeling of a stale wafer in my mouth and then a sip of wine, I felt pure joy, and a sense of being in the presence of God.

When we went home, there was a festive breakfast waiting for me. I felt special and loved that day. I thought heaven would feel something like this. I was also embarrassingly aware that this was an unmerited gift, and a bit of a scandal. For you see, I had only just turned eleven. Let me give you the bigger context.

I grew up in an Anglican family, fairly active in the life of our parish, the Church of St. Simon-the-Apostle, Diocese of Toronto, from the early 1960s. In those days, St. Simon's celebrated the Eucharist—Holy Communion—at 8:30 every Sunday morning, and at 11:00 on the first, third, and fifth Sundays of the month; sung Matins was on offer on the second and fourth Sundays at 11:00. All services were strictly in accordance with the 1959 Book of Common Prayer of the Anglican Church of Canada.

I have no memory of the service of Holy Communion before I was seven years old, my age when I joined the parish choir. Because children processed out of church to Sunday School early on in every service, it is quite likely that I had never been to a celebration of the Eucharist before becoming a chorister. I just can't remember.

What I do remember, however, was how much I looked forward to Communion Sundays as a choirboy. In comparison with matins, Communion Sundays were utterly different. There was much more movement, with the celebrant and the other clergy wearing different colored vestments, marking the liturgical seasons. Singing the classical Anglican service music for Holy Communion touched my soul and stirred my faith; it still does. There was reverent ceremony at and around the altar, especially during the prayer of consecration. And then, there was receiving Holy Communion itself. I remember being fascinated by the choir men and older choirboys going to the altar rail before the rest of the congregation, kneeling to receive Communion. I remember such a longing to receive Communion with them, but I knew that I was too little, and of course, I was not confirmed.

When I was nine years old, I remember asking my parents about confirmation. They, in turn, asked our rector who said that I was too little. But I persisted and when I was ten, I was permitted to attend confirmation classes, and so I was just eleven when I was confirmed. I have no memory of the content of those classes, largely because the goal for me was never being confirmed, but to receive Communion. The bishop of Toronto duly confirmed me with the rest of my class on 22 February 1970, at sung evensong.

The next Sunday, being the second Sunday of the month and thus matins, my father took me to the 8:30 Communion service at St. Simon's, as I described above. From then on at every Communion Sunday, I was fully part of it, and I remember feeling profoundly privileged.

As a child, I had no sense of a diocese, or a national Anglican Church, and I am quite sure that I never heard of the Anglican Communion. I remember experiences of receiving Communion beyond my parish, and thus of a sense of belonging to a wider community. The first were summer visits to my grandparents in the Diocese of Quebec, and receiving Holy Communion in their parish. Their house rule was that no one had to go to church while on summer holidays. My pre-adolescent rebellion was to go to Communion every Sunday on holidays after I had been confirmed. I also remember a choir trip to the United Kingdom in 1971, and again, the sense of being part of something much bigger than St. Simon's by receiving Holy Communion in cathedral churches of the Church of England.

From Communion to Eucharist

When my voice broke at age fourteen, I left the choir and St. Simon's, which meant leaving the church. Six weeks later, however, I was back. I had simply missed Holy Communion too much. I soon became a server, joined the youth group, taught Sunday School, and never looked back.

As a teenager my relationship with the word *communion* evolved. I came to realize that not everyone was welcomed to Communion, not just the unconfirmed, but Christians from other churches who were not Anglican. I became aware that I was not necessarily welcomed to receive at other Christians' celebration of Holy Communion, precisely because I was an Anglican. I discovered that Holy Communion for some churches happened every week, while for others it took place three or four times a year. I noticed that we used different words for the Communion service, such as Mass or the Lord's Supper. As the word communion was becoming more of a church boundary-marker for me, the joy of Holy Communion started to become complicated.

As a teenager I finally started to take note of the literature that I was given in confirmation classes, with other pious primers that came my way, in a decidedly Anglo-catholic direction. These devotional aids took me beyond Communion as a gift of communion with God, to the realization that it had a great deal to do with Jesus, and his sacramental body and blood, his death and resurrection.

There were other developments. I thoroughly reformed my liturgical vocabulary: the "Communion service" became the "Eucharist," or in the right company, the "Mass." This shift in vocabulary was already taking place in the life of the Anglican Communion and its ecumenical partners. For good liturgical and ecumenical reasons, "Holy Communion" in the Prayer Book became "The Holy Eucharist." I went further. Taking "Holy Communion" became receiving "The (Blessed) Sacrament." The word "service" was replaced by "liturgy." My eucharistic piety evolved. The high point of the eucharistic liturgy was no longer the reception of the sacrament in isolation, but rather within the larger context of the prayer of consecration and the words of consecration themselves—"This is my body / This is my blood"—with solemn genuflections and elevations. These things had been part of the liturgical landscape all my life, yet I had barely noticed or understood them. But they became the heart of my evolving eucharistic piety.

Towards Ordination and Eucharistic Presidency

As a sense of vocation to priesthood emerged in my late teens, I noticed a not-so-subtle shift from a pre-adolescent longing to receive Holy Communion, to a post-adolescent longing to say the Eucharistic Prayer.

In 1981 I began my theological studies in the Faculty of Divinity at Trinity College, University of Toronto. It was a thorough pastoral and theological formation that took me apart and put me back together again in new ways that remain with me today. The formation in liturgy shaped and challenged me in such ways that I would later complete a doctorate in liturgy. I understood where the communion rite fitted within the overall shape of the liturgy. I became a champion of the communion of *all* the baptized, which included small children and recently baptized infants; receiving Holy Communion was part of the rite of initiation, and the only repeatable part, at every age.

All of this I brought to my liturgy ministries as a priest, especially as the celebrant of the Eucharist. I am also aware that in terms of the Eucharist, the load-bearing part for me remained the eucharistic prayer, which I would practice, learned by heart, said or sung in its entirety. Communion was important, of course, but like so many clergy, my aim was to find the most creative ways to communicate as many people in the fastest time.

In or Out of Communion

My commitment to the communion of all the baptized had another significant focus from my early twenties: the scandal of Christian disunity and the broken eucharistic communion between divided churches. Even before my theological studies I was already caught up the ecumenical movement, with all the fervor of those heady days in the 1970s and 80s; I still am today. Those years saw the publication—and wide reception—of iconic agreed statements between the churches, such as *The Final Report* of the Anglican-Roman Catholic International Commission (ARCIC) and *Baptism, Eucharist and Ministry* (BEM) of the Commission on Faith and Order at the World Council of Churches (WCC).

These ecumenical times also marked a new phase in my relationship with the word communion, which had become for me almost a juridical concept that described levels or degrees of ecclesiastical relationships, such as broken communion or excommunication, impaired or imperfect communion, limited communion and inter-communion. The human efforts it would take to bring us back to communion with one another, as God intended, seemed daunting. This understanding of "communion" bore no resemblance to the excitement and grace that "Holy Communion" meant to me as a younger Christian.

I became scandalized by divided Christianity, with its living history of broken and impaired communion, the refusals to recognize one another as Christians, and thus a compromised capacity to engage in witness and mission together. Full communion meant lots of work; restoring lost or impaired communion was even more fraught, involving commissions, agreed statements—fully received by all sides—and mutual acts of reconciliation, the work of decades, if not longer. This was the ecumenical movement to which I felt called to serve in my small way, initially the restoration of communion with other global families of churches, and later maintaining communion within the Anglican Communion itself.

As a young adult, I became aware of the Anglican Communion, where the language of "communion" functioned as limit and boundary between other church families at the global level. While I knew that the Anglican Communion at its most basic level is a eucharistic communion with the See of Canterbury, there was little grace and wonder to it. From the 1970s Anglicans started to discover just how fragile that communion could be, easily broken or estranged by disagreements on the remarriage of divorced persons, or the ordination of women to the priesthood and to the episcopate. Later expressions of broken communion emerged around diverging attitudes on the inclusion or exclusion of LGBTQ people within the churches of the Anglican Communion. I was intensely aware that broken communion is the consummate threat that Anglicans continue to hold over one another, as if ecclesial communion was a construct of a resolution of the Lambeth Conference or a General Synod, and a human choice to be made, one way or another.

From "Communion" to *Koinonia*

For a continuous period from 1989 to 2019 I was privileged to be part of a series of bilateral and multilateral ecumenical dialogues, both within Canada and internationally. For most of those years I was a church-appointed member of these dialogues. For seven of those years I gave staff leadership to these dialogues as part of my work as the director of the Commission on Faith and Order at the WCC, and later for four more years as the director for unity, faith and order at the Anglican Communion Office. It was through these experiences of ecumenical dialogue over three decades that I slowly came back to my earliest understanding of communion as a word full of grace and gift.[1]

Let me explain. A major shift in ecumenical theology began in the 1990s that led to a focused study of ecclesiology, that is, the reflection on the nature and mission of the church. Ecclesiologists, theologians, and international ecumenical commissions began to describe the church as communion, in the New Testament Greek sense of *koinonia*.

Being immersed in these ecumenical conversations about the church as communion, and involved with the preparation of their agreed statements and convergence texts had a cumulative and irreversible effect on me. I was truly blessed to have worked with several of the major pioneers of communion ecclesiology.[2] Conversations and insights offered

---

1. In particular, I note four texts from those different commissions: *The Church of the Triune God* (2007) from the International Commission for Anglican-Orthodox Theological Dialogue (ICAOTD), and *The Church: Towards a Common Vision* (2013) from the Commission on Faith and Order. The last text I worked on at the Anglican Communion Office, with a drafting team from the Inter-Anglican Sanding Commission on Unity, Faith and Order (IASCUFO), was a working paper commissioned by the Primates' Task Group, "The Gift, Call and Challenge of Communion" (2019). The Primates' Task Group accepted it in January 2020. The fourth project that shaped me was the draft agreed text of the International Reformed-Anglican Dialogue (IRAD), "*Koinonia*: God's Gift and Calling" (2020), completed after I returned to Canada in 2019. (One the Anglican theologians on the dialogue who gave impetus and direction to IRAD's work when it first met in 2015 is the Rev. Dr. Amy Richter, one of the co-editors of this volume.)

2. In particular, I note the following pioneers of communion ecclesiology with whom I worked on the dialogues. First, I encountered Fr. Jean-Marie Tillard OP on the Anglican-Roman Catholic Dialogue of Canada; he was one of the major Roman Catholic theologians on ARCIC, as well as on Faith and Order. Second, on ICAOTD I encountered Metropolitan John (Zizioulas) of Pergamon, the Orthodox co-chair, and also a member of Faith and Order. Third, was Dame Mary Tanner, whom I first met when she was the European President of the WCC; she is also a former member

by members of various commissions influenced my thinking and gave me hope at a time when within and between the churches of the Anglican Communion, there were acute experiences of challenged, weakened, and broken communion.

The use of the word communion in ecumenical theology comes from a recovery of the biblical understanding of communion, from the Greek New Testament word *koinonia*. The standard English versions of the Bible translate *koinonia* in many different ways that make its meaning easy to miss, along with its profound theological significance. *Koinonia* comes from the verb that means "to have something in common," "to share," "to participate," "to have part in," "to act together."

For instance, when Paul describes the reconciliation between Peter, James, and John with Barnabas and Paul, as extending the "right hand of *fellowship*" (Gal 2:9), the Greek is *koinonia*. When Paul commends the churches of Macedonia and Achaia for having "been pleased to *share* their resources with the poor among the saints at Jerusalem" (Rom 15:26), the word for "share" is *koinonia*. When Paul later refers to this event as a "*sharing* in this ministry to the saints" (2 Cor 8:4), the word is *koinonia*. One the most significant uses of the word *koinonia* in the New Testament is Paul's final greeting to the Corinthians: "The grace of our Lord Jesus Christ, the love of God, and the *fellowship* of the Holy Spirit be with you all" (2 Cor 13:13); again, the word for fellowship is *koinonia*. But here, it is applied to the inner life of the Trinity, thus linking the life of the church within the *koinonia* of the Triune God.

Early in the Acts of the Apostles, Luke writes, "They devoted themselves to the apostles' teaching and *fellowship*, to the breaking of the bread and the prayers" (Acts 2:42), an early reference to the Eucharist, where fellowship in the Greek is *koinonia*. On the Lord's Supper, Paul writes: "The cup of blessing that we bless, is it not a *sharing* in the blood of Christ? The bread that we break, is it not a *sharing* in the body of Christ?" (1 Cor 10:16–17); the word for sharing is *koinonia*. The breaking of the bread—the Eucharist—is the sacramental experience of communion in the body and blood of the risen Christ, united to and grounded in all the

---

of ARCIC and a former Moderator of the Commission on Faith and Order; the dissemination of communion ecclesiology ecumenically and within the Anglican Communion owes much to Dame Mary. Fourth, I worked with the Rev. Dr. Paul Avis on IASCUFO. Paul brought his insights about communion ecclesiology to bear on the Anglican Communion at a time of acute internal challenges.

other expressions of *koinonia* that emerge from within the communion of the Trinity: love, justice, peace, solidarity, reconciliation.

The Church: Towards a Common Vision

While all of my ecumenical work shaped me in one way or another, the project that pushed me intellectually and spiritually the farthest was the multilateral dialogue of the Commission on Faith and Order, which culminated in its 2013 convergence text, *The Church: Towards a Common Vision* (TCTCV). This most broad-based ecumenical reflection on the church as *koinonia* begins with a vision of God's design for creation. Created in the image of God, "every human being bears an inherent capacity for communion with God and with one another." Human sin damages "the relationship of communion between God, human beings and the created order." Yet, the "dynamic history of God's restoration of *koinonia* found its irreversible achievement in the incarnation and paschal mystery of Christ."[3] I marvel at how succinctly TCTCV holds together the life of the church of the Triune God with its mission in and for the world as one ecclesial reality: "Communion, whose source is the very life of the Holy Trinity, is both the gift by which the church lives and, at the same time, the gift that God calls the church to offer to a wounded and divided humanity in hope of reconciliation and healing."[4]

As a communion in unity and diversity, the church is rooted in the *koinonia* of love within the unity and diversity of Triune God. The church is not the privileged keeper of communion or the goal of communion; TCTCV describes the church as "sign and servant of God's design for the world" which is "to gather humanity and all creation into communion under the Lordship of Christ."[5] *Koinonia* is eschatological.

For the sake of this witness to God's design for the cosmos, Christian unity matters. It means that while human beings may reject, distort, and deny God's gift of *koinonia*, we can neither create nor destroy it. For all churches, and for the Anglican Communion, this means that we are never out of communion with one another, however costly ecclesial communion may be experienced, or however limited that communion may be received. The simplest test to find out what Christians really believe

3. TCTCV, §1.
4. TCTCV, §1.
5. TCTCV, §25.

about God's gift of *koinonia* is how they answer this question: "Can communion contain conflict, so that conflict loses its power to divide?"[6]

Whenever Christians are unable to agree with one another, yet choose communion, refusing to say, "I have no need of you" (*cf.* 1 Cor 1:21), then we proclaim that what binds us together is unshakeable, namely God's pure gift of *koinonia*, forever restored in the life, death, and resurrection of Jesus.

Going Back to the Future

One of the unexpected consequences of having worked so long in ecumenical ecclesiology with the accent on *koinonia* was waking up one day to realize that I had shifted from thinking *about* communion, to believing *in* communion in a new way. I became stunningly aware of this shift just after we had finished all the boring editorial work on TCTCV in preparation for its publication in 2013.

Something happened to me during a very ordinary Sunday celebration of the Eucharist in my parish in Geneva, Saint-Germain, a French-speaking parish of the Old Catholic Diocese of Switzerland,[7] that brought it all together for me. On that Sunday, as our priest was distributing Communion to our community standing in a circle around the altar, I had a profound experience. As I was receiving the bread of heaven and the cup of salvation, the body and blood of Christ, I felt within my whole being that I was caught up in an experience of cosmic *koinonia* through communion with the Triune God, with the Christians beside me and around the world, with all humanity and the created order. It lasted only a few minutes, but it was a foretaste of heaven. It was pure joy, and a new sense of being in the presence of, and communion with, God. It was what I remembered as a child at St. Simon's in Toronto on that February day so long ago. In this gift of the Holy Spirit, I had come full circle to where it all began, but bringing everything that I received since with me. And every time I have received the gift of Holy Communion since, there have been wondrous echoes, reverberations, and the *anamnesis* of that particular

6. This question was posed at the first meeting of IRAD in 2015, by the Anglican co-chair, Bishop David Chillingworth, former primus of the Scottish Episcopal Church.

7. The Old Catholic Churches of the Union of Utrecht, including the Diocese of Switzerland, is a small, vibrant European church that has been in full communion with the Anglican Communion since 1931.

experience of Communion in Geneva in 2013 and my first Communion in 1970.

This experience of sacramental *koinonia* transformed me as a Christian and as a priest. I realized that like the biblical translations of *koinonia*, God's gift of communion is all around us, but in different words and experiences. As a priest, I celebrate the Eucharist in a renewed way. Of course, there is the same attention to the eucharistic prayer, but now I take my time with every person into whose hands I place the bread of heaven and the cup of salvation, and say, "The body of Christ, given for you" and "The blood of Christ, shed for you." I believe that gift and encounter with the risen Christ is always a moment of gifted communion for everyone I meet, and in an utterly exceptional way at Holy Communion. Amen.

Bibliography

World Council of Churches, *The Church: Towards a Common Vision*. Faith and Order Paper No. 214. Geneva: World Council of Churches, 2013.

5

Concupiscence

Duane Alexander Miller

THE STUDENT WROTE HIS master's dissertation on demonology. *Demonology!* I am a professor at a Protestant seminary in Spain. I moderated the student's academic tribunal—I'm tempted to call it an inquisition—three professors who determined the grade for this project.

After the defense we had our celebratory meal for the end of the school year. Most of us had been on lockdown until recently, due to the spread of COVID-19, which had caused a number of deaths in Spain. It was extra special, therefore, that students, staff, and some family were able to gather together, while an undergrad was making an enormous serving of paella—the traditional Spanish rice dish. I was talking with Eli, the student who had just successfully defended his dissertation, and another student. The conversation turned to the question, what does Satan think about *himself*? I noted that the best treatise I know on the topic is the final scene from *The Devil's Advocate*, wherein Al Pacino, playing the devil, says to Kevin, his son:

> I'll tell you. . . . Let me give you a little inside information about God. God likes to watch. He's a prankster. Think about it: He gives man . . . instincts. He gives you this extraordinary gift, and then what does he do? I swear, for his own amusement, his own private, cosmic gag reel, he sets the rules in opposition! It's the goof of all time! Look, but don't touch. Touch, but don't taste. Taste, but don't swallow. And while you're jumping from one foot to the next, what is he doing? He's laughing his sick, f—ing

35

ass off! He's a tightass! He's a sadist! He's an absentee landlord! Worship that? Never!

At this point Kevin asks if it is better to reign in hell than to serve in heaven. The devil answers:

Why not? I'm here on the ground with my nose in it since the whole thing began! I've nurtured every sensation man has been inspired to have! I cared about what he wanted, and I never judged him! Why? Because I never rejected him, in spite of all his imperfections! I'm a fan of man! I'm a humanist. Maybe the last humanist.[1]

At this point, you may be thinking, *wait, isn't this called "Saving Words"?* And yes, it is. And my saving word is *concupiscence*.

It's an old-fashioned word that we don't use often anymore. I learned it studying moral theology under Father John Leies—may he rest in peace—of the Society of Mary, STD. We'll flesh out the definition below, but for now let me clarify that concupiscence is not only related to sexual desires.

Concupiscence is a saving word because it unlocks the mystery of humanity—of our great capability for goodness but also for evil at the same time. It reconciles the apparent paradox that we are made in the image and likeness of God, and yet, in spite of all our learning and devotion and piety, we can thoughtlessly ruin our lives or ministries with one catastrophic transgression.

I am thinking of a letter I read last week from a bishop who was disciplined and removed from his position for a year because he had committed adultery. This had just been made public. In this letter the bishop expressed his sorrow and said that he would take time for healing and that he himself did not fully understand why he had made those decisions. I also think of the Rev. Dr. Martin Luther King, Jr.—a great hero of civil rights. But his adultery and fornication is also common knowledge today. Or Karl Barth, arguably the greatest Protestant theologian of the twentieth century: it recently came to light that this man who had profoundly influenced two generations of priests and pastors (sometimes without their even knowing it) had lived in an adulterous relationship for decades. Or John Howard Yoder, pacifist and one-time professor at the University of Notre Dame: this great voice for peace was found to have

---

1. Hackford, dir., *The Devil's Advocate.*

had a long history of sexual predations, especially against young, female students. There is no shortage of examples.

How can good and evil reside side-by-side in the people of God, within each person in the people of God? Clearly, evil is not the will of God. Paul, in his epistles, often concludes with moral exhortations about living lives characterized by purity, holiness, kindness, and humility. But in his masterpiece, Romans, he acknowledges his own struggles, recognizing that they are common to all the people of God: "I do not understand what I do. For what I want to do, I do not do, but what I hate, I do. . . . For in my inner being I delight in God's law; but I see another law at work in me, waging war against the law of my mind and making me a prisoner of the law of sin at work within me" (Rom 7:15, 22 and 23 NIV). How can good and evil, holiness and temptation reside and even operate in the same person at the same time?

There are proposed answers. The optimism (almost extinct now) of the Enlightenment proposed that humans are basically good, and that when we do bad things it is because we lack knowledge that they are bad. So not concupiscence, but ignorance. The solution to what religious folk call "sin" is better education. I'm an educator so I'm certainly not going to say that it is of little value, but knowledge alone does not produce holiness. The best educated country in the world at the dawn of World War II was Germany. Osama bin Laden and self-styled Caliph Abu Bakr both had received fine educations. So, while education *may* help *some* people to overcome *some* prejudices, the answer fails.

There is another answer: humans are basically evil. The idea is that in our fall from grace we became totally estranged from God. Surely sin touches every facet of the human's life, but I don't see how it follows that we are fundamentally or basically evil. For we have, in addition to the problem of evil, what C. S. Lewis called "the problem of good."

The problem of good? Yes. If we are so far gone from any connection to our original creation in the image and likeness of God, then how is it that people—including non-religious people and folks who are not Christians—are sometimes capable of heroic and breathtaking acts of goodness and righteousness?

And there is finally a third answer, and this one is common among some of the New Atheists (a movement on the verge of extinction, it seems) and militant secularists. And that is: there is no such thing as good and evil—they are simply subjective cultural constructs that helped societies to survive in the context of evolutionary biology . . . or something

like that. Really? We read of the slaughter of schoolgirls in Nigeria by ter-
rorists and we are supposed to accept "there is no such thing as evil"? We
see the sacrificial and faithful charity of Mother Theresa of Calcutta and
we're supposed to accept "there is no such thing as good"? And irony of
ironies, this proposal is somehow supposed to be more reasonable than
the proposal that there is a God who is the source of all goodness, and
that ethics, whatever they may be, in some way flow both from and back
to this God?

How can we have two appetites or hungers at the same time? But
we've all been there.

Which brings us back to that monologue in the *Devil's Advocate*.
The devil, in his profound discourse, has a distorted view of good. He
really does believe he is doing what is good. He really does believe that
by never judging man he has done something better than what God did,
does, and will do, which is enact a merciful and mysterious judgment, but
a genuine judgment none the less. The devil exclaims that he's "nurtured
every sensation man has been inspired to have!"

And here is the rub: it can be difficult to discern between love and
concupiscence. Both love and concupiscence are types of desire or hunger for something (or someone) else. Love reaches out to the other on the
basis that one will sacrifice one's own good for the sake of the wellbeing
of the other. There can be no love where there is no possibility of sacrifice
or loss. Concupiscence, likewise, is a hunger and reaches to the other but
in a disordered manner. Being able to differentiate between a desire for
the other that is in harmony with the Creator's personality, and a desire
for the other that places the self at the center of the universe as one's god,
is profound and valuable. The word concupiscence helps us name this
distinction. This is why I believe that it is indeed a saving word.

I was not raised in a Christian household. I knew very little of religion, though I had, like most humans, an innate belief in God. I can't
remember a time when the reality of God did not seem to me to be obviously true. I didn't know that Christmas was about baby Jesus or that
Easter was about the resurrection. I was a typical American kid in the
'80s who was raised on the profoundly destructive (and diabolical, let
us say it) concept that I should do what I *think* is right. There was little
guidance on how to responsibly think through the question.

When I was a teen a friend invited me to his small Protestant church
in Mexico and I attended. I kept on attending. I was sort of mystified: why

were these people here? In Mexico in the '90s you got no social benefits from attending a little evangelical church. But people were friendly and I was curious. It was the first time I had ever heard that there were things that were always right and other things that were always wrong. In other words, that some ethics are not situational. This was a strange idea that I had never encountered before. I was not the cool kid in school, but I wasn't a loser either. And here I was being told that to ridicule and belittle the kids who were losers was categorically *wrong*. I learned that I should treat my parents with respect even if I was certain they didn't deserve it. (The moral of so many Disney movies is this: parents are stupid old people and the young must follow their hearts—that ethical truth was firmly engrained in my brain as an American kid!)

Those are just a few examples, but I was moving into a whole new world of understanding that there was actually a relation between the God who was there and how I lived my life, and I could have a relationship with that God, and that God desired such a thing. I also learned about limits: there were limits that should *never* be crossed. If I wanted to be a Christian I would have to sacrifice certain "rights." I mean, a relationship that went beyond the conviction that God existed to help me when I needed it—the one theological truth I had learned as an American kid.

I am reminded of these events in writing about concupiscence. I would not learn that word or its meaning until some eleven years later. I think that one of the great reassurances of the Christian faith is not only that it tells us the truth about God—not *everything* about God, but the truth—but also that it tells us the truth about ourselves. We're not basically good, full stop. We're not fundamentally bad, full stop. We are creatures with intentions and dreams and appetites, and that is all in accordance with our Creator's loving design. But some of those appetites lead us outside of the original design and tempt us to make our own plans.

Augustine, in his brilliant theological historiography, *City of God*, proposes that, in the end, there are really not hundreds or thousands of tribes and city states and empires. It may look to us like this is the case. But really, the truth—hidden though it may seem—is that there are only two cities:

> Accordingly, two cities have been formed by two loves: the earthly by the love of self, even to the contempt of God; the heavenly by the love of God, even to the contempt of self. The former, in a word, glories in itself, the latter in the Lord. For the

one seeks glory from men; but the greatest glory of the other is
God, the witness of conscience. The one lifts up its head in its
own glory; the other says to its God, "Thou art my glory, and the
lifter up of mine head." In the one, the princes and the nations it
subdues are ruled by the love of ruling; in the other, the princes
and the subjects serve one another in love, the latter obeying,
while the former take thought for all. The one delights in its own
strength, represented in the persons of its rulers; the other says
to its God, "I will love Thee, O Lord, my strength."[2]

And there are two types of loves: a genuine charity that flows from
and to God, and concupiscence, something that camouflages itself as the
former, but is a fraud; it is perverse.

I teach Old Testament here in Madrid. One of my favorite passages
is Genesis 2. The nuance and complexity are breathtaking. I like asking my students: When the serpent says that they will become *like God*,
knowing good from evil, is she lying? (*Serpiente* in Spanish is a feminine
noun, hence the *she*.)

Yes and no. They will become like God in that they will have a
conceptual awareness that evil exists, as does God. But it is a half-truth,
which is usually more dangerous than a lie, because they will come to
know evil by becoming its servants. God is like a doctor who specializes
in cancer and is an authority on the topic without ever having had it.
These first ancestors are like people struck by the disease and dying from
it. But now they know good and evil, now they can compose their own
laws, having shrugged off the friendship of a God who, according to the
serpent, was like a selfish kid, not wanting to share his toys.

Adam and the woman—she has no name until just before they are
exiled from Eden, because to name is to control in Hebrew culture—had
appetites: to see what is beautiful, to eat what is good, to savor what is
delicious. All of that was within the original design. But the serpent says
no, it is not enough. There can be *nothing* forbidden. There can be *no* appetite that must be controlled and disciplined or outright denied. In the
words of the Al Pacino's devil: Look, but don't touch.

> Touch, but don't taste. Taste, but don't swallow. And while you're
> jumping from one foot to the next, what is he doing? He's laugh-
> ing his sick, f—ing ass off! He's a tightass! He's a sadist! He's an
> absentee landlord! Worship that? Never!

2. Augustine, *City of God*, 14:28. The first quotation is Ps 3:3. The second is Ps 18:1.

At the heart of the mystery of good and evil there is the question—as the devil rightly points out—of God's intention. Why does God give us certain appetites but then tell us to reign them in? Is it because God delights in seeing us jump from one foot to the other? What is the devil missing out on? Of what is he ignorant? The devil will side with man, not God: "I'm a humanist. Maybe the last humanist."

I think the answer comes in the final line: "Worship that? Never!" Most of our theological and liturgical words come from Latin or Greek. But *worship* is an old English word, originally derived from the idea of worth-ship. *Worth* denotes the value of something, and *-ship* was a native English suffix denoting character or condition, as in *friendship*.

The devil does not see worth or value in God: he sees limit; he conceives of glory as having no boundaries and being able to compose or improvise one's own laws—the ethic I had grown up with. The devil sees fulfillment in absolute license: "Do what thou wilt shall be the whole of the Law," as the occultist and esotericist Aleister Crowley taught.

Perhaps we Christians have at times taken the commands of God and made them too strict and binding. That is *our* fault, though. Perhaps today, in some places, we have made them too lax. Perhaps *we* have at times been the tightasses—if I may borrow the devil's vocabulary—but God never was. There is worth in God.

There is an irony or paradox we encounter in Christian mysticism. It is much older than T. S. Eliot, but he expressed it better than anyone else writing in English, I think.

> To arrive where you are, to get from where you are not,
>   You must go by a way wherein there is no ecstasy.
> In order to arrive at what you do not know
>   You must go by a way which is the way of ignorance.
> In order to possess what you do not possess
>   You must go by the way of dispossession.
> In order to arrive at what you are not
>   You must go through the way in which you are not.
> And what you do not know is the only thing you know
> And what you own is what you do not own
> And where you are is where you are not.[3]

Appetite. Hunger. Desire. Will. Sensation. The devil taught us love, but a perverse love, an unbounded and limitless love. But to be human is to be limited. Through Eliot in these verses—which draw on the mysticism

3. Eliot, *Four Quartets*, "East Coker," III.

of St. John of the Cross—we are taught to embrace that limitation. In embracing the limitation we will begin to encounter freedom. In order to arrive at a genuine freedom, one founded in knowing God and being with God, we must accept that our desires are suspect, we must scrutinize them, and we must lose them. When we have shed all desires, it is then, says Eliot, that we might meet God. It is then that our desires will be reborn and regenerated. It is then that we will be able to comprehend and in our own imperfect way live out the injunction of St. Augustine: Love God, and do as you please.

I do not claim to have mastered these things. I think most Christians will never do so, not on this side of the eschaton. But let us examine our appetites and desires. Let us seek wisdom in discerning if they are born of authentic, divine love. The bishop who committed adultery wanted good things: companionship, pleasure, intimacy, friendship. But the way he sought them out was perverse, and in retrospect he admitted that he did not fully understand why he had done what he had done, though he did take responsibility for his actions.

We speak of love and charity a great deal. But to discern the real item we must be able to comprehend and name its imposter. *Concupiscence* is a saving word, because without it we may be tempted to mis-take (touch, taste, swallow) the slippery simulacrum for the love that truly saves.

Bibliography

Augustine. *City of God*. https://carm.org/augustine-city-of-god-book-14.htm.
Eliot, T. S. *Four Quartets*. New York: Harcourt, Brace and Company, 1943.
Hackford, Taylor, dir. *The Devil's Advocate*. Burbank, CA: Warner, 1997.

6

Dead

Laurie Brock

I DON'T LIKE TO say the word *dead* aloud.

Given the number of euphemisms we have created for the word dead, I'm not alone.

It lacks the elegance and softness of saying *passed away*, *gone to their eternal rest*, even *lost*, perhaps because they have those soft *s* sounds that slip over you like an unexpected chill that arrives, then slides out underneath a crack in our souls, leaving us slightly unsettled, but not shaken to our core.

Dead is harsh. Dead is blunt. Dead is the uninvited guest that arrives in the middle of our dinner party, kicks over the chairs, and puts out its cigar in the middle of the antique table. Dead throws the silver punchbowl through a window before taking a seat with no plans to leave anytime soon. We are stunned and perhaps even stupefied for a moment or a month or the rest of our lives.

Death has become an indirect reality for many of us. We may sit with loved ones in their final days and hours of life, yet when they have died—when they are dead—others come to usher us away while they handle things, the things that are writ large with the presence of the dead. The body is removed, prepared, and presented for us to pay our last respects. Even the burial is done by others. We come to the site to find the grave already dug, the coffin already in place, and the mound of dirt covered by AstroTurf (as if an AstroTurf hill in a cemetery is less obtrusive than a pile of dirt). Chairs are placed in orderly fashion around the grave. We say prayers, then leave. The tools that will be used to bury the coffin or urn are around the corner, out of sight, held by those we've paid to do the uncomfortable work of the actual burial. The family goes back to the house or their lives, and the dead are taken care of by others.

Our modern world has created ways to encounter the dead in quick visits and avoid the overwhelming presence of death. The tangible acts of being with the dead have been subsumed by professionals—washing and preparing the body, building the coffin, sitting with the dead, and even digging the grave.

This was not always the case.

I have memories of my grandparents talking about the deaths of their previous spouses, both of whom died young in tragic circumstances. In rural southern Mississippi in the early twentieth century, funeral homes were still a luxury for many, an odd luxury, to hear my grandmother speak of them. "Why would you want your dead loved one touched by strangers, dressed by people who don't know them or love them, and then laid out in a room with industrial carpet and furniture that isn't worn from years of family use?" she said, shelling peas with me on the front porch.

I recall my mother and her sisters talking about the last wake they remembered in a home, for their nephew, who died of leukemia. His body was carefully washed and dressed by his mother and some of the women of the community, then laid out in a coffin in the family dining room.

Mirrors were covered, either to make sure the spirit of the dead didn't catch a reflection in the mirror and stay around as a ghost or to remind the family that in the midst of raw grief, not brushing your hair or taking a bath is perfectly acceptable. Ancient superstitions and practical matters are not always separated in the substantial occasions of life and death.

Family and friends were present with the dead in a raw and holy way. They touched death, and in that outward and visible moment of courageous love and grace, they touched it, bathed it, combed its hair and dressed it in its Sunday best. Those who loved the one who had died sat up with the corpse in the family home over the course of three days. The body of the dead was never alone. Neighbors came to pay their respects, often bringing casseroles with handwritten directions taped on the tin

foil with masking tape: *Heat for 35 minutes in the oven at 350 degrees.*
"Don't worry about the dish. I can get it later," they would say as they
placed it on the table, near where the body of the dead person was in
repose. Then they would go look at the body.

"He looks so young," someone would muse. "She loved that dress.
I remember when she wore it to Easter Sunday last year," a member of
her Sunday School class would recall. Some words to soften, perhaps, the
reality that they were looking at the mortal remains of a human, a dead
body, and that is never a comfortable vision glorious. Despite our best
attempts, a dead body looks exactly like that—a dead body. Embalming
softens the edges, but does not alter the reality. And over the course of
three days, death settles in, both in the body of the one who has died and
the souls and lives of the ones who watch and wait.

For generations, families and friends sat with the dead until the
burial. During that time, they prayed, read psalms, reminisced about
"that time when he" or "can you believe she" or the other beginnings of
the stories we tell of the dead to remind ourselves *yes, they did live and
they were here with us.* Often those stories, which, by my childhood were
told out on the front porch of the funeral home at the wake, ended with
words that drifted into silence, then a long sigh as the presence of the
dead settled in a bit more.

Death does that—stops the words and leaves them open at the end,
with us searching for what might come next.

Generally three days after the death, the funeral happened in a
church, usually the deceased's church. If the Baptist Church was too
small, the local Methodists or Episcopalians might offer their space.
Then, after the funeral, they would go to the cemetery and take an active
part in the burial. Local men and older boys participated in the sacred act
of digging the grave, then stood at the back of the graveside service, ready
to lower the coffin and fill in the grave with the help of family and friends
still gathered. The final act of love, perhaps, was casting shovels full of dirt
until the grave was filled, then arranging the flowers on the raw cut of dirt
on the earth. The grave would almost always face east, the direction of the
return of Jesus (Matt 24:27), the rising of the sun or other reasons that
symbolized a home-going.

After the funeral, a few days and a few weeks and a few months, we
would go to see, to watch the grass grow over the dirt, to feel the new life
grow in the muck of grief and loss. *All of us go down to the dust; yet even
at the grave we make our song: Alleluia, alleluia, alleluia.*

The Book of Common Prayer still assumes the body will be buried at the graveside with loved ones present and members of the community, including the family, assisting. During the prayers for The Committal, the part of the burial service where the coffin is placed in the grave, the celebrant (often the priest) is directed to cast earth upon the coffin while saying, "In sure and certain hope of the resurrection to eternal life through our Lord Jesus Christ, we commend to Almighty God our brother/sister, and we commit her/his body to the ground; earth to earth, ashes to ashes, dust to dust."[1]

In almost twenty years of being ordained, I have seen few graves filled. I often have to bring my own dirt to the cemetery to cast on the coffin, which is almost never lowered into the grave when I pray this prayer. I asked one funeral director why. "Too hard on the family," he explained.

Death is hard. Period. Even when the death is one that feels more merciful than tragic, like a death after years of Alzheimer's, death is still cautiously welcomed and then encouraged to leave quickly. In the Book of Common Prayer, the Preface for the Commemoration of the Dead says "For to your faithful people, O Lord, life is changed, not ended," but what a painful change death brings.

Some faith traditions and cultures still engage in this direct participation. The family or religious leaders gather to wash the body and prepare the person for burial. Ministers come to pray in the home. Those mourning wear black or white. Particular prayers are said in the presence of the body. Incarnations and expressions of honoring the dead, burial, and mourning are varied. We humans over time and over cultures have our own ways of meeting death when it comes and being in the presence of grief when it settles in for a while.

Historians suggest the rituals between the death and the burial developed as a way to ensure the dead were truly dead in a time before medical tests could ensure they weren't in a prolonged unconscious state. These rituals also claimed the liminal space death always brings. Wakes, funerals, Masses for the Dead helped family members and friends move from the place where a loved one was alive into the new reality that arrived with death. From the business and legal matters of property transition to the very important life matters of how will we go on without them, the liturgies of the dead give us time and words to help us reconfigure our life.

1. The Book of Common Prayer, 501.

And yet far more of us have replaced the directness of death with indirect passivity. We meet at a funeral home and discuss plans. We hire people to do the work of being present with the dead. We show up to view the body, if there is a viewing. Funerals are rebranded "Celebrations of Life." Even the time between the wake (now almost exclusively called the visitation) and the funeral has been condensed, often to the same day. "It was hard on the family," one funeral director replied, when I observed the loss of the traditional three-day wake.

That again.

What might happen, I wonder, if we gave death its place again, not as an event that we try desperately to protect people from, but as a tangible reminder of our Christian faith that is expressed even in times of grief and sorrow? What might happen if we sat with the dead again, if we put our hands in the dirt and buried our loved ones? How would our faith and grief and joy of the resurrection be deepened because we recognized the holy place of the word dead in the Christian life?

The Episcopal Church names our funerals "Burials of the Dead." Within the service, as we celebrate eternal life, we say the words: *dead, death*. Also mentioned are the words *body* (as in corpse), *grief*, and *mourn*. We even try to create, as we can, a way to ease into a holy death, which may seem akin to the headwinds that convey the imminent arrival of a hurricane. The breezes begin to move us with the Prayer for a Person near Death: "Almighty God, look on this your servant, lying in great weakness, and comfort them with the promise of life everlasting, given in the resurrection of your Son Jesus Christ our Lord. Amen."[2]

Thus begins the series of prayers commonly known as last rites, but titled in the Book of Common Prayer, "Ministration at the Time of Death." This time of prayer has its roots in the practice of giving Communion to the dying—*viaticum*, which means provisions for the journey. These prayers, lamentably not used as frequently as they once were, remind us that death is a journey for all involved. Death moves the person dying from life to death to eternal life. Death also moves those who remain into a particular journey of grief. This journey for those who have a dead loved one takes time. It takes time because this journey is hard, difficult, and challenging. Life is realigned. Love is transformed. Faith is challenged.

---

2. The Book of Common Prayer, 462.

"In the midst of life, we are in death" are not merely words we say. They are words with a reality, one that our culture tells us must be avoided, mitigated, and softened because they are hard, difficult, and even crushing. Our Lord agrees, hands us a tissue, and asks us to remember and believe with our whole heart and soul and mind, "I am Resurrection and I am Life. Whoever has faith in me shall have life, even though they die."[3]

Maybe in our attempts to soften death, to mitigate its abruptness, and to avoid its pain with niceness, we are inadvertently running a race to flee a grief that will not be outpaced. Our detour to avoid the valley of the shadow of death has landed us lost and unable to venture out at all. Dead is a word we whisper, if we say it at all. And sadly, because we cannot give death its space in the holiness of God's creation, we also limit our ability to celebrate the joy of the resurrection.

For Christians, death is with us in the expressions, confessions, and sacraments of our faith. In holy baptism, we are buried with Christ in his death, and by it we share in his resurrection. In the celebration of the Holy Eucharist, we remember Christ's death and celebrate his resurrection as we await the day of his coming. *Death, dead,* and *buried* are all words in both the Apostles' Creed and the Nicene Creed.

In the midst of life, we are in death. In the midst of the words of our faith, we speak of death and dead. For Christians, the joy of resurrection happens only through the gate of death. And as fearful, as crushing, and as overwhelming as it can be to be present in the moments and days and months when someone we love walks through that gate, our faith boldly proclaims that nothing, not even death, shall separate us from the love of God, which is in Christ Jesus our Lord.

Our faith dares us to be present to death and to those who have died because doing so is an affirmation of our faith. Caring for the dead, attending to them and our grief and sadness, is an act of profound love. A Jewish colleague said that caring for the dead—sitting with the body, saying prayers, washing it, dressing it—is one of the purest acts of love we can do because the one who has died can never repay us. Our actions of being present and caring for the dead are outward and visible signs of the inward and spiritual grace of sacrifice, of love, and of faith.

Byron Stuhlman notes that when planning for the Burial of the Dead, the songs we sing should express joy and sorrow, Christian hope in the resurrection and grief and sorrow at death. "A false note is stuck if

---

3. The Book of Common Prayer, 491, with inclusive pronoun.

either of these elements is avoided in music or the texts of the rite," he observes. When we avoid saying the word *dead*, when we avoid the tangible spiritual and emotional chords our souls need to sing in its presence, we are left with false notes.[4]

The word itself has been buried under our own desire to mitigate death, to relegate it to the fringes of a world that doesn't particularly care for the way it arrives, usually uninvited and unwelcome, always leaving evidence of its presence and a stark reminder of how we are not God. Our actions have followed our words. We leave the dead to others for reasons that likely sound very logical and helpful. We avoid speaking of death.

Perhaps the time has come to touch death again, to sit with it, to see it in the bodies of those we love who have died as their lives are changed but not ended. We can sing songs of joy and grief as we cast shovels full of dirt on the coffin, casting our cares on God in grief at the same time. We can remember that dead is a foundational word of our faith, for without it, we have no sure and certain hope of the resurrection in our eternal life with Christ.

Maybe that's why, every Sunday, the Nicene Creed has us say aloud, so that everyone can hear, whether I like or not, "We look for the resurrection of the dead."

Bibliography

Episcopal Church. *The Book Of Common Prayer and Administration of the Sacraments and Other Rites and Ceremonies of the Church.* New York: Church Publishing, 1979.

Stuhlman, Byron D. *Prayer Book Rubrics Expanded.* New York: Church Publishing, 1987.

4. Stuhlman, *Prayer Book Rubrics Expanded*, 171.

7

Doctrine

Ian Markham

ONE CURSE OF MAINLINE Christianity is that the word *doctrine* has gone out of fashion. Doctrine feels dogmatic or doctrinaire. Doctrine exudes a self-confidence about the metaphysical that feels unrealistic. Doctrines draws lines; these religious adherents are right, others are wrong. Doctrine sits alongside the word "heresy" as divisive. At an extreme, the word reminds us all of the medieval debates about the number of angels that can dance on the head of pin.

For many, the word doctrine needs to be replaced. *Spirituality* is popular. *Pluralism* is good. *Inclusivity* is often used. Instead of explaining what God is like (the work that doctrine aspires to do), we need to enjoy the "feeling" of being religious; and we need to recognize our connection with all religious people.

In my judgment, if we do not recover the word doctrine, then mainline Christianity deserves to disappear. Doctrine is key to our survival. To do this, we need our conservative sisters and brothers to be honored and included. We need to tell the story afresh of our faith and be able to demonstrate its coherence and beauty to others. This is the work of doctrine.

After Virtue Had a Point

Alasdair MacIntyre's masterpiece *After Virtue* starts with a famous thought-exercise. He invites his readers to imagine a world where there is a sudden and complete reaction and rejection of science. Scientific books are destroyed; scientists are persecuted; and scientific labs are demolished. Then some three hundred years later, fragments of scientific papers are found. People begin using scientific terms again. But the usage is completely different from the original meaning. People use the language to describe their feelings instead of using the language to describe the universe. Language that was intended to be objective and to accurately describe the way the universe really is had become subjective and simply described how we felt about the world.

MacIntyre concludes his thought exercise by explaining that this, in his judgment, is what has happened to the language of morality. MacIntyre explains: "What we possess . . . are the fragments of a conceptual scheme, parts which now lack those contexts from which their significance derived. We possess indeed simulacra of morality, we continue to use many of the key expressions. But we have—very largely, if not entirely—lost our comprehension, both theoretical and practical, of morality."[1] For MacIntyre, moral language was in the past part of a holistic and coherent system that described, objectively, how we should relate to the universe; now in the twentieth century (when the book was written) the meaning of moral terms has been reduced to individual preferences. The word "right" used to mean "true for all people"; now the word "right" means "something I approve of." People use moral words but have no idea how they all connect together.

What is true of moral language is also true of theological language. People use the words "God," "incarnation," "sin," and "salvation," but they have no idea how they connect together. They do not appreciate that these words are part of a coherent narrative—a claim on the world that describes how best the world should be understood. Our task is to recover the coherent narrative. This is the work of doctrine.

Becoming Aware

The idea that the survival of mainline Christianity depends on the recovery of the concept of doctrine is one that came slowly to me. My fundamentalist upbringing made me nervous about strong doctrinal systems. Academic interests are often biographical. A central theme of my work has been "plurality" and "toleration." Given a world where the entire human race was in error save for our sect (in my case the "Exclusive

1. MacIntyre, *After Virtue*, 2.

Brethren"), questions around "how do you live with difference?" were central to me.

It was Hartford Seminary in Connecticut that changed my worldview. It was 2001, and I was appointed academic dean of this extraordinary and imaginative graduate school in Hartford. Under the leadership of President Heidi Hadsell, there were already a significant number of Muslims studying at the Seminary. Along with Dr. Ibrahim Abu-Rabi, Heidi Hadsell created links with Indonesia, Syria, and Turkey. Muslims from these countries came to study; suddenly, there was a significant Muslim presence in the student body, comprising over one third of the whole.

The other two thirds of the Seminary tended to be liberal Roman Catholics and members of the United Church of Christ. Every class was fascinating. The liberals were delighted to be in such a diverse class; but they were often appalled when they learned exactly what their new Muslim friends believed. Where the buzz words for the liberal Christians were "spirituality" and "love," the key words for the Muslim were "Qur'an," "judgment," and "mercy." It was not just the discourse that was different, but so were the practices. Most of the classes were in the late afternoon and evening. At the start of every class, I would ask the Muslims what time should we have a class break so they could leave and say their prayers. The time for the break would come; the Muslims would go to the Chapel to pray; the liberal Christians would go and get a coffee and a snickers bar from the machine.

There were many moments that were deeply ironic. In a class that I was teaching with Dr. Yehezkel Landau (our professor of Jewish Studies) called "Abrahamic Partnerships," I was trying to explain the doctrinal diversity of Christianity to the class that was comprised of ten Christians, ten Muslims, and ten Jews. I put on the board a list of beliefs—God, incarnation, Trinity, resurrection of Jesus, the virgin birth, heaven, hell, angels, demons. I then turned to the Christians and asked them to indicate which ones of these beliefs they personally affirmed. Almost everyone believed in God (we had one person who was post-theistic and had sympathies with the writings of Don Cupitt),[2] but by the time we got down to virgin birth there were only three believers out of the ten Christians present. Turning to the Muslims, I said "Just out of curiosity, how many

2. Don Cupitt was famously described as the "atheist priest." Although he would reject the label, it is true that he does not believe assertions can be treated as descriptive of reality. For a clear statement of his position see Cupitt, *Taking Leave of God*.

Muslims believe in the virgin birth?" Ten hands shot up, with one Muslim commenting "Have to, it is in the Qur'an." Christians and Muslims stared at each other utterly puzzled by the other.

This was my epiphany. This was the moment when I knew how important the word "doctrine" was. Muslims get that they are making a claim about the world. Their practices are intelligible within a wider narrative of conviction.

At Hartford Seminary, a significant community of Muslims was from Turkey. The Nur community, who were inspired by the Muslim theologian Bediüzzaman Said Nursi, were deeply committed to pluralism and conversation with the other. But unlike liberal Christians, they did not commit to dialogue because they were unsure about their own convictions. They committed to the conversation because they were sure about the authority of the Qur'an and that from the Qur'an they knew they had to be involved in dialogue with their neighbor. Dialogue was not a result of their skepticism but was inspired by a confident affirmation of their beliefs. They believed in dialogue with Christians *because* they believed in Muhammad and the Qur'an, not despite their beliefs. Like a child much loved by her family, they embraced the other in the world with a self-confident engagement. They knew who they were. As a result, they were engaging with the other out of a self-confident identity.

The problem with the anti-doctrine movement inside mainline Christianity is that it creates a god out of its whims and preferences. It is a "make-up-your-own" theology based on one's own likes and dislikes. "I don't like that sort of God" is a refrain. There is no serious theological work. Many in this group are universalists (i.e. they take the view that everyone is saved). But the basis for their affirmation of universalism is utterly unclear. To the simple question: how do you know this or that idea is true? They have no answer because this is the realm that is covered by the word doctrine.

Recovering Doctrine

Once you discuss doctrine, you will be driven to acknowledge an authority. How exactly do we know what God is like? How do we know what God wants? Given that humans are small and the universe is massive, any talk about the creator of the universe is going to depend on revelation.

We need to trust that somewhere, somehow, God has spoken and is speaking.

Now, at this point one can take several routes. There are scholars who believe that through the application of reason you can work out that Christianity is the true revelation. Harold Netland and Richard Swinburne[3] take this approach. Netland lists some twelve rational criteria that he believes, if applied to all the world religions, will only vindicate Christianity.[4] The difficulty with this approach is that it ignores the way knowing is heavily shaped by culture and vantage point. There is no Archimedean point; there is no transcendent perspective outside all the different cultures from which we can access and determine that this is indeed the truth.

Another route is to opt for a non-realist, loosely postmodern, account of the Christian faith. This is the position of Don Cupitt, whom we met above. Christianity is a narrative; it tells a story that provides meaning to my culture. One should not imagine that the narrative is true—in the sense that it is descriptive of the way the world is. Instead, the narrative is a pair of culture-imposed spectacles that shape our experiences. One must hold one's narrative with humility; it is neither better nor worse than alternative narratives. All narratives are legitimate—the Buddhist, the Muslim, the secular, and the Christian. There is no way of getting outside your narrative to determine which narrative is really closer to the reality, because we are all trapped in our respective cultural perspectives.

Now the obvious difficulty with this approach is the problem of ugly and destructive narratives. The narrative of the antisemitic Nazi and of the white supremacist racist are just competing narratives. On what basis do we resist these narratives? The standard response is to appeal to a set of ethical values. Narratives, advocates of this approach respond, should be judged by their ethical impact. The problem here is consistency: how is it that we can have ethical truth but not metaphysical truth?

In between these two extremes is an alternative. It is not that Christianity is just self-evidently true nor is it that Christianity is just one narrative among many in a sea of relativism. Instead, Christianity is a world perspective that meets sufficient rational and experiential factors

3. For Richard Swinburne see his initial trilogy: *The Coherence of Theism, The Existence of God, Faith and Reason*.

4. Netland, *Dissonant Voices*, ch. 5.

to justify the act of trust.[5] Trust is quite beautiful. We trust another person when there might be much that we do not know or about which we are not sure. From the car mechanic, whom you have gotten to know over many years, who tells you the "catalytic converter is broken," to your son, whom you just know did not get involved in the act of bullying at school, trust is the mysterious factor at work. Now, trust does need some type of justification. If the car mechanic is a fraud or the son is good at lying, then the trust can be misplaced. However, trust, by definition, is never definitive. It is always based on a certain impression, sometimes a gut instinct, and repeated encounters.

Doctrine begins with an act of trust that Jesus is the eternal Word. The support for this act of trust is the church. It is through the church, which reads holy scripture, that we hear of Jesus as the Word. We meet this Jesus in the liturgy. We learn of the stories, the parables, the miracles, and the teaching. We learn that almost all of those closest to the resurrected Jesus were martyred for their witness. We learn how the values of Christ have shaped a certain political agenda, where justice is central and the poor and marginalized are valued. We learn of a teacher who constantly calls us to be better than ourselves; but we also see a teacher who spends much of his time with those who find his teaching hard and he never seems to give up on them.

J. B. Phillips, the New Testament translator, entitled his biography *The Ring of Truth*. This lovely phrase captures the nature of trust. The picture emerging from the New Testament of Jesus Christ has the "ring of truth." As we acquaint ourselves not simply with the historical Jesus in the text of the Gospel, but with the Jesus who comes to us through liturgy and the church, we find ourselves saying that this life is worthy of trust. It is perfectly rational to stake your life on this act of trust. This is what marriage involves; this is what any close friendship involves. One is never completely sure (because such complete certainty is unavailable, for none of us is omniscient), but there are sufficient grounds for trust for us to build our lives on such relationships.

The act of trust in Jesus is the conviction that Jesus really shows us what God is like. Jesus is the eternal Word made flesh. When we look at Jesus, we see God. Once we say this, we are committed to the work of doctrine. It is from the claim that Jesus is the embodied "thought" of God

5. This is a theme of my *The New Apologetics*.

(after all, a word is simply a thought made manifest) that we are led to the doctrine of Trinity. The logic is simple: if Jesus is the embodiment of God on earth, then presumably there must be a way that God is still sustaining the universe. If this is the case, then we must be committed to talking of at least two persons of God. Add in the claim in scripture that all of God's interactions with the world involve the Spirit of God, then it becomes easy to understand why Christians adopt the language of the Trinity.

The work of "reading" the words and deeds of Jesus of Nazareth is hard. Certain big themes are clear: we are called to be persons of holiness engaging with love for all we encounter, with an emphasis on justice and inclusion of the poor. We are called to be disciples who make God the highest priority in our lives. But other themes are less clear. Where exactly does the reading of Christ leave the church in respect to the use of force for a just cause to bring about a just peace? What exactly does the reading of Christ teach about divorce, remarriage, and LGBT inclusion? So one does the work of doctrine in conversation. It is in conversation with the past (hence the importance of tradition) and with the church catholic, especially those Christians who are living with the questions at stake. Some doctrinal conversations can be "firmer" than others. Others are held with some humility, aware that doctrinal conversations can be less sure and open to the possibility of change.

The doctrinal edifice moves out from the incarnation (the authority for doctrinal claims) to scripture to encompass the entire drama from creation to eschatology. From the teaching of Christ (and the witness of the New Testament), we learn that death on the cross was transformative for God's relations with the world. We learn that our human vanity leads to a destructive egoism that can be damaging. We learn that, especially in the cross, God has the authority to forgive. We learn that the resurrection of Jesus from the dead creates legitimate expectations for humanity and, according to Paul in Romans 8, all creation. So the traditional doctrines—creation, sin, atonement, resurrection of the body—are all part of this narrative.

Doctrine becomes a frame that justifies any assertion about God and God's relations with the world. Instead of the "make-up-your-own theology" grounded in your preferences, there is a basis for the assertion. With some doctrines, any claim about God may be right; without any doctrines, there is zero reason to believe that the claims being made about God may be right.

Recovering Doctrine in the Church

The major mistake of many mainline Christian churches is that they feel the solution to decline is to invite everyone to be anywhere they choose. The result is that mainline congregations are full of seekers, sharing very little in terms of identity, and having zero confidence that the words being taught by the preacher are true. Adherents of these mainline churches cling to faith by their fingernails.

A church that teaches doctrine is a church that can create a congregation that has some confidence that their worldview is true. This will be a congregation that has reasons for their claims about God and how God relates to the world. The secret is education and formation. Space needs to be created for members of the congregation to understand the basis of Christian claims about metaphysics. From the course in Lent or at Advent to Bible study materials, ways need to be found to encourage a literacy about the drama of faith.

To advocate for doctrine does not mean that one need be intolerant or narrow. The tradition encourages a pluralism. If you read St. Thomas Aquinas from the thirteenth century closely, then you can see that he is in certain fundamental ways disagreeing with St. Augustine of Hippo from the fourth century. They both share certain fundamentals, but they also disagree on certain topics (e.g., the relationship of faith to reason). Doctrine requires conversation. Doctrine requires learning from those who see things differently. Certain doctrinal claims need to be held more lightly than others.

One need not become a heresy hunter to believe in the importance of doctrine. One can welcome those who challenge orthodoxy in imaginative and creative ways. Although it is true that what is "official" church teaching must have some type of boundary (I would leave The Episcopal Church if, for example, General Convention denied the truth of the bodily resurrection of our Lord), one can welcome the debates in the church and in the academy about the "social trinity" and the more "classical trinity." This is good and healthy.

A doctrinally literate congregation is one where there are genuine conversations about the Christian worldview. It is one that understands why the tradition teaches the Trinity and the resurrection of the body. It is one that is open to different understandings of eschatology and atonement. Such a congregation will take doctrinal literacy into the world and engage differently with the world. When questions are asked about this or that, answers will be given. When people are seeking for some answers to their fundamental needs, this congregation will be able to provide those answers.

Doctrine is not a word to be feared. Doctrine is not the cause of our demise. Instead doctrine is our hope. We can do this. We need to do this.

Bibliography

Cupitt, Don. *Taking Leave of God*. London: SCM, 1980.

MacIntyre, Alasdair. *After Virtue: A Study in Moral Theory*. 2nd ed. London: Duckworth, 1985.

Markham, Ian. *The New Apologetics: At the Intersection of Secularism, Science, and Spirituality*. Lanham, MD: Lexington/Fortress Academic, 2020.

Netland, Harold. *Dissonant Voices: Religious Pluralism and the Questions of Truth*. Vancouver, BC: Regent College Publishing, 1999.

Phillips, J. B. *The Ring of Truth: A Translators Testimony*. London: Hodder and Stoughton, 1977.

Swinburne, Richard. *The Coherence of Theism*. Oxford: Oxford University Press, 1977.

———. *The Existence of God*. Oxford: Oxford University Press, 1979.

———. *Faith and Reason*. Oxford: Oxford University Press, 1981.

8

Father

CATHERINE RICKETTS

IN THE DARK OF the hospital room, it's three a.m. and Austin and I have been taking turns staying awake to watch our newborn breathe. He was born yesterday at just this time. He's a healthy boy, but we've never had a child before and it will take us weeks to believe that he'll keep breathing on his own, that the will to live is innate and strong. So Austin holds him, and watches, while I doze.

They're in a chair beneath a wide window. The city blinks behind them. My eyes open now and then, and I see the same thing: Rodin's *Thinker* with an infant in his arms. My eyes close. Though the boy is awake they make no noise, and I sleep deeply, elated and sore. When I open my eyes again, the sky has brightened to indigo, our son sleeps, and Austin studies. His posture is fixed, but his face has changed. It seems softer, for he is discovering deep, surprising kinship. Day breaks, and Austin is transfigured into a father.

Does God watch us this way, with such urgency of attention? As if we are brand new to him? As if our life depends on it?

Watching Austin become a dad has made me want to get to know God again as *Father*. This name for God was meaningful to me when my dad was alive, for I could imagine God with a body: Dad's hearty frame, spry through his sixties, his earnest blue eyes, his hands tenderly cupped when he listened. He's been gone six years, and I haven't thought much of God in this way. The language feels abstract, trite. And as critique of patriarchal systems sweeps through my workplace, my church, and our nation's common life, I've wondered if a name like Father for God hurts more than it helps. Misunderstood, this language causes spiritual harm, narrowing our view of God as male, justifying abuses of power by fathers and clergy, tempting us to map our dads' flaws onto God and disfiguring God in our eyes. There can be great healing in dethroning Father from its dominion over theological language, omitting male pronouns from our liturgy, dusting off other metaphors for God: mother bear, nursing woman, hen gathering her chicks. Rediscovering such ancient but unfamiliar language gives us a more expansive lexicon of imagery to help us behold the expansive nature of God.

Father, though, is the name Jesus gives us. He tells his disciples, "Therefore, pray in this way: 'Our Father'" (Matt 6:9).[1] It's the relationship he shares with God and the relationship he invites us to share, too. I want to discover anew what this kinship feels like. Might there be some expanse *within* this tired word? I look to the Gospel of John, where Jesus speaks of God almost exclusively as his Father. I choose a translation that David Bentley Hart published three years ago because it's new to me, and I'm looking to be surprised. What I discover between Jesus and the Father is extraordinary intimacy, like that between a young man and a newborn son. I recall Austin in the hospital room and wonder: Is God, eternally, a new dad?

I'd been pregnant fifteen weeks when I recognized the sensation of champagne bubbles popping in my belly to be "the quickening," the first of the baby's discernible movements. Two weeks later, in bed, when Austin casually cupped his hand over my navel, he sensed on his palm the miniature thud. "Did you feel that?" we said in unison, incredulous. Then we were silent, lying on our backs. His palm stayed upon me, and he began to cry.

Austin doesn't cry often. He cried at my father's deathbed, his palm then pressed against my back. He cries during movies for acts of courage at war. When he cries, it's silent. Tears only. His face doesn't twist; his lip doesn't tremble. But his eyes change. Welling slightly, they become a small cosmos of passion, full of awe and pity, the way Rembrandt drew the eyes of Christ.

1. Unless otherwise noted, all quotations from the New Testament are from Hart, *The New Testament.*

I turned my head to smile at Austin, whom I abstractly knew to be the father of that little flick, and I was surprised to see his eyes wet with wonder.

What is God but a new dad when, in the creation narratives, God stops again and again to wonder at all that is becoming? "It is good" is God's joyful refrain. Did God's own eyes brim as the waters rushed to fill oceans, rivers, and rivulets? As the land surged verdant? Wonder seems an almost universal quality of new fathers. Likewise, wonder gives rise to our very existence. God made you, me, the moss, and the octopus, not for utility but for *delight*. The world was not, and then it was, because it delighted God. I was not, and then I was, because it delighted God. When we look to the faces of new fathers, we see that God our Father, worthy of highest reverence, also reveres us.

What does it feel like to be the child of such wonder? To hear, spoken plainly, "You are my Son, the beloved, in you I have delighted" (Luke 3:22)? Jesus lives and moves and has his being in God's delight. He knows he's come from God's gladness, and that he is ever entering into God's gladness. It grounds him confidently in his mission; it raises him to glory. Looking to his death and resurrection, Jesus prays, "Father, glorify me by your side with that glory I had by your side before the cosmos was" (John 17:5). He knows in his bones that he's been basking in God's delight since before the stars burned or the angels were born. In the same prayer, he remembers, "You loved me before the foundation of the cosmos" (John 17:24). Austin loved his son when the boy was only a patter on his palm. God loved his Son before all things came into being, and, through Christ, loves me the same.

By Christmas, our son is seven months old. My aunt gives him a plush rabbit, a hand puppet. It's not cartoonish, but lovely, its coat a natural brown, its belly the color of cream. Austin names him Oxford Rabbit, and begins a routine at the foot of the bookshelves where tugging volumes onto the floor is a regular stop on the boy's rounds through the apartment. Oxford Rabbit speaks in an exaggerated British accent, holds books between his paws, and gives the baby brief reviews: "A fine choice, my boy. This here is *The Varieties of Religious Experience* by the unmatched American Pragmatist William James. James was a Harvard chap, not bad if you can't be an Oxford man like myself."

Silliness is not Austin's everyday demeanor. Austin has a serious face: dark hair parted on the side, dark beard shaved close, dark eyes that do not always light when they greet you. His eyes light and his smile softens for those he knows best: his sister, his college friends, my cousins. He's chatty with people who turn conversation toward him, who ask thoughtful questions, who seek his expertise or wonder about his upbringing. But we've sat through entire dinners with friends where he hasn't said more than a sentence. He comes by it honestly, from a family of people who don't like to call attention to themselves. Once, when we worked together, a colleague in her sixties told me that Austin was hard to read and it made him seem arrogant. Those more charitable to introverts know him as calm, quiet, smart as a whip, and wise.

But since becoming a dad, Austin's not afraid to appear foolish. Silliness was always within him, I knew, but he reserved his improvised songs, put-on voices, and bad puns for the private society of our marriage. Now, our son at his side, he feels free to sing and speak baby in front of others. His eyes become big and his mouth stretches across his face as he babbles to our boy. Fatherhood loosens him, and he is coming to be generous with his whole self.

Traditional notions of masculinity limit male expression to stoicism and anger. These align with classical conceptions of God: Men are aloof; God is unknowable. Men are impassive; God is unchanging. Men are violent; God is prone to wrath. But in John's Gospel, the Father is characterized in no such terms. Instead, we learn of God's generosity of spirit: the Father gives all of himself to the Son. John the Baptist tells us, "The Father gives the Spirit without measure. The Father loves the Son and has placed all things in his hand" (John 3:34–35). Jesus proclaims, "All that the Father has is mine" and "For the Father loves the Son and shows him all the things he does" (John 16:15; 5:20). Such generosity frees the Son to be generous in return: "All that is mine is yours, and what is yours is mine," he prays (John 17:10). It inspires him to be generous toward others: "Knowing that the Father had placed all things in his hands . . . [he] began to wash the disciples' feet" (John 13:3). What's more, Jesus's presence among us is the Father's lavish revelation of his very self to the world. John writes, "No one has ever seen God; the one who is uniquely God, who is in the Father's breast, that one has declared him" (John 1:18). In Christ, God is an effusive new father, babbling to us with extravagant expression so that we might understand who God is.

Another three a.m. Our living room. The baby is eight months old and wakes in the night. Austin's unwilling to let him cry himself to sleep, in spite of my urgings and those of our doctor and the books and online forums. I've stopped nursing overnight in hopes that Austin will get tougher about crying. Instead, each night, when the crying starts, Austin rises uncomplaining, scoops our son from the crib, and carries him to the couch. He lies on his back and the boy drops his cheek to Austin's chest and immediately settles. Streetlights give an ambient glow. Cars pass below with an occasional *hush*. The two lie together, Austin foregoing restorative sleep, until light dawns patiently over the city.

A persistent theme of scripture is the patient presence of God. God makes covenant after covenant, vowing to remain with his people. God comes to be with men and women as a wrestling angel,[2] within a burning bush,[3] in a flame.[4] People don't always recognize how very near God is, though, and they act badly, afraid, at heart, to be alone, and God becomes vexed. A commitment to patient presence does not preclude moments of vexation; some nights, if our son keeps crying in his father's arms, I hear Austin through the walls, groaning the boy's name. But in his groaning he remains present, desiring and seeking our child's best. God is this way. Finally, the Father sends his Son into the world, the ultimate gesture of his presence.

Unlike other people, Jesus knows deep in his heart that the Father is with him, and this knowledge bolsters him through difficulty. When he's questioned in the temple, he explains to his critics, "I am not alone. I stand with the Father, who sent me" (John 8:16, NIV). When he foretells his betrayal to his disciples, he says soberly, "An hour is coming—has indeed come—when you are scattered, each one to his own home, and you leave me alone; and I am not alone, because the Father is with me" (John 16:32). Heartened by the Father's presence, Jesus passes through fear to bear his cross.

This week, our son is teething and he cannot sleep alone. From midnight on, he wakes every hour and calls out. We try to soothe him and return him to the crib; he wakes again soon after. But when he's lifted up and laid down with his dad, he sleeps deeply. His pain becomes bearable when he's in good company. Does the presence of another actually alter our bodies, our brains, changing the way we experience pain? The Father's presence emboldens the Son to face the cross. The Father becomes present to humankind in the broken body of Jesus. This is the body of a

2. Gen 32:24.
3. Exod 3:3.
4. Judg 13:20.

good dad, lying down with his child in radical compassion, the sharing of suffering.

Austin and our son, now ten months old, are in the tub. I'm in our room preparing for bedtime, and I hear their voices sound from the tiled bath: "Get those toeskies, get behind the kneeskies, get those handskies, don't forget the earskies!" The boy chirps with gladness. Tonight, like every night, Austin has undressed, sat in the tub, filled it a few inches, and waited for me to place the naked child in his hands. Every night he asks, "Is it too hot?" as our son's feet and legs and butt slide into the water. Every night he sings as he brushes the bamboo cloth over the boy's shoulders, between his fingers, beneath his chin. Then it's time to play, and I hear splashing and infant laughter, a sound more soothing than rainfall.

There may be no more intimate a time between father and child than in infancy. Before words, the body speaks; it is gentle, handling this fresh and precious form. Before the busyness of childhood, the language barriers of the teenaged years, and the renegotiation of ties between parent and adult child, the communion of a father and an infant is free and pure. Through this window, the light shines all the way.

Bodily intimacy between a mother and her child is a cultural assumption: Our son came to be within my flesh. He nursed a year at my breast. He will always feel some fundamental kinship with my skin. Intimacy with fathers is not culturally assumed. If I look to the male archetypes at hand, it's hard for me to understand the extraordinary intimacy between God the Father and Jesus the Son, or the intimacy that Jesus invites me to share with the Father. But when I look to the father of an infant, I glimpse something of what Jesus means when he says, again and again, "I and the Father are one" (John 10:30). I see union. I see chest pressed to chest, or forehead to forehead, or temple to nose. I see bodies relating to each other without the barrier of shame or the rift of a hurried life. I see a vivid physical expression of Jesus's prayer, "You, Father, are in me and I in you" (John 17:21). I see what John meant when he called Jesus the one "who is in the Father's breast" (John 1:18). More intimate than two beings who are *with* one another, the Father and the Son are *in* one another.

Jesus opens up this strange, mystical union and welcomes me into it. For me, and for all who believe his disciples' testimony, Jesus prays, "Just as you, Father, are in me and I in you, that they too might be in us" (John

17:21). By Christ's invitation, I am held and washed and known—*my fresh and precious form*—in God the Father.

•

Hart's translation of John stays close to the Greek in order to bring twenty-first century readers into the mind of a first-century author. Most translations only do this in footnotes, but Hart brings that spirit into the lines themselves. He does so at the risk of phrasing that sounds clumsy to modern ears, like the phrase above, "in the Father's breast." But in some sense, the language of fatherly intimacy that Hart pulls from the historic text feels familiar to my contemporary sensibilities. Here's why: Austin's presence with our son is evidence of a larger trend that I see among fathers in my circles. New dads are up in the night, diapering their children before placing them in their wives' arms to be fed. They're pushing strollers around the neighborhood, taking afternoon hikes with the baby on their backs, and visiting the pediatrician. They're eager to match their wives' efforts at nursing; when the baby begins eating solid foods, they flip omelets and cut pancakes into teeny pieces, hungry to nourish their kids. In our middle-class urban households with two working parents, whether Black or Asian or White, chef or pastor, in finance or biology or tech, the new fathers among my friends are seeking to be as involved in infant care as are new moms. In a time when male authority is scrutinized for bad behavior, with the dangerous leadership of the Trump White House, excessive violence perpetrated by police, and testimonies of sexual abuse exposing the shadow side of even beloved spiritual figures, the present young father is a welcome glimmer in the dark landscape of male leadership. It is a picture of the kind of Father Jesus knows, and bids us come and know.

Finally, the boy is one and is learning to speak. His favorite word is *hammer*, probably because of the plastic tool set Austin gave him. He says this word over and over; now when he cries in the night, he soothes himself, saying, "Hamma, hamma, hamma." He was napping the other afternoon when our upstairs neighbor nailed a frame to the wall at the opposite end of the apartment. I heard a small voice from the bedroom call out, "Hamma!" His other favorite words are hammer's phonetic cousins: hummus, lama, mama, challah.

Austin is a keen interpreter of our son's speech, in part because he has a good ear for language, but mostly because he is thrilled about this stage of development. Austin recognizes something that I did not: Our son repeats *hammer* not because he loves hammers or because he wants his hammer but because it's exciting to be able to communicate. Austin finds pleasure in our son's pleasure in being able to speak to us. Is this how God feels when we are learning how to pray?

I am learning how to pray by watching my son speak to his daddy. In this spirit, I pray not to be given some prize I desire, but simply to be in my Father's company, and to be heard by him. "I knew that you always hear me," the Son prays (John 11:42). This is a prayer of confidence and familiarity, born of the Father's delight, generosity, and faithful, intimate presence. I don't pray very often, largely because, if I'm honest, it's hard to imagine that God hears me. But I try to picture God listening, laughing a little just to hear my voice. Maybe the Father is grinning at Jesus in his glory, the way Austin catches my eye when our child goes on and on about that hammer, the two of us just over the moon to hear him speak. Imagining this, I want to start talking to God again. Maybe my prayer is a single word, repeated when I wake and when I dream. Maybe it's as simple as *Abba*.

As I imagine God as a new father, I am beginning to feel intimately loved by the Father. I pray that my son would feel this, too. Jesus knew in his bones that he was loved from the beginning. I pray that this child would know, in a deep, inchoate, bodily way, the love of his father at the start, and that this would make plausible the love of God, whom Jesus teaches us to call our Father.

Bibliography

Hart, David Bentley. *The New Testament: A Translation*. New Haven: Yale University Press, 2017.

9

... As We Forgive Those
Who Sin Against Us

ANTHONY BASH

IN ALMOST EVERY ANGLICAN service I can think of, we say the Lord's
Prayer, with the words, "Forgive us our sins, as we forgive those who sin
against us." Sometimes we say "trespasses" instead of "sins." The words are
familiar, and I suspect we rarely stop to think what they mean because
they are so familiar.

In many services, when there is a confession of sin, a priestly absolution follows. Deep down, I am not sure I can absolve anyone of their
sins—I think absolution is the gift of God, and the gift of God alone—but
as a loyal Anglican I treat the words I say as modeling the assurance that
God offers to those who, in the words of the Book of Common Prayer,
confess their sins "in penitence and faith." I say the words as much to
myself, who stands in need of forgiveness, as I do to the members of the
congregation whom I hope are listening.

One of the things that has bothered me for a long time is why, in
the Anglican Church, there is such a strong emphasis on confessing one's
sins to God, but not on admitting upfront how rotten, mean, selfish, and
altogether unpleasant we can sometimes be to people around us. True,
we need to be "in love and charity" with our neighbors when we come to
Holy Communion, but there is little more than that in Anglican liturgies
when it comes to the wrongs we do to other people. In contrast, God gets
a rather better "look in": in the same prayer that reminds us that we need

to be "in love and charity with our neighbors," we say we "acknowledge and bewail" our "manifold sins and wickedness" against God, with no words of lament about wrongs against "neighbors."

Around the time this book will be in print, Wipf & Stock will also publish a book of mine in the Cascade imprint called, *Remorse: A Christian Perspective*. In the book, I explore why it is that the Christian church has so little good theological thought about remorse for the wrongs we do other people. (This is not a shameless "plug"; it is relevant to what I say.) We are quick to say we should forgive "those who trespass against us" but rather less quick to say to the "trespassers" that they should repent and be ashamed of what they have done.

Don't get me wrong. I am an unapologetic enthusiast of forgiveness as a defining and radical ethic of Christian discipleship—so long as the forgiveness we advocate is biblically framed. Such forgiveness is essential for human flourishing personally and in communities, and it is one of the identity markers of the kingdom of God. As we shall see, biblically framed forgiveness is transformational, ecclesial, and eschatological, and for these reasons profoundly evangelistic. But before we explore what biblical forgiveness is, we must first clarify what forgiveness is not, so that we can get right what it is.

What Forgiveness Is Not

In the popular mind, forgiving and forgiveness are among the greatest moral goods, with examples of selfless forgiving in response to appalling wrongs by unrepentant wrongdoers often held up as examples of virtue and godliness. The roots of this way of thinking seem to come from the supposed forgiveness that Jesus offered on the cross: Jesus's words in Luke 23:34, "Father, forgive them for they do not know what they are doing," are sometimes taken as paradigmatic for all people to practice.

A careful reading of Luke 23:34 indicates that when he was dying on the cross, Jesus did *not* forgive those who were crucifying him. He prayed for his enemies and asked that God would forgive those who were crucifying him, in line with the traditions of the Old Testament that God forgave those who sinned in ignorance. But he himself did not forgive, though of course it is true that, in the midst of the profound suffering he was enduring, he loved his enemies and prayed for them (see Matt 5:44). In keeping with the (non-)example of Jesus, the message of the gospel is *"repent* and believe," as John the Baptist preached it, and as is often repeated later in the New Testament (e.g., Luke 24:47). I think we ought also to say, "Be sorry and remorseful when you repent . . . ."

To suggest that it is a moral good to forgive the unrepentant can make forgiveness, in the eyes of some, objectionable and distasteful, as forgiveness offered this way appears to let wrongdoers "get away with" what they have done. Forgiving the unrepentant runs the risk of failing to give due regard to the trauma, brokenness, injustice, and sense of violation that can arise from having been wronged. Anecdotally, many who apparently "forgive" the wrongs of unrepentant wrongdoers often find they have to revisit the supposed forgiveness they have offered, or subconsciously deny to themselves that they still bear anger and resentment towards the wrongdoer. In short, forgiving the unrepentant asks too little of wrongdoers and too much of victims.

Of course, with the minor "knocks" of life, it is often best to do the equivalent of shrugging one's shoulders, to let go of one's anger and resentment, and to move on. Such a response is not forgiveness, in the true sense of the way the New Testament intends the term; it is more like forgetting, an idea expressed well in other contexts (but never in relation to forgiveness) by the New Testament words *epilanthanomai* (to overlook, forget) and *lanthanomai* (to forget). The same approach may even be appropriate of other hurts that do not have life-changing consequences. But when it comes to what Stephen Cherry calls "shattering" hurt, that is, harm that "undermines the health, integrity or identity of the victim,"[1] tolerating, overlooking, or forgetting the wrongdoing is neither possible nor pastorally wise, and not holding the wrongdoer to account overlooks the part that justice and fairness have in wholesome human relationships.

Transformational Forgiveness as Evangelistic

To understand the true radicalism of forgiveness in its New Testament context, we need first to understand the framework of Jewish thought out of which the New Testament developed. Forgiveness is one kind of response to wrongdoing;[2] there are others. In the context of Jewish and other ancient Near Eastern laws in the period of the Old Testament, the typical response to wrongdoing is not to forgive but to exercise a

1. Cherry, *Healing Agony*, 19.
2. Bash, *Forgiveness and Christian Ethics*, 1.

measured right to retribution or retaliation. The retaliation can be "an eye for an eye, a tooth for a tooth,"[3] but no more. Forgiving one's neighbor for wrongdoing is neither celebrated as a moral good nor commanded by God.

As Jewish theology developed, a new approach to responding to wrongdoing emerged. We see from Matt 18:21 evidence of an established practice of interpersonal forgiveness among the Jews in the time of Jesus: Peter quotes an existing, and presumably well-established, tradition that victims should forgive those who wronged them up to seven times. An earlier record of the new approach is in the deuterocanonical book, Sirach (ca. 196–175 BCE): Sirach says that anyone desiring God's forgiveness must first show forgiveness to personal enemies (28:2–5).

Jesus developed these new patterns of thought about interpersonal forgiveness and explained them with new clarity in the parable of the unforgiving servant (Matt 18:21–35). He does this in response to Peter's question about how many times a person should forgive a wrongdoer. Jesus illustrated that forgiving others is the result of an experience of the transformational grace of God and, unlike in the tradition quoted by Peter in Matt 18:21, he insisted that forgiveness is to be offered lavishly and without limit.[4]

In the parable, a servant owes his master 10,000[5] talents, an impossibly and absurdly large sum. Though the servant offers to repay the sum, the master decides to waive it. He "releases"[6] the servant and "forgives" the debt. Shortly after, the forgiven servant meets a colleague who owes him, the forgiven servant, a relatively small sum. The forgiven servant refuses to postpone payment of his colleague's debt. When the master of the two servants hears that the forgiven servant has refused to postpone

3. As in Exod 21:23–25 and Lev 24:19–21, in the Old Testament, and in the Code of Hammurabi, a Babylonian code of law dated ca. 1754 BCE. In the case of the Code of Hammurabi (and unlike in the Old Testament), the severity of a penalty sometimes depended on the social status and gender of the offender and the victim.

4. The Greek is ambiguous about the number of times forgiveness is to be offered. The Greek could mean forgiveness should be offered seventy-seven times or 490 times. The point is that the offer must be lavish and (in effect) without limit.

5. The word for 10,000 is *murioi*, the largest numerical unit in Greek arithmetic, perhaps corresponding to what people today might mean by "trillion." The word is used in secular Greek of countless numbers.

6. This is the word that is translated "forgive" in Luke 6:37. It occurs in this sense only once in the New Testament. Etymologically it is made up from two components and means to "loose [something] from [someone or something]."

repayment of the debt, the master berates the forgiven servant for his lack of mercy and the master not only reinstates the original debt but also inflicts dire punishment on the unforgiving servant.

The parable points to the nature of forgiveness as it is understood in the Gospels and probably in its earlier, intertestamental setting. The word for forgiveness that is used both in Sirach 28:2–5, in Peter's question in Matt 28:21, and about the cancellation of the debt in Matt 28:27, 32 are forms of the verb *aphiēmi*.[7] The word is a compound of *apo* (which means "from") and a verb, *hiēmi*, which means "release, let go, send."[8] When the word is used of debts, it refers to the right of the victim to choose to forgo the right to repayment of money owed. When *aphiēmi* means "to forgive" in an interpersonal setting in the Gospels, I suggest it points to a victim choosing to forgo the right to retribution and revenge. In other words, in the context of both debt and forgiveness, people forgo the right to exact something (money, in the case of a debt, or retribution, in the case of wrongdoing) to which they are entitled. Seen this way, it becomes obvious that the forgiveness the parable seeks to explicate is different from what people mean by "forgiveness" in the contemporary period, as this latter sort of forgiveness is not usually set in contrast with revenge and retribution.

The second point to note is that forgiveness, if properly received, is transformational: it is regenerative and life-changing, causing those who are forgiven to reframe their outlook and behavior so profoundly that they are transformed into forgivers by nature and outlook, giving what they have received. It is palpably absurd to be unchanged by the waiver of a debt that is the equivalent of a trillion dollars, and if one is unchanged by such a gift, we can say that such a person will have accepted the gift but not the grace with which it comes. To put it in modern terms, forgiveness should be *transformational*, changing the recipient, and not *transactional*, like receiving the benefit that comes, for example, from handing over money to buy a loaf of bread or a jar of honey.

This interpretive approach now explains why Jesus says, in the Lord's Prayer, that people are to pray, "Forgive us our debts, as we forgive our debtors" (Matt 6:12) and "Forgive us our sins, for we ourselves

7. This is the characteristic verb in the Gospels to describe (among other things) the action of forgiving. The word is in widespread use in Greek and usually means "to leave, let go, permit, allow."

8. *Hiēmi* occurs in the New Testament in other compounds with the prepositions *syn-*, *kath-*, *ana-*, and *para-*.

also forgive all who are indebted to us" (Luke 11:4). Despite what people think, divine forgiveness is not contingent on antecedent personal forgiveness (whether of sins or debts); rather, the people Jesus speaks to and urges to pray are Jewish and *already* the recipients of divine love and the grace of God's forgiveness. Their forgiveness of others is evidence of their transformational experience of God's forgiveness, and so they rightly can point to their own practice of forgiveness as the basis of their petitions for forgiveness. It is not that they are asking for the forgiveness they have not already received or that they are afraid of losing the forgiveness God has given them. Rather, it is a prayer—perhaps even a celebration—that their present practice of forgiving others is the ground of their certainty that God *is* a forgiving God and that they *have* been forgiven. Were God not a forgiving God, and were they not forgiven, they would not have had the grace to forgive others.[9]

For all these reasons, the practice of interpersonal forgiveness—in the sense that one renounces revenge, retribution, and retaliation, as well as the emotions that go with them—is constitutive of what it means to be a recipient of the forgiving grace of God. It is a form of behavior that is a defining identity marker of someone who has experienced the grace of God. Just as "We love because God first loved us" (1 John 4:19), so we might now also want to say, "We forgive, because God first forgave us." In these senses, to forgive is a profoundly evangelistic act, for it incarnates God's forgiveness in interpersonal relationships: the watching world can see a model of the love and transformative power of God's forgiveness that the forgiver has already received. Perhaps we can go so far to say that an unforgiving Christian is an oxymoron, impossible, and even absurd because to be such is to not to have been transformed by the irresistible power of God's forgiveness.

Of course, forgiveness is not straightforward or easy, and there are many people who, though they have experienced the forgiving grace of God, are nevertheless so battered and broken by their experiences of hurt that forgiveness is a long process effected—sometimes incompletely— over many years. Glib talk of forgiveness to such people is folly, but they may still recognize the need to forgive, and perhaps eventually be able to say (to adapt Mark 9:24), "I do forgive—but help me to overcome my unforgiveness." Stephen Cherry traces the journey that such people can make in *Healing Agony*—and recognizes that the journey is never easy.

9. I am not suggesting that only those who have experienced the grace of divine forgiveness can forgive others!

The journey of forgiveness may be likened to peeling off the layers of an onion. There are many aspects to hurts, and we may think we have dealt with the hurt we have experienced, only to realize later that there are more aspects to the hurt. Without wanting to make light of some of the dreadful hurts people face, the following illustration may help to make the point. Some years ago, I was one of two candidates interviewed for a job. Very quickly at the interview for the job, it became apparent to me that I was not the preferred the candidate and the interviewers had made up their minds whom they wished to appoint, well before the interview itself. I felt used, angry, upset, and treated unjustly. I thought I had dealt with the hurt until, two years later, I met the chair of the interview panel at a social event. I felt my anger and resentment return, and I found it difficult to be in a social setting with the chair of the panel. Meeting him made me realize that there were aspects to what I had experienced that I had not addressed or dealt with.

Ecclesial Forgiveness as Evangelistic

In Paul's thought we see the same rationale for interpersonal forgiveness that we saw above. The pattern is (to put it simplistically), "You have been forgiven, so forgive others." In Eph 4:32, for example, Paul urges the Ephesians to forgive one another "as God in Christ forgave you." We also see same pattern in Col 2:13 and 3:13.

Paul writes relatively little about forgiveness and he tends not to use the verb *aphiēmi* or the cognate noun, *aphesis*. So, in Eph 4:32 and Col 2:13, 3:13, for example, he does not. This is probably because these words do not adequately express what Paul means by forgiveness and the underlying rationale of forgiveness as he understands it.

We know that the center of Paul's theology is justification, with an emphasis on what John Barclay calls God's gift of "unconditioned grace."[10] Of course, forgiveness is implicit in what Paul means by being justified, as Paul himself recognizes in Rom 4:7–8. For Paul, justification is a gift of grace (*charis*), and the pattern of his thought is that as people have received God's *charis*, so in their relations with others, they are to show *charis*—an action expressed by the verb *charizomai*, a verb that describes the action of giving, being gracious to, or giving gifts to others.[11]

---

10. Barclay, *Paul and the Gift*, 391.
11. The verb can also be used of cancelling a debt (Luke 7:42–43).

In the context of the New Testament, *charizomai* is sometimes translated as "forgive," a new meaning for the word at the time. When *charizomai* is translated this way, it often refers to God's gift of forgiveness that its recipients are themselves to enact in interpersonal relations, typically (but not always) in a context of community relations in churches. So, in 2 Cor 2:7, 10 Paul refers to the forgiveness he and the Corinthians are to offer to an offender whose wrongs seem to have affected the whole church community. In Eph 4:32, forgiveness is included with kindness and tenderheartedness as typical of community-building and community-enhancing virtues. In Col 3:13, Paul stresses the importance of forgiveness—as well as other virtues, such as love, compassion, thankfulness—for the good of the unity and harmony of the "one body" that is the church community (Col 3:15). In short, the graciousness Paul expects people to show in the community-setting of the church is expressed through virtues to do with forgiveness, patience, longsuffering, and kindness towards others. It is therefore perhaps only a modest exaggeration to say that in many of the places where Paul uses the word *charizomai*, what is uppermost in his mind is not so much interpersonal forgiveness between two individuals, a wrongdoer and a victim, as individuals being gracious, generous, and lavish in their relations with other people.

What we can also say is that the Pauline ethic of forgiveness is the result of Paul's own experience of unconditioned grace that leads him to rethink for diaspora churches what in other contexts might be thought of as some aspects of Greek virtue ethics. Christian communities are to model the grace of God that its members have experienced in justification.

Understood in this framework, forgiveness is an example of the grace of the gospel incarnated in the context of the way people live and worship in a community together. Those who see Christians together should see an enactment and model of the gospel in day-to-day living. Forgiveness is part of what builds loving, peaceful communities, authenticates the message of the gospel, and demonstrates the transformative power of God's grace in human relationships. It also models the message of the gospel, and proclaims and confirms the reality and power of God's grace in communities which, because they have been transformed by God's grace, are distinctively different from other communities or associations.

Eschatological Forgiveness as Evangelistic

In Luke's account of Jesus's rejection at Nazareth (Luke 4:16–30), Jesus read from Isa 61:1–2 and in verse 21 says that Isaiah's words "have been fulfilled" in the hearing of his listeners. By this, Jesus indicates that the *eschaton*, the period of the last days as well as the end of time, begins with his coming and ministry. Commentators have long noticed that the words Jesus quotes provide many of the recurring themes in the Gospel of Luke and in the second volume of Luke's writings, Acts.

Often not much commented on is the word *aphesis*, the cognate noun from the verb *aphiēmi*, that occurs in the words from Isaiah that Jesus quotes. *Aphesis* is translated "release" in the phrase "release to the captives" and "set free" in the phrase usually translated as "to set free the oppressed"[12] in Luke 4:18. The ideas that *aphesis* are intended to communicate are freedom and release. These ideas are set in the context of coming of the kingdom of God. The kingdom, still set alongside the present order of reality that one day will be superseded, will bring freedom and release from injustice and oppression in the many different forms, literal and metaphorical, that injustice and freedom take.

Understood in this framework and context, the meaning and scope of the word *aphesis*, which is sometimes elsewhere translated "forgiveness," take on new significance. True, *aphesis* does refer to forgiveness as an ethic of interpersonal relations; it also refers to a categorically different type of existence in the kingdom of God—a category of existence that is without the oppression, suffering, poverty, and cruelty that characterize so much of human society without Jesus and outside the kingdom of God.

For these reasons and set in this context, to forgive another person is to act in a way that proclaims and models the ethics of the kingdom of God. It is more than simply to choose not to seek retribution and revenge. It is to model as well as to give a foretaste of God's loving initiative with sinners. It is to offer a recreative opportunity to put the past behind and to begin a different future without oppression and injustice. If we give *aphesis* to people, we are helping them to experience what the kingdom of God is like and in small measure giving them a preview of and insight into God's greater *aphesis* that will be established at the consummation of the *eschaton*. I now like to call such ministry "aphetic" to highlight how striving for forgiveness, release, and freedom for others in our actions

12. The phrase is literally, "to send away the oppressed in (or 'by') release."

and thoughts is an essential part of what it means to live out and practice the ethics of the kingdom of God.

In Closing

Surprisingly, examples of forgiveness are hard to give because forgiveness usually heals and puts right fractured relationships. We tend to forget quickly former hurts after forgiveness, for the narrative of life continues to be rewritten and we make new memories. The words, "I'm sorry," especially if they are coupled with remorse and with appropriate acts of restitution, can have what seem to be miraculous effects. You will probably be able to call to mind such examples of healing forgiveness.

Sadly, and I suspect more easily, you will also be able to call to mind examples of unforgiveness—and the rupture to relationships that unforgiveness brings. It is sometimes said of bereaved people that they must do their "grief work" if they are to experience healing from their loss. In many ways, unforgiveness is like grief, and so unforgiving people must do their "forgiveness work" if they are to experience healing in their relationships.

I am writing these words during the coronavirus pandemic, and I can give an example of what I mean. Almost daily I hear or read about people whose lives are polluted by the unforgiven and unresolved wrongs of the past that resurface in the close-knit experience of living together in the "lockdown" period. We may bury or ignore our unforgiveness, but it does not go away. Likewise, we can ignore the effects on others of the wrongs we have done, but the effects of those wrongs will continue to be felt in our relationships until we put right the wrongs.

The Anglican Church therefore needs to be more alert to the importance of interpersonal forgiveness, and not treat it in its liturgy as an adjunct to divine forgiveness. Dire consequences await those who do not forgive others (Matt 18:35), as interpersonal and divine forgiveness stand in a reciprocal relationship (Matt 6:12, 14–15 and Mark 11:26).

Forgiveness is much more than an interpersonal ethic, wonderfully attractive and important though that ethic is. Forgiving others is one of the identity-markers of those who live out the ethics of the kingdom of God (e.g. Matt 18:23), for thereby they practice *aphesis*—release and freedom not only for themselves but also for the recipients of their forgiveness as well as the communities of which forgiven people are members.

Forgiveness is also a practical outworking of the grace of God's greater *aphesis* that will mean freedom from oppression, injustice, and suffering. To forgive and be forgiven is to experience the kingdom of God in the present. The grace that justifies people transforms them so that they have grace for *aphesis* in their relationships and communities. To forgive is to model and thereby proclaim the *aphesis* of the gospel for salvation, ecclesiology, and eschatology, that is, for the whole range of Christian experience, both in the present and in the future. There is no lived-out gospel without "aphetic ministry." To adapt Archbishop Tutu's famous book title, there is "no gospel without forgiveness."[13]

Bibliography

Barclay, John. *Paul and the Gift*. Grand Rapids: Eerdmans, 2015.
Bash, Anthony. *Forgiveness and Christian Ethics*. Cambridge: Cambridge University Press, 2007.
———. *Remorse: A Christian Perspective*. Eugene, OR: Cascade, 2020.
Cherry, Stephen. *Healing Agony: Re-Imagining Forgiveness*. London: Continuum, 2012.
Tutu, Desmond. *No Future without Forgiveness*. London: Rider, 2000.

13. Tutu's book title is *No Future without Forgiveness*.

Obedient to the Earth

Learning Humility from the Humus

RAGAN SUTTERFIELD

ON SUMMER DAYS, WHEN the heat settles like a blanket and even the mornings bring sweat, my garden sprawls in raucous rebellion. In the spring the beds were nicely bordered, the plants laid out in neat patterns, all well mulched. Even the edges of my lawn that I leave intentionally wild, seemed tame, prairie fleabane hosting skippers, delicate grasses pushing up beneath the elderberries. But by late June and on through September, it all falls into a messy mix of growth and weeds and pledges to mulch more next year, to get out and fight the Bermuda grass before it gets the best of me once again.

Still, as I take my hori hori, a small Japanese tool, out among the plants, digging here and there in the soil, my feet bare upon the mulched ground, I feel a peace and acquiescence—a remembrance that though I tended this garden and planted much of it, its life is beyond me. I can only serve it and keep it, as best I can.

When I am in my garden, my blood pressure lowers. I feel happier the more time I spend with humus. There are many reasons for this, but among them is what is in the soil itself. Amid the myriad microbes, the billion or so creatures found in a small handful of garden soil, are organisms like *Myobacterium vaccae*, a bacterial strain that has been shown to

act as an effective antidepressant. Its presence in the body releases sero-
tonin—flooding my brain with the same sense of happy contentment that
comes with any good pleasure.

If a natural high from digging in the dirt weren't enough, the soil
also contains organisms that help maintain healthy skin. A company
capitalizing on these bacteria calls itself "Mother Dirt." You can buy a 100
ml bottle for $49 or work in your garden and hold off on a shower.

These soil microbes reflect the larger reality that any human life is
intertwined with the earth, living from it, dependent upon it, and one
day returning to it. If we want to get at the truth of who we are as human
beings, beginning with the humus would be a good start.

To seek the truth about who we are is at the heart of the virtue of
humility. And that truth is not a wide-ranging search, but a return—a
living into the fact that human life is humus life; that if we are to find our
fullness we must go down toward the soil.

This reality is found in the very etymology of our being. Human
comes from humus—we are literally earthlings and humility is that path
whereby we come close to the earth. Such a connection does not only
belong to those languages that draw on an Indo-European root. Hebrew
makes the same link between the *adam*, the human, who is formed from
the *adamah*, the humus soil. These words come from people who knew
our basic truth—from earth we come and to earth we will return.

But such truth can be hard to take. We have, from the beginning,
been in rebellion against our humanity, our soil-bound lives. From the
ziggurat of Babel to the infinite life-extension projects of Google, we have
sought to be more than human, more than lives rooted in the earth. We
have continued the rebellious search to transcend our earthbound lives
and become "as gods" and it is manifest in our world through everything
from the creation of "whiteness" to the reduction of creation to "resources." We need to live into the truth of who we are and that life is what the
Christian tradition has called humility. Our forgetting of this virtue is the
forgetting of our truth.

Part of our difficulty with humility is that we have come to understand it as a virtue for those who are not also brave, or strong, or
bold. When we think of humility we do not typically think of life lived in
fullness. Think of a humble person, and most likely the image provided
from the storehouse of culture will be someone who doesn't stand up for
themselves or anyone else, someone who goes about afraid of stepping

on toes, someone who willingly gets stepped on themselves—a doormat. We needn't join in Nietzsche's assessment that humility is one among the perverse virtues of Christianity that elevates the low and lowers the strong to think that humility does not belong among those other more easily promoted Christian goods such as love, kindness, and joy.

Our non-Christian forebears in the Greek and Roman worlds valued such things as love and kindness and joy, they valued generosity and self-control, but humility was absent from their goods. As Alasdair MacIntyre wrote in *After Virtue*, "humility . . . could appear in *no* Greek list of the virtues."[1] Humility is a uniquely Christian contribution to Western values. It belongs to the great reversal that is at the heart of Jesus's teachings—the death that turns to life, the going down in order to rise again.

If we are going to reclaim humility for our time, freeing it from its misrepresentation and returning it to its place as a key stance of Christian life, then we should return humility to Christ, who even Nietzsche had to admit was a powerful figure, someone who was no doormat, someone who appeared on the scene of human life with such decisiveness that people were divided about who he was as if by the strike of a sword. If Jesus is the ultimate embodiment of humility then a humble person is one who looks a lot like Jesus—a person dedicated to living in the truth, no matter the cost.

And what is that truth? I think that perhaps the best way to understand Jesus is to see him as St. Paul and St. Athanasius both clearly saw him: Jesus Christ is the new Adam, the reiteration of what a human life is to be. As Athanasius puts it, "You know what happens when a portrait that has been painted on a panel becomes obliterated through external stains. The artist does not throw away the panel, but the subject of the portrait has to come and sit for it again, and then the likeness is re-drawn on the same material. Even so was it with the All-holy Son of God."[2]

To fully understand how Christ can be the new Adam we must take a look back at the old Adam—the model upon which we must shape our vision of Christ and of the humble path toward wholeness that Jesus modeled for humanity. As we've already said, Adam is the one who is formed from the *adamah*—a mix of earth and divine breath. As such, Adam shares a certain form of life with all other animals—literally the

---

1. MacIntyre, *After Virtue*, 136.
2. Athanasius, *On the Incarnation*, §14.

spirited/breathing ones—those creatures who are made of soil and share in God's breath.

The biblical story of humanity's beginnings use two words to describe our relationship with the soil: *adamah* and *afar*. *Adamah* is what we would call humus, compost—the living and life-giving soil of the earth. Modern soil ecology has seen what the ancient authors knew without the use of microscopes, that the kind of soil that is good for growing new life is that which is full of living, breathing creatures, and made from the organic matter of what were once living plants and animals. In fact, soil biology is a greater determining factor for the life-giving potential of soil than its chemical makeup. Most soils in fact have the basic chemistry necessary for plant growth and health. The problem, more often than not, is that those nutrients are not available for the plant. It takes microbes such as bacteria and fungi to break down the nutrients in the surrounding material and make it available for growth. Soil is the earth that is rich in this teaming and varied life.

Not all earth, however, is rich in soil biology. It was no surprise to the Yahwist that much of the ground could bear no life. To this dead earth the biblical writers gave the name dust—*afar*. "All of these look to you, in due season O LORD, you send forth your breath and they are created, when you withdraw your breath, they return to their dust," writes the Psalmist. Adam, after the fall, becomes one who will turn to dust—he has become alienated from the breathing ground, the living soil of *adamah*. To lose this relationship to the earth, to the full and true source of who he is as a creature, reflects a loss of contact with the animating reality of it all—God whose breath brings life. To be an *adam*, to be a human being, is to be a creature who needs and relies on God's breath. When the *adam* (human) is alienated from this breath the *adamah* (humus) turns into the *afar* (dust).

Such a transformation is at play throughout the world where living soil is rapidly being transformed into dust. It is among our most difficult challenges. Because human society is living in rebellion against the truth that we are creatures, we are cutting off the breath by which all creation is sustained and so the world's soils are dying. "Cursed is the ground because of you," has become a fact of human life upon this planet. It is especially present in what ecologists call desertification, the process through which soil dies because of various abuses, from overgrazing to ploughing. Once the soil has died, it is difficult to restore it so that it can give life again. And because soil life is itself a complex interplay of relationships with plants and animals, the death of the soil is combined with a more generalized death of whole ecosystems. The ecosystems of the world which are entangled with the lives of humans (*adam*) who have turned toward dust (*afar*) is a world that is also turning toward dust. This is why we need a new way, a new example of how to be an *adam*, someone who can help us recover our relationship with the living breath of God and usher in the reanimation of the world.

This new Adam is Jesus Christ, who becomes enfleshed with what Paul calls the "dusty body" of Adam, but brings to that body the Spirit or Divine Breath that comes from God (See 1 Cor 15:42–49). This path of the Divine Breath entering into the dust of the earth and giving life can be seen as a return of the Spirit of God to the ground, once again making it living, once again making it fruitful for more life. But this time the breath is more than simply an animating presence—now it is a breath of life that brings all who share in it into the life of God. We move from the merely animating breath of life and into the empowering breath of the Holy Spirit.

The journey that Jesus takes toward inhabiting the dust and reviving it is the path of humility that is so beautifully put to verse in the "Kenosis Hymn" of Philippians 2. There Christ Jesus is shown as one who is equal to God and yet went down, humbling himself, aligning his life with the powerless and disinherited people of the dust. But it was through such a descent that Christ is now elevated, and it is through such a descent that we also now can go down in order to go up into the full flourishing of our personhood. But in order to do that we must "have the same mind that was in Christ Jesus." We must learn to live into the way of humility so that our lives can be renewed into the fullness of what human life was always supposed to be.

Fr. Nivard Kinsella defined humility as "nothing more or less than the attitude of the creature in the presence of his Creator, and the way of acting which results from such an attitude."[3] This is something very different from a groveling servitude, but it carries with it a call toward a form of life that is alien to so much of our current human situation. We are far more familiar, as Bernard of Clairvaux rightly remarked, with pride than we are with humility. This means that we are more familiar with an alienation from our nature as creatures than we are with a life lived in the full embrace of our dependence. Rowan Williams once wrote

3. In Bernard, *How to Become a Saint*, 37.

that "being a creature is in danger of becoming a lost art."[4] Yes, now more than ever, but it has been in danger since Adam. It has been lost since the time that ploughs first cut into the life-giving ground and began their onslaught of the soil, turning it from life to dust.

So how do we cultivate a humility that enables us to live as creatures? How do we return our humanity to its roots in the humus by following Christ's humble example? The answers are varied, but among them I think we should include a new spiritual discipline of soil—cultivating it, working with it, living from it, spending time bent near it. When we attend to the soil and submit ourselves to its schooling, we will begin to learn the necessary humility that will help us live as creatures once again. And when we turn as creatures to our Creator, acting in full dependence upon God, then we will start to truly and fully live human lives.

It can be difficult to know where to begin practicing such humility. There is certainly much that can go wrong if the virtue is taken up without the proper orientation. No one has been more influential in defining the practice of humility than St. Benedict of Nursia, whose twelve-rung "ladder of humility" has served as the starting point for everyone from Thomas Aquinas to Bonaventure to Joan Chittister. Among his many steps, Benedict often returns to the importance of obedience for the humble life—several steps could really be subcategories of this one important practice. We might think this convenient for an abbot of a monastery and much of the practice Benedict outlines is meant for such a context, but I think Benedict is right that learning obedience is one of the first aspects of learning to be humble. In the great hymn of Philippians 2 it is Christ's obedience that is the mark of his humility for it was through obedience that he entered into solidarity with humanity. For my part, this obedience is learned not in the monastery but in my garden—the small urban lot that is my yard.

A couple of years ago now I sat in a stuffy classroom on the top floor of the Episcopal church where I serve as a priest, with a mix of urban gardeners, church members, clowns (seriously, though not in costume), and activists. We were all taking part in a ten-day, seventy-two-hour permaculture design course. Our teacher, the one who had attracted such a diverse group, was a permaculturalist named Chris Grataski. Chris is one of those rare people who can talk about gender theory and its theological implications and then give some really good advice on how to cultivate

4. In Wirzba, *The Paradise of God*, 15.

the soil microbes surrounding your tomato plants. He's a farmer philoso-pher with a deep passion for social justice. Most of us in the room had come to learn permaculture from him because we wanted a vision for healing the world that involved both compost and compassion.

Permaculture is a somewhat nebulous concept but, to put it simply, it is a form of human interaction with the landscape that seeks to create a diverse and flourishing human habitat that works with and sustains the local ecosystem. It is marked by a very different way of interacting with land than is typical, even in what is now called sustainable agricul-ture. While sustainable agriculture might approach a pest problem, for instance, with the question of what kind of organic pesticide we could use to control it, permaculture would instead ask, why is this pest here? Is there an imbalance in the soil that is inviting pests to feasts on vulnerable plants? What are the natural predators of this pest? How can I attract them? As one designer has said, you shouldn't say "I have a slug problem" but rather "I am missing ducks from my system." With ducks, the slugs will be turned to eggs, another source of food and life for the farm.

Permaculture, at its best, is a kind of obedience. Many permacul-turalists say, for instance, that before doing anything to a landscape you should observe it for a year. Attention of this kind requires a great deal of patience. While I often want to mold the landscape to my desires, I am asked instead to learn from it, to have the land be my teacher. In doing so I enter into a kind of ecological catechesis. The questions answered in such a catechesis are varied, and as with the best education, many of them only push toward new questions. Some of these questions are: Who lived here before me, both myself and my ancestors? What was this place in geological time? If no humans were here what would grow here? Who would be the primary creatures forming this place? Whose bodies lie in this soil and give it life? What damage has been done here? What healing can happen here?

To sit with these questions in my own place, my yard and neighbor-hood and on into the larger watershed that forms the ecological com-munity of my place, I am enabled to be "put in my place." And this is where the best obedience begins. To be put in one's place must not be a violent act of the kind exercised by those who step out of their own place in order to seize idolatrous authority (as in patriarchy, whiteness, authoritarianism of all kinds). Rather, the placing found in humility is an invitation into a relationship of fitting; a welcome into the community in which we find our wholeness. Humility is that virtue by which we find

our humanity, discovering that in being human we are not alone as atom-
ized individuals the way the modern state and corporation would have
us believe we are, but we are rather always already members of a creation
of which we are a part and upon which we are dependent. To possess the
virtue of humility is to live in the realization of this truth, a truth that
includes our ultimate dependence upon God.

In my garden I learn the lesson that I am not alone, that my power
is limited and my ignorance vast. The more I learn about soil ecology the
more I learn that what makes soil good and life-giving is the community
of life within it. This community, as I pointed out in the opening, is also
deeply tied in with the human body. We are made up of more living cells
that do not properly belong to "us" than those that do. More than 0.3%
of your body weight is made up of the cells of bacteria that live throughout your anatomy. Of the cells in your body, at least half belong to non-
human organisms at a ratio of 1.3 (bacterial) to 1(human). These facts,
and the necessary functions those "other" organisms provide, call into
question the very idea of our individual bodies. What they remind us of
is that, just as Paul well knew, the body is made of many members—we
are never healthy or whole alone.

Humility, a life oriented toward the ground, keeps us in the presence
of that truth. When we remember that we are but dust, we know that
without the varied whole of creation our lives will never support growth;
without breathing in God's presence, we will never return that breath into
the great exchange of life. If we hope for any healing in our world then
humility must be our way—the downward path toward our truth, the site
of death and decay that is transformed into the soil of all life.

Yesterday evening, after the summer sun had begun its westward
descent and the ground began to cool, I worked in my garden, pulling
weeds, harvesting fruit, tilling and keeping this garden in some nod to
the original human vocation. As I pulled the weeds and trimmed some
plants growing beyond their bounds, I put all of the green materials into a
bin to turn to compost. In my harvest, any fruits that were insect-pocked
or damaged, I took inside to feed to the teaming worms that transform
my scraps into soil. As I was putting the tools away from this evening
gardening session, I realized that I had achieved something I'd been seeking. I realized that my life had become oriented toward the soil—its good,
its health, its wholeness. In realizing this I knew better than to think that
I had achieved humility, but I did feel like I was getting closer to something, some truth about who I am as a human being. So it was that I

ended my time in the garden, not proud of my harvest or the abundance of life I'd cultivated there, but thankful for the soil, grateful for what this place is teaching me. Gratitude is its own kind of obedience.

Bibliography

Athanasius. *On the Incarnation.* Translated by a Religious of C.S.M.V. Crestwood, NY: St. Vladimir's, 1998.

Bernard, Jack. *How to Become a Saint: A Beginner's Guide.* Grand Rapids: Brazos, 2007.

MacIntyre, Alisdair. *After Virtue: A Study in Moral Theory.* 3rd ed. South Bend, IN: Notre Dame University Press, 2007.

Wirzba, Norman. *The Paradise of God: Renewing Religion in an Ecological Age.* New York: Oxford University Press, 2003.

II

Impassibility

Jane Williams

GOING TO BOARDING SCHOOL as a small child gave me two important theological insights. It also taught me quite a lot about original sin, but that's another story. The first insight was that God goes with you wherever you go, unlike your parents. It was a first, significant, step into a personal commitment of faith that has needed to be regularly renewed, but has never gone back to being "cultural," merely what I happened to grow up with.

The second insight took longer to articulate, but was none the less deeply felt. Lying sobbing quietly at night in a dormitory full of little girls doing the same, I was, without realizing it at the time, disagreeing with Bonhoeffer that "only a suffering God can help."[1] I was already surrounded by people sharing my suffering and although that offered the consolation of shared desolation, rather than desolation deliberately and personally targeted, it also made it seem as though this was the inevitable reality of the whole world. A suffering God in a world of suffering simply confirms that this is the way things are and always will be.

The two insights were, I now realize, connected. God is not limited by time and space; nor is God limited by emotion. God can simultaneously be fully present with those who weep and those who dance. In my sad and smelly dormitory, it became clear that God could be with both me at boarding school and my parents back at home. Despite all

1. Bonhoeffer, *Letters and Papers from Prison*, 361.

87

appearances to the contrary, there was an abiding connection between us, held safely in the reality of God.

The upshot of my insights was not that God did not care about me. Rather, I came to see that God had resources to draw upon that were greater than mine, like omnipresence, and that gave God a freedom in which I could at least fleetingly participate. God could inhabit both my homesickness and my parents' at-homeness, with equal fullness; God could inhabit sorrow and joy simultaneously. Whichever state each of us was in at the time, the other state had reality, validity, because of God. The other state still existed, even though I might not then be inhabiting it.

God's ability to connect different states of being was most vividly present to me when I read the Bible or heard it read—it was a boarding school run by Christian missionaries in India. I knew that those words were also being read by my parents and read in the little whitewashed church, open at the sides, where they worshipped, as we sat in the dim, Anglican pews at school. This insight was profoundly consoling, because it meant the reality I could not be part of still existed, together with the possibility of inhabiting it again.

It would be some years before I came to see my childhood insights in terms of the theology of God's *impassibility*. When as an adult I began to study theology and read the church fathers, however, the concept instantly resonated, and took me back to the sense of God's freedom and God's resourcefulness as among the key attributes of impassibility. Such insights put me at crosscurrents with streams of contemporary theology. From at least the mid-twentieth century onwards, the tide has been turning against the notion of God's impassibility as a "saving word."[2] Like Bonhoeffer, increasing numbers of theologians argue that a God who does not suffer is an irrelevance. Immensely strong arguments are put forward to suggest that proper attention to the biblical witness demands that Christians speak of the passionate God.

In his classic book, *The Crucified God*, Jürgen Moltmann writes, "When the crucified Jesus is called the 'image of the invisible God,' the meaning is that *this* is God, and God is like *this*. God is not greater than he is in this humiliation. God is not more glorious than he is in this self-surrender. God is not more powerful than he is in this helplessness. God is not more divine than he is in this humanity. The nucleus of everything that Christian theology says about 'God' is to be found in this Christ

2. Richard Bauckham traces this development in an article, "Only the Suffering God Can Help."

event. The Christ event on the cross is a God event."[3] Moltmann's theology is unashamedly a "theology after Auschwitz": "Shattered and broken, the survivors of my generation were returning from camps and hospitals to the lecture room. A theology which did not speak of God in the sight of the one who was abandoned and crucified would have had nothing to say to us then."[4] In an illuminating conversation in the Jerusalem Chamber of Westminster Abbey, Moltmann said that theories of the atonement nearly always seem to be addressed to the needs of the sinner rather than the victim of sin, and that insight lay behind his emphasis in *The Crucified God*.[5] In Moltmann's theology, as in most theologies that defend the passibility of God, the crucified Christ is identified with those broken and rejected by the powerful. God in Christ is in solidarity with victims over against oppressors.

Moltmann's trinitarian theology is explicit in saying that Jesus's suffering on the cross is not "just" human suffering, but is suffering at the heart of the Godhead: "The Son suffers dying, the Father suffers the death of the Son."[6] For Moltmann, suffering cannot be confined to the humanity of Jesus, but lies at the core of the inner-trinitarian relationships. This is who God *is*—the God of suffering love.

Moltmann's emphasis on God's self-identification with the victim and the outcast has been extremely influential in recent theology. James Cone, for example, says, "black theology believes that God's love of humankind is revealed in God's willingness to become black. . . . This means that to love blacks God takes on black oppressed existence, becoming one of us."[7] Moltmann and others therefore believe that impassibility is an alien concept, imported into Christian theology and never fully integrated with it.

The world in which the early church fathers lived, it is argued, had as unexamined aspects of its cultural and intellectual life concepts of the divine as changeless and passionless. The fathers so took these for granted that they could not see that the God of the Bible, the God revealed in Jesus Christ, shattered such abstract notions. Moltmann describes the overriding Christology of the fathers as one that is dictated by a theology

3. Moltmann, *The Crucified God*, 205.

4. Moltmann, *The Crucified God*, 1.

5. Conversation with invited guests, 2 March 2020, Westminster Abbey.

6. Moltmann, *The Crucified God*, 243.

7. Cone, *A Black Theology of Liberation*, 78.

of salvation as participation in the divine life: "The non-transitory and immortal Logos takes mortal, transitory human nature upon himself, so that transitory and mortal human beings may become non-transitory and immortal."[8] This culturally derived concept then overrules a more straightforward reading of the biblical texts. "Attributes are ascribed to the divine nature of Christ which the God of Abraham, Isaac, and Jacob, 'the Father of Jesus Christ,' never knew. His faithfulness is transformed into a substantial immutability, his zeal, his love, his compassion—in short his 'pathos,' his capacity for feeling—are supplanted by the essential apathy of the divine."[9] God can no longer be said to love with passion or to suffer, because of a concept of God that is not innate to the Jewish and Christian scriptures. Richard Bauckham sums up this approach: "It seems increasingly obvious that the Greek philosophical inheritance in traditional theology was adopted without the necessary critical effect of the central Christian insight into the divine nature: the love of God revealed in the cross of Christ."[10]

These critiques of the concept of impassibility need to be taken seriously. In particular, it is vital to note the ways Christian theology has side-lined the voices of marginalized and oppressed people. Churches have done more than simply neglect the powerless—they have actively colluded in maintaining the status quo. If that is what impassibility means—that God is as indifferent to the suffering of the victim as most of us are—then impassibility is clearly a theological tool for the powerful and the comfortable.

It is not clear, however, that the concept of God's impassibility has to be interpreted in this way. Moltmann states, "Were God incapable of suffering . . . then he would also be incapable of love."[11] The words pack a powerful emotional punch, which can divert the attention from the fact that they are not necessarily true. We know that to be true of human beings, but we do not know that it must be true of God, because God is not an object in the universe but the creator and sustainer of all. If we were to change the phrase to something less emotive—"If God is incapable of sleeping, then he is incapable of refreshment," for example, it is easier to see that we have simply extrapolated from human experience to divine.

8. Moltmann, *The Way of Jesus Christ*, 48.

9. Moltmann, *The Way of Jesus Christ*, 53.

10. Bauckham, "Only the Suffering God Can Help," para. 33.

11. Moltmann, *The Crucified God*, 230.

The fathers, whose deliberative work gave us our creeds and our traditional understanding of the characteristics of God, did not think that God had to suffer in order to love. This was not because they had less experience of suffering and horror than modern theologians. Many of the church leaders who gathered at Nicaea in 325 had shepherded their communities through times of severe persecution and torture. Their memories of the arena or the salt mines were still fresh; members of their churches had lost limbs and eyes, to say nothing of family members and property.

The fathers were also dedicated expositors of the Bible, week by week teaching and preaching through the same texts that they are now supposed to have so misunderstood. Nor were they unaware of the problem. Various solutions were suggested, most of which were ruled to be heretical because, ultimately, they threatened the great, non-negotiable insight of the Council of Chalcedon, which is that the life, death, resurrection, and ascension of Jesus is the interaction of the full reality of humanity and the full reality of God, in full and complete co-operative existence, yet neither altering the nature of the other.[12] The Chalcedonian definition insists that humanity and divinity co-exist in Jesus Christ "without confusion, without change, without separation, without division." No third category of being is created here, which is a bit God and a bit human but not really either.

That the Chalcedonian definition is difficult is obvious. Cyril of Alexandria discusses it at some length, emphasizing that the suffering of Jesus truly "belongs" to God, because of the union between humanity and divinity in Jesus, but also that this does not affect God's impassibility.[13] It is possible Cyril's complex argument is simply culturally conditioned, and that he would have done better to abandon the attempt. But it is also possible that Cyril is onto something worth exploring. For one thing, Cyril helpfully reminds us that when we talk about God we always have to remember the limits of our language. Limits do not make our talk about God untrue, rather they make it more mystical than didactic.

The theology of the first few Christian centuries was deeply distasteful to the philosophical culture of the day. The insistence on God's unchanging commitment to the created world, the personal terms in which God is described, the dependence upon the love of God all flow from a

12. The "patripassian" heresy was one such solution: that the Father suffers in the sufferings of Jesus Christ.

13. Cyril of Alexandria, *Scholia on the Incarnation of the Only-Begotten*, para. 36.

Christian theology profoundly shaped by the gospel, and yet committed to the unchangingness of God. God acts but is not acted upon. God cannot be made to be unmerciful, unloving, uncreative, lifeless. God's impassibility is not a negative quality, describing what God is not able to do, but a force of life, describing the reality of God's sheer act.

This theology enables a much stronger apprehension of what the incarnation is for. It is not that God needs to become human in order to share human experience and therefore to understand and empathize. God is the one who creates "out of nothing." There is nothing in all of creation that exists beyond God's comprehension and action. God does not need to go on a fact-finding mission to understand the reality of creation, because God is the one on whom the whole of creation is dependent. John 1:3 says: "All things came into being through him, and without him not one thing came into being"; Colossians 1:16 says, "for in him all things in heaven and on earth were created"; and Hebrews 1:3 says, "he sustains all things by his powerful word." God does not need to become human to fulfil some lack in God. God becomes human for our salvation.

God does not need a human body in order to act in creation. All of creation exists only because of the ongoing creative activity of God. The sobering reality of the Christian doctrine of creation "out of nothing" is that God does not need creation in order to be fully God. Creation adds nothing to God's reality.[14] That remains the case even in the incarnation. God does not become more God, or in any way different because of the union of divine and human in Jesus the Son. As Thomas Weinandy says, "Within the Incarnation, the Son of God never does anything as God."[15] The suffering that Jesus undergoes is fully human suffering, fully owned, inhabited by the Son of God, but not made into a drama about God and God's pain. The "feelings" of God are not changed on the cross, giving God a previously unfelt experience of pain. Something much more wonderful is going on here: God cannot be forced to let go of humanity, even in death and suffering.

What the theology of God's impassibility insists upon is that in the incarnation we see the unchanging action of God. God is impassible because God is love; unbreakable, unalterable, unfailing, never quenched, unassailable even by sin and death. Nothing changes God. All God's other attributes flow from this fundamental reality of God as love.

14. For a full and beautifully clear exposition of the theology of creation from nothing, see McFarland, *From Nothing*.

15. Weinandy, *Does God Suffer?* 205.

This is the logic of divine "simplicity." God is not made up of a competing desires, God is not tossed about by different forces. God is whole, of a piece, utterly full of integrity. Under all circumstances of our encounter with God, God is "impassible": nothing can act upon the love of God to alter it. Before creation, God is Father, Son, and Holy Spirit, an eternal life of love.

All the ways in which God acts towards creation flow from this unchanging nature, and find their fullest exposition in the life, death, resurrection and ascension of the human being Jesus, who is fully embraced by the life of the Son of God. Jesus shows us our created call, destiny, and reality—to be drawn into the fullness of the love of God. The resurrection of the crucified Christ is our assurance that nothing the world of creation holds can undermine the saving action of God. And if it is our eschatological goal to share Christ's risen life, it is also our daily discipleship, not an abstract desire to be like God, but an enfleshed, sacramental reality of the indwelling of the Holy Spirit, enabling us to say "Abba, Father" (Rom 8:15). What we glimpse in the incarnation is the astonishing promise that the divine reality does not decimate the human, and that the human reality has a God-given dignity and purpose. God in Christ tells humanity its story, makes and remakes, creates and recreates, atones, and redeems, impassible to the deathly narrative that humanity tells itself.

A theology of impassibility is, in practice, a much stronger defense of the love of God than one that assumes God must suffer. Moreover, the two theologies are almost certainly doing different things. Moltmann and others are doing what might be called "theodicy": in a world of injustice and suffering, both innocent and culpable, how is it possible to believe in a good and loving God? And of course, it is not wrong to say that the cross is at the heart of any Christian ability to go on believing and trusting in the face of the apparent absence of God.[16] But without a corresponding theology of the impassibility of God, what we are left with is a God who is as broken as we are, rather than what we actually have, which is the God whose love can never be overcome. This is the God who is able and willing to be fully immersed in the terrible reality of the world, to be with us in faithful and transforming power.

It is argued that the theory of impassibility is an improper importation into the Christian belief in God as passionately committed to creation. But perhaps it is also worth examining the cultural norms that

16. Weinandy, *Does God Suffer?* 205.

drive our modern tendency to believe that God has to suffer if God is loving, and to notice their evolution. Bonhoeffer, for example, in the much-quoted passage in which he discusses the suffering of God, appears to be musing about the whole Enlightenment project that increasingly worries the Christian establishment by apparently eroding the necessity for God "as a working hypothesis in morals, politics, or science."[17] Bonhoeffer is exploring the idea of a "world come of age,"[18] in which God refuses to be a kind of fairy godmother for human religiosity, but instead insists on defining God's own character and action.

The *Letters* are tantalizing in drawing us into Bonhoeffer's work in progress, rather than a systematic doctrinal study. But I would argue that only an "impassible" God, one not acted upon by human need and longing, can allow for a humanity "come of age." This is the humanity that is seen in Jesus Christ, fully human, fully co-operating with the action and presence of the divine Son. There is nothing in the nature of God that requires human subservience because there is nothing in the nature of God that needs anything from creation. It is not that God is trying to control and subjugate human beings, but the other way round. Thus, although Bonhoeffer's phrase is frequently cited in defense of a "passible" God, it would appear to be doing a very different theological task, driven by a profound reflection upon a culture that had domesticated God, and whose practice of Christianity might be characterized as an offer of "cheap grace,"[19] requiring no conversion, no repentance, no change of life.

That is not the task most passibilist theologies now undertake. The cultural reflection that drives this neo-orthodoxy is perhaps one that rejects a false and patronizing representation. We are not willing for others to speak on our behalf, if they do not share our experience. This is a profoundly important insight, born out of the centuries in which white, male, well-off European articulation of reality was largely assumed to be the norm, and was assumed to be God's viewpoint, too. "We" can speak on behalf of God. To that extent, there are shared roots with Bonhoeffer's project—human beings are always trying to make God in our own image, and powerful human beings are always trying to impose that image on others, claiming divinely sanctioned authority. Theology needs to repent,

---

17. Bonhoeffer, *Letters and Papers from Prison*, 360.
18. Bonhoeffer, *Letters and Papers from Prison*, 361.
19. Bonhoeffer, *The Cost of Discipleship*, 44.

and make space for diverse voices to speak truly of differing experiences and priorities because otherwise it cannot truly speak of God.

But humanity also needs to be able to speak of God together. Christianity remains unalterably a "metanarrative," speaking with passion of one source and one telos for the human family, even if we are not yet able to tell that story truthfully or with any profound vision of each other's reality and our impoverishment without it. The tone of the human telling of this story has to be one of repentance and greater and greater depth of attention to one another. Passibilist theologies are in danger of undermining this by their apparent assumption that God, too, cannot tell the human story unless and until God experiences it. Such a theology risks being tempted back into making God in our own image, but this time in multiple images. "My" God cannot be the same as "your" God because we are too different; "your" God can only speak about your reality, not mine.

This is a recipe for disaster, theologically. If it is only possible to believe in God if God suffers as I do, if it is only possible to believe in God's love because, like human love, it is vulnerable and responsive, rather than absolute and impassible, then God would need to become incarnate over and over again. It is not logical to assume that the suffering of God on the cross gives God empathy with all human suffering. God does not suffer dementia or childbirth or rape or starvation, therefore, on this showing, God does not know what it is like to be "me." If the point of the incarnation and death of Jesus Christ is to assure us that God knows what it is like to suffer, then surely this is a significant failure on God's part.

And it is an unnecessary failure. God is closer to us than our own breath. God knows us and is with us from our mother's womb. In every instance of suffering and joy, we are sustained only by the breath of God. Every hair of our head is numbered. God knows our coming in and our going out. At the heart of the biblical witness to God is this unfailing certainty of the intimacy and inerrancy of God's love.

The impassibly loving God is the source of hope for those who suffer in a way that a suffering God cannot be. In the omnipresent love of God, the oppressors cannot separate themselves from those they oppress. There is nowhere to flee from God, there is no deed done in darkness that is hidden from God. Moltmann's insight is surely right: that the atonement must act as powerfully for the victim as for the oppressor, but it does so not because God, too, is a victim, but because God's unflinching love raises Jesus from the dead. Human injustice, violence, and hate do not define reality: God does.

The theology of the impassibility of God says that we do not know ourselves, but God does. We battle constantly to make God small enough to serve us, but God moves, with no deviation or distraction, to invite us to be fully ourselves in the body of Christ, our home with God. This is why impassibility is a saving word. It tells us that God is forever for us, with us, loving us with unchanging, purposeful love.

For the five-year-old at boarding school, though she did not know it, God's impassibility was a way into understanding that God is not overwhelmed by human suffering. If God is not defined by suffering and God is the reality of all creation, then suffering is finite, and hope, love, and purpose are not. Jesus is with us as a tangible promise that "nothing can separate us from the love of God in Christ Jesus," even if we are apparently separated from human love. And if human love is a reaction, derived from the love that holds the universe, then that greater love encompasses and mediates the lesser. Then, when my parents were far away, and now that they are dead, still their love is mine, in the love of God.

The concept of God's impassibility is, as the fathers surmised, the best way to talk about the faithful, unbreakable, inexorable love of God. The Bible shows us God's unswerving faithfulness, over and over again. God "remembers" the love and promises made to those long dead—Abraham, Isaac, Jacob, David—but alive in the love of God. This is the active impassibility of God and so it is the source of hope. Violence, hatred, death, and destruction do not force themselves upon God and God's reality, and so they cannot finally dictate our reality, either. God acts to save because God is love, world without end. Amen.

Bibliography

Bauckham, Richard. "Only the Suffering God Can Help: Divine Passibility in Modern Theology." *Themelios* 9.3 (1984), 6–12. https://www.thegospelcoalition.org/themelios/article/only-the-suffering-god-can-help-divine-passibility-in-modern-theology/.

Bonhoeffer, Dietrich. *The Cost of Discipleship.* Edited by Eric Metaxas. New York: Simon and Schuster, 1995.

———. *Letters and Papers from Prison.* London: SCM, 1953.

Cone, James. *A Black Theology of Liberation.* New York: Orbis, 2010.

Cyril of Alexandria. *Scholia on the Incarnation.* http://www.tertullian.org/fathers/cyril_scholia_incarnation_01_text.htm#C35.

McFarland, Ian A. *From Nothing: A Theology of Creation.* Louisville, KY: Westminster John Knox, 2014.

Moltmann, Jürgen. *The Crucified God.* London: SCM, 1974.

———. *The Way of Jesus Christ.* London: SCM, 1990.

Weinandy, Thomas. *Does God Suffer?* Edinburgh: T. & T. Clark, 2000.

Williams, Jane. *Why Does Jesus Have to Die?* London: SPCK, 2016.

12

Lamentable

AMY E. RICHTER

MY HUSBAND JOE AND I walk to the grocery store. Cloth shopping bags hang limp over our shoulders. Mine is imprinted with the Episcopal Church logo, useful swag given to us by the Global Missions department before we came here to Makhanda (formerly known as Grahamstown) in the Eastern Cape of South Africa. Two empty blue plastic five-liter water bottles dangle from my left hand, my fingers laced through their thick white handles. They periodically thunk against each other or against the ones Joe carries, like a tuneless windchime or a randomly tapped drum.

At the Pic'n'Pay, we thread our way through the produce section and baked goods to the back of the store where three clear water tanks the size of hot water heaters are raised on a platform against a black wall. A light above the tanks makes the water sparkle. If there's no line, we can set a jug under each tank's spigot and finish our task quickly. When there is a queue, one of us waits with the empties and our cart while the other gets the other items on our list. There are things here it is a pleasure to buy, foods that at home in the eastern United States are expensive or seasonal or both, but here can be staples: avocados, mangos, pineapples, cashews, butternut squash, and rusks, like a puffier, crunchier version of biscotti and our nightly dessert. But buying water is an uncomfortable habit. I can't shake the feelings I've brought with me from home, that it's extravagant, a giving in to convenience or laziness when I could just fill my own container from the tap.

We started drinking bottled water when we arrived because people warned us that the municipal water wasn't safe for drinking. But not long after our arrival a shortage of water in the area turned into a genuine drought. The municipal supply was periodically shut off, sometimes with a warning ahead of time. Limits were placed on water usage (fifty liters per day per household, sometimes decreased to twenty-five). Charts were posted all over town with guidance on how to allot water for drinking, cooking, flushing, cleaning, bathing. The municipality's website claims that everyone is using way more than each household's limit, but it's common knowledge that the city's infrastructure is crumbling. The pipes leading from the pumps at the reservoir to our faucets were laid in Victorian times and the pumps often need repair. There isn't enough water for daily needs, but water seeps from streets and runs along crumbling curbs.

It was the water source in town, plentiful enough at the time for the British troops, that led John Graham to choose the site as a garrison post in 1812, and, prior to that, presumably had made the place attractive to the Xhosa chief who kept his kraal (cattle enclosure) here. Now, with the population several thousand times bigger, and no substantial rain for months, the reservoirs were almost dry, and the local spring where people could fill containers for free had slowed to a trickle.

With the drought, my feeling odd about buying water gained a patina of virtue. I thought our purchase meant we decreased our use of the municipal water supply. Since we had the means to buy water—at a tiny fraction of what it would cost us in the United States—we were leaving more in the municipal system for the people who couldn't afford it. Until I found out we weren't. A comment on the town resident association's social media page revealed what was probably obvious to others, that our bottled water also came from the municipal supply; it was just purified by a local company before it was sold to us. I had assumed it was shipped in from some other place where springs still flowed and water shortage wasn't an issue. My ignorance about our water matched my ignorance about where most of our consumables originate. Even on a missionary's stipend, I was well off enough not to give it much thought. To the grief I felt about the difficulty the water shortage caused for people, I added shame about my wishful thinking that our purchase of water was somehow helping.

Our walk to the store is downhill. Our walk home with full bags and bottles is uphill. I break a sweat and my heart beats faster. But today

I also get a blow to my gut as a line from the biblical book of Lamentations comes to mind: "We must pay for the water we drink" (5:4). I don't know what makes me think of the verse just then. Maybe it's the weight of the jugs. Maybe it's wishing I could shower when I get home. Something shakes this verse loose in me today. Here is an indication of how bad things are. Here is something worthy of crying out to God: we must pay for the water we drink. The situation in our town is not just hard, not just sad. It is *lamentable*.

The context of Lamentations is the destruction of Jerusalem in 587 BCE. The description is dire, terrifying: the city is in ruins, the people search for bread among fainted and fallen bodies. They contemplate cannibalism. Can our drought, something I'm personally experiencing, be as bad as all that?

I will come to find hope and power in this word "lamentable," but my first reaction is, I don't want any part of it. I have seen the word used as a synonym for "regrettable" or "unfortunate," when people want to express a feeling of resignation about a negative situation. Something has gone wrong, but they don't want to take responsibility or their hands are tied. It's beyond their control. But I've read enough biblical laments to know that "lamentable" is not a shrug of the shoulders, while it is an admission or confession that we are incapable of solving the problem. "Lamentable" is for people who know that only God can help. I don't want to admit that kind of dependency or desperation, even as we trudge past the skinny donkeys who graze in town, who sweep their muzzles across the brown grass that crackles underfoot like frozen snow.

I like thinking that there is something I can do. (Organize a fundraiser. Cut back even further on my consumption. Stop eating foods that need boiling or soaking or rinsing.) I like thinking there is something they should do. (They: government officials, reservoir managers, wasters of water; should do: act, manage, stop.) Linking our water scarce situation and the label "lamentable," at least at first, heightens my fear of being powerless. If this is lamentable, if this is really worthy of lament, this situation is something neither I nor my good ideas for others' actions will fix. It will not change without some serious intervention.

When we get home I look up the verse from Lamentations. Is there anything on the page that would soften the sentiment, or, honestly, distance me from a Bible verse that labels the situation as desperate?

I read the whole chapter, which begins:

> Remember, O LORD, what has befallen us;
> look, and see our disgrace!
> Our inheritance has been turned over to strangers,
> our homes to aliens.
> We have become orphans, fatherless;
> our mothers are like widows.
> We must pay for the water we drink;
> the wood we get must be bought. (Lam 5:1–4 NRSV)

The chapter in which my gut-punch verse is found is a final plea to God to set things right, things like the threat of violence when people are trying to get food (v. 9), the rape of women (v. 11), young men and boys being forced to work (v. 13). Having to pay for water is one part of the larger catastrophe, one whose other horrors are also too familiar. At this moment I can only contend with the water crisis.

I look the passage up in Hebrew, and verse 4 in the original language is no less alarming. A possessive pronoun identifies the water: *our* water we buy. Wait, I think, trying to apply the brakes to the acceleration of my sinking heart. Maybe it is "ours" like I call the glass of water mine to distinguish it from yours on the table. I breathe deeply, then read the passage again. It seems more likely that the people regarded the water as their own possession and now they have to pay someone else to have what is rightfully theirs, theirs by rights. "Our water we must buy." It isn't supposed to be this way. This is lamentable.

I think of the ease I have experienced of getting potable, even temperature-adjusted water straight from the tap, which now seems like a luxury, and realize that during our lifetime, we've always paid something for our water. Someone has to collect it, treat it, pipe it. There's always a bill. I would later read that South Africa and India are the only countries with constitutions that guarantee free water to their citizens. The "Free Basic Water Entitlement" in Section 27 of the South African Constitution guarantees every citizen twenty-five liters of usable water per day or six kiloliters per household per month. The disconnect between what is supposed to be and reality must sting even more for the people who dreamed and worked for this right.

In my life, it's only those times when potable water has not been available, or, perhaps worse, has been toxic that I've thought of some price that's been paid by victims, or should be by perpetrators. I think of the cryptosporidium outbreak in Milwaukee's water, the toxic levels of lead in Flint's water, Baltimore city schools relying on water coolers rather than drinking fountains because of lead pipes. When I think of the people who died, the children who have suffered, those who suffer now, the word "lamentable" begins to burrow into my heart. I soften against its dire weight. I stop resisting. The reservoir of tears opens and flows.

There are people for whom the action of lament is not unfamiliar. There are countless people for whom the cry to God to put things right, for God to hear and remember and intervene, for God to repair the breach between the way things are and the way they ought to be, is, as Brian Blount has preached, "as natural and as regular as the beating of our hearts."[1] Perhaps for such people, my need to reflect on the label "lamentable" would be laughable. But "lamentable" opens my eyes. The tears "lamentable" shakes loose from me remind me of the words of Archbishop Christopher Munzihirwa of Bukavu in Eastern Congo: "there are things that can be seen only by eyes that have cried."[2] The sight "lamentable" makes possible is a first step on the path leading from illusion or aversion and into the particular kind of prayer that is lament.

Lament, in the Bible, is not mere complaint. It's a cry to God to act.[3] Having taken, or been confronted by an unblinking look at reality, we see the disconnect between what *is* and what *should be*. We notice that God's creation has been marred, broken. Present reality is dislocated from God's intention. Rains haven't come. Reservoir levels are dropping. Water needs treating or it is toxic. Governments do nothing. People thirst. Diseases spread. Our water we have to buy.

Lament begins with a cry for God's attention, a plea for God to remember, or to see what we see, or both:

Remember, O Lord, what has befallen us;
    look, and see our disgrace! (Lam 5:1)

I say to God, my rock,
    "Why have you forgotten me?
Why must I walk about mournfully
    because the enemy oppresses me?" (Ps 42:9)

1. Blount, "Breaking Point," 148.

2. In Katongole, *Born from Lament*, 33.

3. On the content and forms of biblical lament, see Westermann, *Praise and Lament in the Psalms*; Brueggemann, "The Costly Loss of Lament"; Hall, "Suffering and Soul Care."

> How long, O Lord? Will you forget me forever?
> How long will you hide your face from me? (Ps 13:1)

The prayer of lament calls God to remember, to see, and to act because we remember who God is and what God has done in the past. Lament Psalms abound with these statements of faith, which serve to remind both God and the ones lamenting of God's steadfast love. For example,

> Answer me, O Lord, for your steadfast love is good;
> according to your abundant mercy, turn to me. (Ps 69:16)

> Yet you are holy,
> enthroned on the praises of Israel.
> In you, our ancestors trusted;
> They trusted, and you delivered them.
> To you they cried, and were saved;
> In you they trusted, and were not put to shame. (Ps 22:4–5)

Just so, in the book of Lamentations, the one lamenting pours out grief, but takes comfort clinging to a creed:

> The thought of my affliction and my homelessness
> is wormwood and gall!
> My soul continually thinks of it
> and is bowed down within me.
> But this I call to mind,
> And therefore I have hope:
> The steadfast love of the Lord never ceases,[4]
> his mercies never come to an end;
> they are new every morning;
> great is your faithfulness.
> "The Lord is my portion," says my soul,
> "therefore I will hope in him." (Lam 3:19–24)

Lament calls to God because God is the one who can address the situation, end suffering. God has in the past. God may do it again.

But the lamenter cries out, because God has not acted yet. So lament feels risky, because it contains a complaint, a challenge to God, an argument: Do something. Be who you are. Unless you no longer care . . .

---

4. The NRSV notes that this is the Syriac Targum's claim. The Hebrew text too is hopeful: "Lord, we are not cut off."

> My tears have been my food
> day and night,
> while people say to me continually,
> "Where is your God?" (Ps 42:3)

Those who lament may even express that their faithfulness is the cause of their torment or that all their faithfulness has gotten them is the scorn of their neighbors:

> All who see me mock at me;
> they make mouths at me, they shake their heads;
> "Commit your cause to the LORD;
> let him deliver—
> let him rescue the one
> in whom he delights!" (Ps 22:7–8)

> Because of you we are being killed all day long,
> and accounted as sheep for the slaughter (Ps 44:22)

Lament demands honesty and what may feel bold, even brazen, in our speech to God. Who am I to complain? Who are we to question God?

Who are we? Lament says we are those who stay in relationship with God rather than plummeting into despair, those convinced of God's presence even when God is silent or hidden. Lamenters are those who have heard the record of God's mighty acts, of God's covenant faithfulness, God's power to save. So we are those who can turn to that same God in prayer that calls into question the goodness and mercy of God. If God is good, why do the faithful suffer? If God is steadfast in mercy, why does our pain continue?

Lament is the prayer of the persistent, the dogged, those who, even though the possibility exists that God will neither remember nor repair, refuse to conclude that God is not God or that God is not good. Those who lament remain in relationship with this God and their prayer reads like a dare for God to prove something. *You are our gracious God. Then act like it. Unless we are wrong about you and you have ceased to be that God.* Therefore they persist in the prayer, proclaiming a confidence that God will respond, act, make right, and prove worthy of glory and praise:

> Consider and answer me, O LORD my God!
> Give light to my eyes, or I will sleep the sleep of death,
> and my enemy will say, "I have prevailed";
> my foes will rejoice because I am shaken.

> But I trusted in your steadfast love;
>   my heart shall rejoice in your salvation.
> I will sing to the LORD,
>   because he has dealt bountifully with me. (Ps 13:3–6)

Lament does not hold back tears, complaints, or confidence that God is the one who can fix things and that God will act.

These are the usual contents of a lament—a cry to God for help, a complaint, a statement of trust in God, praise of God for God's response or future response and remedy. We see these elements in the conclusion of Lamentations, from where my wake-up call came to lament the drought. The ending of the book contains its own mini-lament with most of the familiar components. The writer confesses belief in God's eternal sovereignty:

> But, you, O LORD, reign forever;
>   your throne endures to all generations. (Lam 5:19)

Therefore this is the God who can act, but God so far has not acted and the lamenter returns to the theme of God's apparent amnesia:

> Why have you forgotten us completely?
>   Why have you forsaken us these many days? (Lam 5:20)

The writer makes the book's final plea for God to act and come to people's aid:

> Restore us to yourself, O LORD, that we may be restored;
>   renew our days as of old— (Lam 5:21)

But then, instead of confidence in God's future action or praise for rescue now accomplished, comes the book's stark final verse:

> unless you have utterly rejected us,
>   and are angry with us beyond measure. (Lam 5:22)

The lamenter expresses openness to the possibility that this time, God's rejection is final and there will be no restoration. Maybe just such a bleak statement may rouse God from sleep or amnesia, may turn back God's anger, may summon God to bring those suffering once again into God's healing embrace. The book ends. The lamenter's voice falls silent. Or the lamenter's words and tears are exhausted and the prayer continues in silence. What will God do? We wait.

Lament is a prayer for God to act. But, as with other kinds of prayer, lament acts on the one who prays as well, and this may be the strange alchemy of lament. To cry out to God is to take action. But those who lament also express a new feeling of agency in and through their prayer. Lament engenders new possibilities, not just that God will act, but that neither is the lamenter powerless. Lament "articulates the inarticulate. Tears become ideas," writes Denise Ackerman.[5]

In all this calling upon God to see and remember, our memories and eyes are trained. Lament schools us in proper affections. Do we grieve the right things? Rejoice only in things worthy of rejoicing? Lament is not just calling on God to see, but calling on God to notice that we notice, perhaps what God has known all along. Whether it's our complaint that "our water we must buy" or "the waters have risen up to my neck" (Ps 69:1), we dare to say these things to God because it is godly to pray these things. They are, in fact, lamentable, and not to lament them is to remain blind to reality or lost in delusion, where we will not pray for God to do something new amongst us.

But, in order for new life to spring forth, something must die. Walter Brueggmann writes, "The lament Psalms . . . do their work of helping people to die completely to the old situation, the old possibility, the old false hopes, the old lines of defense and pretense, to say as dramatically as possible, 'That is all over now.'"[6] Something comes to an end, dies, with "lamentable" and that makes room for something new. With defense and pretense stripped away, there can be room for imagination. Perhaps that imagination can include some way to turn copious tears, through the filter of lament, to abundant potable water.

We gather in the Anglican cathedral for an interdenominational prayer service to pray about the drought. It is noon, but the large neogothic stone church, the work of English architects that feels like it belongs and doesn't in this place, is dim and cool. The service is a mix of readings, prayers, and comments. Our prayers are polite, our comments addressed to one another, not so much to God. People test waters, gingerly naming how this present crisis lays bare wounds from Apartheid that haven't yet healed, how much worse this drought is for people who live in the townships on the hill above the cathedral. People say how hard

5. Ackerman, "Mission in the Midst of Suffering," 167.
6. Brueggemann, *Praying the Psalms*, 21.

it is for municipal workers, that there are people who are trying to help, that we can all do our part, that it is good to be together in this place praying for rain. Perhaps all-out lament demands too much vulnerability for this gathering. Can we weep, make demands and risk that God will deny them, and admit that something must die in front of people we don't worship with on other days? Still, this is prayer and we are on our knees with our neighbors. The thin crimson kneeling pad feels like a flat rock, the still cool air like a desert at evening.

The cathedral dean, a gracious and compassionate man who has become a dear friend, told me that this building was constructed on top of the very spring that once attracted the Xhosa chief and the British general. The dean has appealed to a charitable organization to fund a pump to bring the spring water back to the surface and make it once again accessible. The charity's test of the water reveals that it is the only potable water in the downtown area. They agree to move forward with a borehole, a fountain, and a reservoir. But there are challenges: roads will need to be closed and traffic rerouted. The municipality will have to begin a process that typically takes years to complete. The charity gets frustrated with red tape and what they identify as corruption. They leave town.

"Lamentable" is a saving word. It set me on a path of appropriate grief and appropriate crying out to the God who hears our laments. "Lamentable" continues to set me on these paths, as new causes for lament, and familiar, seemingly unshakeable old ones, become apparent to eyes that have cried. "Lamentable" demands over and over again that I give up illusion, ignorance, and false hopes, and learn the humility that comes from knowing I cannot solve these problems on my own; indeed, even together we cannot solve them; God's intervention is required. Why on earth would we try to fix things on our own when God wants to hear our lament? And why, if earth could speak, would earth trust the ones who have caused the problems in the first place?

I need this place to begin. It is lamentable.

Bibliography

Ackerman, Denise. "Mission in the Midst of Suffering: The Bleak Immensity of HIV/ AIDS, a South African Perspective." In *Waging Reconciliation: God's Mission in a Time of Globalization and Crisis*, edited by Ian T. Douglas, 135–70. New York: Church Publishing, 2000.

Blount, Brian. "Breaking Point: A Sermon." In *Lament: Reclaiming Practices in Pulpit, Pew and Public Square*, edited by Sally A. Brown and Patrick D. Miller, 145–53. Louisville, KY: Westminster John Knox, 2007.

Brueggemann, Walter. "The Costly Loss of Lament." *Journal for the Study of the Old Testament* 36 (1986) 57–91.

———. *Praying the Psalms: Engaging Scripture and the Life of the Spirit*. 2nd ed. Eugene OR: Cascade, 2017.

Hall, M. Elizabeth Lewis. "Suffering in God's Presence: The Role of Lament in Transformation." *Journal of Spiritual Formation & Soul Care* 9 (2016) 219–32.

Katongole, Emmanuel. *Born from Lament: The Theology and Politics of Hope in Africa*. Grand Rapids: Eerdmans, 2017.

Westermann, Claus. *Praise and Lament in the Psalms*. Louisville, KY: Westminster John Knox, 1981.

13

Lose Not the Things Eternal

STEPHEN SPENCER

THESE WORDS, BOTH ENCOURAGING and challenging, come from the Collect for the Fourth Sunday after Trinity from the Book of Common Prayer of 1662 (hereafter, BCP):

> O GOD, the protector of all that trust in thee, without whom nothing is strong, nothing is holy: Increase and multiply upon us thy mercy; that, thou being our ruler and guide, we may so pass through things temporal, that we finally *lose not the things eternal*: Grant this, O heavenly Father, for Jesus Christ's sake our Lord. Amen.

I have known the BCP since attending early morning services of "Holy Communion" as a teenager. I remember turning up to a sparsely attended chapel and finding the service both strange and strangely comforting. It was strange because the book, a handy closely printed volume of dense texts and tiny rubrics in italics, with pages and pages of short extracts from the Bible, clearly came from another age. The service itself seemed to be taken from a random selection of pages located somewhere in the middle of the book. It was a pared-down service, beginning in silence with everyone on their knees, followed by an uninterrupted monologue by the priest, composed almost entirely of set text from the book, with no music, no servers, no human interaction apart from a "good morning" at the end. In many ways it was exactly *not* what an act of worship should be for an impressionable teenager.

109

Yet, as I attended the service over a period of time it became strangely comforting. The prefaces and notes revealed how old it was, stretching back behind the emblematic date of 1662 to the reign of Edward VI and specifically to the first edition of the book in 1549, which was broadly Catholic in its theology, and the more radically Protestant edition of 1552. Here was a form of worship that connected the present with the past. While social contact with fellow worshippers was minimal, it felt as if a deeper connection was being forged with generations of Anglicans from the past, so creating a kind of spiritual anchor within the accelerating change of contemporary life. It felt as if the service as a whole, so quiet and spare, as well as so full of words, with layered meanings, was a sacrament of the eternal presence of God, the "things eternal" mentioned by the collect.

This experience was repeated years later, after my ordination training, in which contemporary service books had dominated college worship and church placements. I became a parish priest and found myself responsible for leading early morning Sunday services for longstanding and faithful congregations. The liturgy they used was from the BCP, the edition of 1662 authorized for use in the Church of England, or in Zimbabwe (where I served for five years) from A Book of Common Prayer from the Church of the Province of South Africa of 1954, with a rearranged Communion rite closer to the order of Holy Eucharist I in The Episcopal Church's Book of Common Prayer of 1979.

This time, however, as I was the priest, I had the privilege of speaking the words of the liturgy and of getting to know every rolling sentence and phrase, so suited to be recited "with a loud voice," as instructed by the BCP. The repetition every week allowed the words to become familiar and nourishing and, again, a sense developed of the way they transcended this moment in history and somehow tangibly connected us to previous generations of worshippers in their communion with God and, through that, with "the things eternal."

The way the BCP generates this sense of connection has been very well described by others:

> Cranmer, architect though not exclusive author of the 1549 and 1552 books, can be credited with the extraordinary achievement of expressing a fairly radical Protestant doctrine of dependence upon grace at all points in a language not only weighty and authoritative in itself but also evocative of ancient and medieval piety. Protestant theology is made to speak a dialect deeply rooted

in Greek and Latin liturgy, and so acquires an added depth and seriousness; this, it seems to say, is what the true tradition of the Church has been saying all along.[1]

Now that the Joint Declaration on the Doctrine of Justification has been made between the Lutheran and Roman Catholic Churches,[2] we might adjust the phrase "a fairly radical Protestant" to "a fairly radical Protestant and Catholic doctrine of dependence upon grace," another reason for the BCP's continuing authority.

To return to the collect, then, and to the phrase quoted above, it implies that the things of God, the things eternal, are present and available for all. My experience of BCP worship had shown, in a small but tangible way, that this was true: through handling the book and being part of an act of worship rooted in history I had been connected with previous generations of worshippers and, as the quotation above argues, made some kind of connection with the worship of the early and medieval church. All this lifted me out of the present moment and gave a glimpse of an even bigger dimension, stretching backwards and forwards. In my imagination this then became a kind of sacrament of the reality of God's eternal presence in past, present, and future. The words of the collect and especially the phrase, then, in their affirmation of the truth of this experience, can therefore be described as not only comforting but as saving words.

The phrase, however, is also challenging in at least two ways. There is an interpretative challenge and a personal challenge. The interpretative challenge comes from the way the phrase and, behind it, the collect holds together two propositions about the "temporal," which at a corporate human level can be named as "history" and at an individual level can be named as "the course of our lives." On the one hand, it provides a ringing description of the sovereignty of God over this domain: he is the one who can be a "protector" and "without whom nothing is strong," he is the one who can be "ruler and guide" who can secure for us "the things eternal." On the other hand, the collect implicitly acknowledges that we have the freedom and the capacity to turn away and "lose" those eternal things. By asking God to be our "ruler and guide" (a doubling of words typical of Thomas Cranmer's style) it is acknowledging that we are quite capable of making sure he does *not* rule and guide us.

1. Rowell and Williams, *Love's Redeeming Work*, 10.
2. See https://www.lutheranworld.org/jddj.

The interpretative question is whether this makes sense. Is it possible to hold together these two propositions? How can God be both eternally sovereign over everything and yet allow us to reject and deny that sovereignty? Are we not always bound to end up back in his presence? Here lies a challenge for interpreting the doctrine of the collect.

There is, of course, an extensive literature in philosophical theology on this question. This is not the place to engage with that, but, instead, maintaining the autobiographical thread within these reflections, I will quote one philosophical theologian whom I have studied and written about and who faced this question at several points in his life. William Temple at the end of his life served as Archbishop of Canterbury but at the start of his career he was a philosophy lecturer at Oxford who published several books in this area. The most developed treatment was in his Gifford lectures of 1932–34, *Nature, Man and God*, delivered in Glasgow.[3] As a philosophical theologian influenced by British idealism, which in turn had been influenced by Hegel, the challenge of understanding the relationship of human history with the eternal sovereignty of God was very much to the fore. In the seventeenth lecture on "The Meaning of History" Temple helpfully offers two analogies, different yet complimentary, to understand the relationship. It is important to register that he does not use inclusive language, being typical of his time in this way. He begins with a note of caution:

> In entering on this task let us premise that we do not expect complete success. The essence of the enterprise is that we who are finite are seeking to comprehend the infinite, in order to define its relation to our finite selves. In such an attempt apparent success must be certain failure. Further, our method must be one of analogy and not of demonstration; for the Eternal ever eludes us, and we cannot without certain error form a definition of it which might be the starting-point of logically cogent argumentation. But by analogy we may make progress, and our hope will be that if we reach a stark antinomy, this may arise in regard to that which we know we cannot comprehend, and that at all other points our difficulties may be such as to give way before us even though we never reach their ultimate solution.[4]

3. For an introduction to his life and thought with extracts of his writings, see Spencer, *Christ in All Things: William Temple and His Writings*.

4. Temple, *Nature, Man and God*, 441.

What Temple will offer, then, will depend on the imagination making a reasonable leap from the detail of the analogy to something that, ultimately, is beyond human comprehension.

He then describes how the analogies will help make sense of the relationship between "the complete and all-controlling supremacy of the Eternal" and "the ultimate importance of History and its moral choices," amongst other things. He introduces the first analogy, which is the relationship between the writer of a play ("the dramatist") and the characters and plot of the play itself. He begins by focusing on the second of these and the way they acquire an independence from their creator: "Dramatists have declared that when once they have set their several characters in motion, they have no further control over the conduct of those characters. Indeed in so far as a dramatist creates after the fashion of those poets who apprehend their own thought in the act of expressing it, it must be so."[5] In other words, in great drama the characters shape and form the way they interact with each other and the direction of the play as a whole. This is where the analogy corresponds with real life.

The dramatist, though, remains sovereign:

> Yet in another sense the dramatist retains an absolute control, even to the extent of cutting short the composition and destroying it. His thought, active in self-expression, is immanent in the play; the play is made by it, and apart from it no episode in the play takes place; further, the vitality of every episode comes from the relation of that episode to this thought. Yet the dramatist himself is absolutely transcendent in respect of the play. Upon him it depends whether there shall be a play at all. The play depends upon him for its existence; he does not in that sense depend upon the play at all.[6]

Yet in a deep way he *does* depend on it: "But because his vocation is to be a dramatist, he fulfils his nature by writing plays; if he did not write them he would be untrue to himself. The self-expressing thought through which the play comes into existence is part of the principle of his being. Consequently the play itself, and its content, is of vital consequence to him."[7]

5. Temple, *Nature, Man and God*, 441.
6. Temple, *Nature, Man and God*, 441–42.
7. Temple, *Nature, Man and God*, 442.

For Temple, then, the dramatist is like God the creator in these respects, one who is complete within himself but who creates the world out of the abundant generosity of his love and who comes to care vitally about those he creates, beings who live out their lives in their own ways. Yet, ultimately, they depend entirely on him.

Temple then introduces his second analogy, again using the non-inclusive language of his time, an analogy that gives greater scope to the freedom of those whom God creates. He begins with the role of a creator, this time a parent:

> We now turn to another form of human creativity, which we have the highest religious sanction for regarding as an analogue of the divine. The father in a human family is to his children at once the source of their existence and a present Providence. Because . . . of his love for them, prompting him to give up what he values most if so he can serve their welfare, their doings are of vital concern to him. He gave them being; to a great extent he shapes their circumstances; perhaps his influence over them is so great that they will never knowingly act against his wishes . . . .[8]

Then, very briefly, he describes the freedom of those he has helped create: "yet they are free to respect his wishes or not; if they do so, it is because it appears to them good to do so; when he controls them, he does not coerce them, because his control is effective through their wills and not either apart from or against their wills."[9] The children, then, are free to live their lives in whatever way they choose, in real life and not just in the text of a play. If they do what their father wants they do so out of their own free will.

Finally, Temple describes the limits of the analogies, showing that they are analogies and not similes: "The analogy of the dramatist breaks down because his creations are not substantially alive; the analogy of the human father breaks down because the father himself is only another finite spirit, subject to successiveness in the same way as his children. But if we can think the two analogies together we find ourselves adumbrating a conception which seems to meet some at least of our requirements."[10]

So do these analogies succeed in holding together the sovereignty of God and the reality of human freedom? They do if the ultimate meaning

8. Temple, *Nature, Man and God*, 442.

9. Temple, *Nature, Man and God*, 442.

10. Temple, *Nature, Man and God*, 442–43.

of history, as Temple believes, "is found in the development of an ever wider fellowship of ever richer personalities. The goal of History, in short, is the Commonwealth of Value."[11] This would clearly uphold the sovereignty of God, but to many it will seem much too idealistic about the future of humankind. They will prefer the opposite point of view, which Temple acknowledges, the possibility that

> if there is no such condition, or if finite spirits cannot reach it,
> then History is indeed
> a tale
> Told by an idiot, full of sound and fury,
> Signifying nothing. (*Macbeth* Act 5)[12]

This would clearly undermine the sovereignty of God's purposes.

But almost as an afterthought, at the end of the chapter, Temple suggests a third way of looking at these things, one that is able to recognize that at the present moment the course of history and, similarly, the course of our personal lives may well lack a sense of meaning and purpose. Things may be bad and getting worse. Yet the analogy of the play can accommodate this: within the action of each act it is hard and sometimes impossible to see where the play is going. The best dramas have the capacity to surprise and even shock the viewer with their twists and turns, as villains become heroes and heroes become villains, and sometimes we can be left thinking that all hope has been lost. Yet, Temple argues, "From the standpoint of the end, necessity governs the whole; from any earlier standpoint, there is contingency and indeterminacy."[13] In great dramas, in other words, when the curtain comes down at the end the unity of the whole is revealed: each character and episode has contributed to the total life-affirming experience. And this is why we keep going to the theatre or watching dramas, because of their powerful combination of freedom and necessity.

So, in a similar kind of way, "We are living out such a drama—the drama of which the plot is the creation of finite spirits by divine love, and the fashioning of their initially selfish individualities into the Commonwealth of Value."[14] As mentioned, this may seem too idealistic to some, who prefer Macbeth's view. Yet when it is recalled that for the Christian

11. Temple, *Nature, Man and God*, 448.
12. Temple, *Nature, Man and God*, 450.
13. Temple, *Nature, Man and God*, 451.
14. Temple, *Nature, Man and God*, 451.

faith "God is love" and that love has a great paradox at its heart, that the more it is given away the greater it becomes, so that however bad the course of events turns out to be the power of God's love is not undone, Temple's third way becomes a contender. It provides a way of responding to the interpretative challenge of the collect, based on his two evocative analogies, showing how one who is a sovereign creator can also be one who bequeaths freedom to those he creates, a freedom that they can abuse and reject but which is not undone by that abuse and rejection, only strengthened!

So to the personal challenge. The collect implies that while "the things eternal" are given to all, we are perfectly capable of losing them, so much so that we need his "mercy" as "ruler and guide" to prevent this from happening. The challenge, then, is to find ways of allowing God to "increase" and "multiply upon us" this mercy so that we will *not* lose them and that he remains "our ruler and guide."

How, then, can we do this? At one level the answer is simple and straightforward. Someone who has been given a precious gift must avoid letting go of it and losing it! This may happen if they become distracted and preoccupied by other kinds of possessions. They need, instead, to be continually remembering and giving thanks for the great gift they have been given.

Saying the collect often helps with this, because it makes the person saying it shift their attention from their own desires to the one who has given them life, enabling them to place their trust entirely in him and his protection. This happens in the first line: "O GOD, the protector of all that trust in thee, without whom nothing is strong, nothing is holy." This creates an awareness of dependence on God that is needed for hearts to be open to receive his mercy, a mercy that keeps us united with his eternal things.

But for most people reciting the words of a collect is not enough. They need help and support to allow this shift to take place. Often examples of others can be a great help, especially of those who have been this way ahead of us and can show how it is possible to do this. A figure who exemplifies such a journey, not least for Christian ministers, is the priest and poet George Herbert (1593–1633). Like many others I have found the story of his life as reflected in his writings to be moving and empowering, more so as the realities of parish ministry have become part of my life in both England and Zimbabwe. It provides an inspiring example of what the collect and the phrase is encouraging us to do, and recalling it therefore provides a good way of drawing the exegesis of this chapter to a close.

Herbert is widely regarded as one of the greatest of Anglican poets. He was a complex person who began his adult life as a successful academic at Cambridge. He then became a member of Parliament and could have become a courtier serving the king but, instead, under the influence of Nicholas Ferrar (who had founded a community of devout lay people at Little Gidding) decided to seek ordination and become an ordinary parish priest. He eventually became Rector of Fugglestone with Bemerton near Salisbury, from 1630–33. He came from an aristocratic background but chose to live a life of prayer and service. In one of his poems he contrasts the life of wealth and fame with a life devoted to prayer. Philip Sheldrake has suggested that this poem shows why Herbert chose the latter:

> I value prayer so,
> That were I to leave all but one,
> Wealth, fame, endowments, virtues, all should go;
> I and dear prayer would together dwell,
> And quickly gain, for each inch lost, an ell.[15]

As is well known, he published two very influential works. The first is *The Country Parson* in 1632, a prose portrait of a committed and caring parish priest as he goes about his daily rounds. It is in his other book, a collection of poems published as *The Temple* in 1633 shortly after his death, that he reveals the inner struggle for purity of faith and assurance of salvation. Herbert's biographer, Isaak Walton, reports that when Herbert handed the poems to Nicholas Ferrar for safe keeping, he wrote that the poems are "a picture of the many spiritual conflicts that have passed betwixt God and my soul before I could subject mine to the will of Jesus my Master; in which service I have now found perfect freedom."[16] Nevertheless modern commentators point out the poems also have a rhetorical purpose that shows they are not only autobiographical but have also been written to move and encourage the reader. They are organized into three sections: "The Church Porch," "The Church," and "The Church Militant," which broadly corresponds with the way a Christian

15. Sheldrake, Philip, ed. *Heaven in Ordinary*, 4. An 'ell' is a measurement of forty-five inches.

16. Sheldrake, Philip, ed. *Heaven in Ordinary*, 11.

moves from justification by grace (The Church Porch), through gradual sanctification and growth in personal holiness (The Church), to fulfilled sanctification in the next life (The Church Militant). It is the middle section that is the longest and most dynamic, revealing the inner struggle mentioned above.

Herbert had no pretensions for his verse. It was written for private use and he instructed Ferrar to burn it "if it would not be useful to some poor soul." But it has gained timeless significance, as John Drury has eloquently written:

> Occasion of sorrow or happiness, regret, sensual pleasure, hope and resignation arise in the ordinary course of day to day life, often and over and over again. Most of us let them pass, but the poet seizes upon them and with truthfulness and imaginative craft—an interesting and demanding combination—makes them into works of art. These are the points, common to humanity at large, at which Herbert's readers feel closest to him: points at which his accuracy and sympathy make him, they may feel, a friend. . . . Poetry comes from life: from the contemplative life of the imagination as well as the active life, both of them historical or "in time." From there it addresses other lives in their own particular times.[17]

For many ministers, including myself, one of his poems does this especially powerfully, the poem called "Aaron." It is about the need of the priest to rely not on his or her own powers but to be clothed with God's mercy. It uses the figure of Aaron from Exodus 28:4–37, especially of the way he was magnificently dressed with priestly robes, which included small bells sewn onto the robes. In Herbert's Jacobean English, with his characteristically concise and rhyming verse, centered on the word "drest" (that is, dressed), it begins with a description of how this priest appeared to others, referred to as "the dead" (that is, those yet to be saved):

> Holiness on the head,
>> Light and perfection on the breast,
> Harmonious bells below raising the dead
>> To lead them unto life and rest.
>>> Thus are true Aarons drest.

But the author, himself a priest, then looks at his own life with searing honesty and finds something very different, represented by a different kind of clothing:

17. John Drury, *Music at Midnight*, xvii–xviii.

Profaneness in my head,
Defects and darkness in my breast,
A noise of passions ringing me for dead
Unto a place where is no rest:
Poor priest! thus am I drest.

It is clear from this that Herbert honestly believes he is also one of "the dead," who lacks within himself the true robes of a priest. But such honesty allows him to know in his heart that his priesthood does not come from his own person but from the one who clothes him with another head and heart and breast:

Only another head
I have another heart and breast,
Another music, making live, not dead,
Without whom I could have no rest:
In Him I am well drest.

Then, as the poem reaches its last two joy-filled verses, the "Him" is named and praised for allowing the sinner in Herbert to die and the one who is saved, to rise:

Christ is my only head,
My alone only heart and breast,
My only music, striking me e'en dead;
That to the old man I may rest,
And be in Him new drest.

Now that he knows his "defects and darkness" are as good as dead and that he depends on Christ alone, Herbert realizes how much he has been given of God's mercy and therefore how God is truly his "ruler and guide" and how, therefore, he will no longer lose "the things eternal," to use the language of the collect. In the final verse, triumphantly, he realizes how well he is dressed and able to teach doctrine in word and action, providing a beautiful example and encouragement to all who minister in Christ's name:

So holy in my Head,
Perfect and light in my dear Breast,
My doctrine tuned by Christ (who is not dead,
But lives in me while I do rest),
Come, people; Aaron's drest.

Bibliography

Church of England. The Book of Common Prayer according to the use of the Church of England. Cambridge: Cambridge University Press, 2004.

Drury, John. *Music at Midnight: The Life and Poetry of George Herbert*. London: Allen Lane, 2013.

Rowell, Geoffrey, et al. *Love's Redeeming Work: The Anglican Quest for Holiness*. Oxford: Oxford University Press, 2001.

Sheldrake, Philip, ed. *Heaven in Ordinary: George Herbert and His Writings*. Norwich, UK: Canterbury, 2009.

Spencer, Stephen. *Christ in All Things: William Temple and His Writings*. Norwich, UK: Canterbury, 2015.

Temple, William. *Nature, Man and God*. The Gifford Lectures 1932–34. London: Macmillan, 1934.

14

Partake

Malcolm Guite

MANY YEARS AGO, IN the eighties, I heard Stephen Sykes, then the Regius Professor of Divinity in Cambridge, give a lecture on the Communion service in the Book of Common Prayer. It deeply informed my understanding not only of that service, but of liturgy itself, as a journey from isolation into communion, from a fragmented life into a communal and participative life; a transformation of our whole way of knowing that moves us from spectating to partaking.

A central strand of that lecture was a reflection on the importance of the word *partake*, both in the service itself and in the many passages of scripture on which Cranmer had been meditating when he came to form that liturgy. Sykes began by remarking: "The key word of the rite is 'partake,' the word which English translations of the Bible used with great frequency to translate a range of Greek terms, including of course *koinonia*. This partaking is conceived in the text as the high point of the ritual . . . ."[1]

After delineating the way that service takes us through ritual acts that confess separation and draw us towards aggregation, Sykes returned to the word "partake." He pointed out that it is used first in the

---

1. This and other extracts from this unpublished lecture are taken from Stephen Sykes's own typescript and his further manuscript notes. My wife, the Rev. Dr. Margaret Guite, is his literary executor and has kindly given me access to these manuscripts. Sykes, "The Communion Service in the Book of Common Prayer" (unpublished lecture, manuscript and notes).

Antecommunion, in the prayer for the whole state of Christ's church, which concludes—as it remembers those separated from us by the narrow stream of death—with the petition: "that with them we may be *partakers* of thy heavenly kingdom," so even before we arrive at the intimate partaking of the sacrament our eyes are lifted to that final consummation, our partaking in the kingdom of which the sacrament will be our foretaste. Although the word itself does not occur in the Prayer of Humble Access, Sykes argues that the word *partake* is crucial to the sense of what follows. He says,

> this is a prayer for the intimate partaking of the life of God himself. Furthermore the only petition contained in the prayer of consecration which follows is in terms of *partaking*: "Grant that we receiving these thy creatures of bread and wine . . . may be partakers of his most blessed body and blood." The words of distribution announce that the bread and wine are indeed a partaking of the Body and Blood of Christ.[2]

These words struck deeply into me at that time, into my heart as well as my head. Most of the other students in that lecture hall were ordinands, and were perhaps already partaking and belonging in the life of the Church of England in a deeper and more committed way than I was.

I was there at the lecture as an outsider in a way. I was a school teacher, not a theological student, but my wife was teaching doctrine to some of those students at Westcott House and she invited me along to hear Professor Sykes because he had been an important person in her own life. So in one sense I attended that lecture as a spectator, but there at the core of it was a call to move from merely spectating to a deeper partaking. And although Sykes was talking specifically about the liturgy of Communion, and he certainly renewed the familiar words of that liturgy for me, I began to feel that the invitation to partake went much wider. My subject was not theology but literature, and I had become very disenchanted with arid analytical literary criticism, with all its structuralism and critical deconstruction, which seemed to distance the reader from the text, to disenchant both text and reader, to be suspicious of engagement. As a teacher I was resisting my desire to teach poetry as a form of deeply personal and participative engagement, and here, unexpectedly in this lecture, was someone trying to do the same thing for theology.

2. Sykes, "The Communion Service in the Book of Common Prayer."

There was a wider cultural context too. This was the eighties and so many of the common bonds, the immemorial modes of our mutual participation in a common society were being dismantled and cast aside on both sides of the Atlantic. It was the era of privatization, of untrammeled individualism, in which Margaret Thatcher had notoriously said, "There is no such thing as society." Even prayer and spirituality seemed to have been privatized, but here was a great scholar unveiling for me new depths in a book that was significantly called the Book of *Common* Prayer. Looking back I realize that this lecture was also part of another call for me, a call to partake even more fully in the life of my church, which I eventually discerned as a call to priesthood, a call to offer myself, body and soul, as a physical part of that liturgy, a call to take these words of consecration, and invitation on my lips not only in receiving the sacrament but in giving and sharing it.

So Sykes's lecture on the crucial importance of this single word changed me. I found that not only did I partake more wholly in the service, "not only with my lips but in my life," but also I became aware of the range and power of the word "partake" in scripture, particularly in the earlier translations, and the more I meditated on these places in the Bible, the richer and more important the cluster of ideas around that word seemed to be.

In Hebrews for example, where we are addressed as "partakers of the heavenly calling" (Heb 3:1, KJV) and then a little later told that by being a partaker of the calling "we are made partakers of Christ" (Heb 3:14, KJV) and then the partaking, the participation, deepens further for we "have tasted the heavenly gift and were made partakers of the Holy Ghost" (Heb 6:4, KJV).

There are myriad places in which what begins as an invitation to partake in calling, to partake in suffering, to partake in sacrament, eventually reveals itself to be an invitation to partake in God himself, as the Second Epistle of Peter pithily and shockingly puts it: "Whereby are given to us exceeding great and precious promises: that by these ye might be partakers of the divine nature" (2 Pet 1:4, KJV).

These few passages, chosen from among so many, give us some sense of the theological reach of the word "partake." It goes far beyond outward participation in an event, a church, a congregation, beyond sharing a creed in the sense of mutual consent to a set of intellectual or historic propositions, but is a word that calls and draws us beyond every barrier of separation, into the life of God himself, and through that partaking, that participation, into a new communion, a new *koinonia* with one another.

It was an important word for the compilers of the Book of Common Prayer in their day, because, as Sykes has argued, they were trying to achieve a complete transformation, a paradigm shift in the way people participated in the liturgy. They wanted people to move (quite literally) from being passive spectators of a distant priestly ritual to active and equal participants in, partakers of, a calling. So this active word "partake" was crucial, in its most simple other sense of "take part"! But if Cranmer needed, at a particular moment of church reform, to shift people from the passive to the active, from the detached to the involved, then that is even more important now, when we live so much in a culture of detached spectators, and important not only for liturgy but for all the interlinked spheres of our knowing and being and participating in the world.

When I later trained for ordination and became a priest, partly as a result of seeds sown in this lecture, Sykes's insight here into true participation, the reintegration of being and knowing, and of both with mutual interdependence, mutual participation, became a vital part of my understanding of ministry. And not only the ministry of word and sacrament within the walls of the church, but the much greater challenge of reintegration for the disintegrating society beyond those walls. The clichéd view of those days was a contrast between supposedly fuddy-duddy sacramentalists on the one hand, who had no engagement with secular society, and "trendy vicars in jeans" who were social workers manqué but were presumed not to care about the church or its traditions. But for me the word "partake" was a key both to sacramental and societal transformation. The Eucharist was both a mystery and a social manifesto calling for action.

Western thought since the Enlightenment has become more and more detached from the world, separated, analytical, non-participatory. This splitting and detachment begins perhaps with Descartes's distinction between *res extensa* and *res cogitans*, which already implies we don't participate in the world we observe. This view was developed into an approach to the world that the philosopher of science Mary Midgely called "scientism," and characterized as "an unbalanced fascination with the imagery of atomism—a notion that the only way to understand anything is to break it into its ultimate smallest parts and to conceive these as making up something comparable to a machine."[3] In that sense we might argue that the opposite of partake, in its sense of "taking part," is "taking *apart*." In order to atomize in this way we must presume ourselves utterly distinct from, not partakers of, the nature we seek first to analyze and then to dissect.

This detached and desiccated way of knowing, this false "science," which claims to be impartial but is in fact a very partial form of knowledge, is being challenged and modified on every side. We are remembering that there are other older and wiser ways of knowing that make a necessary complement to our proper scientific achievements. Over against the reductive position that runs from Bacon and Descartes through Hobbes and Locke to the Wittgenstein of the *Tractatus*, there is a counter-movement, emphasizing both knowledge and language as tacit, trustful, ambiguous, imaginatively shaped, and capable of self-transcendence. This is a line that goes back into and behind the beginnings of modernism and runs from Augustine into writers like Donne and Hooker, from Coleridge to F. D. Maurice and Newman, and in historians and philosophers of science like Michael Polanyi, the later Wittgenstein, and the later writings of George Steiner.

If there is one thing that characterizes that tradition it is participation, involvement, *partaking*. It grasps that certain things can only be known from within, by involvement, that there must be some trusting as well as some testing. There are certain realities, like love, for example, that we cannot, properly speaking, know at all unless we also partake, participate. Coleridge, who was of course soaked in the language of the Bible and the Book of Common Prayer, pioneered, in the midst of the most detached period of eighteenth-century philosophy, a path back into this earlier and more balanced way of knowing. He does so, for example, in his restatement of Augustine, in *Aids to Reflection* where he says: "To believe and to understand are not diverse things but the same thing in different periods of growth."[4] And again in his reflections on knowledge as a journey undertaken in faith he writes in his *Notebooks*:

> Try it, travel along it, trust in it and . . . obey in all respects the
> various guideposts both at its entrance and those which you will
> find along it—and this is the method, nay this is from the very
> nature of the thing the only possible method of converting your
> negative knowledge into direct and positive Insight . . . .[5]

3. Midgely, *Science and Poetry*, 2.

4. Coleridge, *Aids To Reflection*, 194.

5. Coleridge, *Notebooks*, 4, 611. This passage is cited in Avis, *God and the Creative Imagination*, 31, in his helpful summary of what he calls the fiduciary tradition.

To try, to travel along, to trust are all forms of partaking. As I worked on my book *Faith, Hope and Poetry*, a book originally suggested and encouraged by Stephen Sykes himself, I began to realize that poetry and liturgy between them were not only transforming my vision whilst I was "partaking" of them, but that they offered the potential to transform my vision of the world at large, that they modeled a way of participating in truth, which was the missing element in the reductive materialism of our current worldview. We cannot know truly unless we first love and to love we must engage; risk losing the supposed invulnerability or "objectivity" of our detachment, and dare to become part of something more.

This link between knowledge and love, with mutual participation as the key of its movement, became central not only to my life as a priest but also to my work as a poet. Some years after my ordination I wrote a semi-autobiographical poetry sequence called *On Reading the Commedia*, which took the form of a response to Dante, a kind of reader's journal, and in one of those poems, "Circle Dance," commenting on the moment in the *Commedia* when Dante meets Boethius, I tried to sum up what I had learnt in those Cambridge days, including of course, Sykes's lecture on partaking:

2 Circle Dance
A sun-warmed sapling, opening each leaf,
My soul unfolded in your quickening ray.
"The inner brought the outer into life,"

I found the light within the light of day,
The Consolation of Philosophy,
Turning a page in Cambridge, found my way,

My mind delighting in discovery,
As love of learning turned to learning love
And explanation deepened mystery,

Drawing me out beyond what I could prove
Towards the next adventure. Every chance
Discovery a sweet come-hither wave,

Philosophy a kind of circle dance,
Weaving between the present and the past,
The whole truth present in a single glance

That looked on me and everything in Christ!
Threefold beholding, look me into being,
Make me in Love again from first to last,

And let me still partake your holy seeing
Beyond the shifting shadow of the earth;
Minute particulars, eternal in their being,

Forming themselves into a single path
From heaven to earth and back again to heaven,
All patterned and perfected, from each birth

To each fruition, and all freely given
To glory in and give the glory back!
Call me again to set out from this haven

And follow truth along her shining track.[6]

As these thoughts, originally sparked by that memorable lecture on
the Book of Common Prayer, began to take shape, I also began to see
the importance of two other writers very much neglected by mainstream
theology, the two less famous "also ran" members of the Oxford literary
group known as the Inklings. C. S. Lewis and J. R. R. Tolkien have justly
become widely known to the world, but Owen Barfield and Charles Williams, writers whom Lewis and Tolkien held in great esteem and who
influenced them strongly, have been less noticed and explored, though of
course that may change.

The emphasis on "partake," the journey towards a true partaking, a
real participation in one another and in God, which Sykes had revealed
in liturgy, seems very resonant with Barfield's ideas, set out particularly
in *Poetic Diction* and *Saving the Appearances*. Close study of the evolution
of language led Barfield to believe that human consciousness itself was
evolving. Early poetry, he believed, indicated a time when we were less
islanded in our own skulls and when we participated in a wider, diffused
consciousness within nature itself. He cites the word *pneuma* as meaning both wind and spirit, experienced simultaneously, whereas a later
more detached form of consciousness splits the two and has meaningless

6. Guite, *The Singing Bowl*, 122–23.

nature on the outside and a mere metaphor drawn from nature on the inside. An original mutually participative unity has been split into two, labeled "subjective" and "objective." Barfield called the earlier stage of consciousness, before this split had occurred, "original participation" and he believed humanity was on a journey from that original participation, through a necessary period of detachment and separation, which allows for individual consciousness and culture, towards a hoped for "final participation," in which we would no longer passively or detachedly observe realities other than ourselves but truly partake of their natures from within, yet without losing our own identity.

But Barfield was also very conscious of the danger that this middle period of detachment might lead to total alienation and a complete loss of meaning. He writes,

> Amid all the menacing signs that surround us in the middle of this twentieth century, perhaps the one that fills thoughtful people with the greatest foreboding is the growing general sense of meaninglessness. It is this which underlies most of the other threats. How is it that the more able man becomes to manipulate the world to his advantage, the less he can perceive any meaning in it?[7]

And again, in another essay, he says,

> The vaunted progress of "knowledge," which has been going on since the seventeenth century, has been progress in alienation. The alienation of nature from humanity, which the exclusive pursuit of objectivity in science entails, was the first stage; and was followed, with the acceptance of man himself as part of a nature so alienated, by the alienation of man from himself.[8]

What is needed, Barfield argues, is not a retreat into a romantic nostalgia for a less alienated past, but a recovery of participative consciousness, which brings its new knowledge with it. He says,

> It remains to be considered whether the future development of scientific man must inevitably continue in the same direction, so that he becomes more and more a mere onlooker, measuring with greater and greater precision and manipulating more and more cleverly an earth to which he grows spiritually more and more a stranger. His detachment has enabled him to describe,

7. Barfield, *The Rediscovery of Meaning*, 11.

8. Barfield, *The Rediscovery of Meaning*, 216.

weigh, and measure the processes of nature and to a large extent to control them; but the price he has paid has been the loss of his grasp of any meaning in either nature or himself. Penetration to the meaning of a thing or process, as distinct from the ability to describe it exactly, involves a participation by the knower in the known. . . . Signs are not altogether wanting that there is such a possibility . . . .[9]

Here again Barfield calls us to participate in the known, not just observe it, to take part and be a partaker.

As Barfield was advocating what one might call a participative epistemology, knowledge as partaking rather than detachment, his friend and fellow Inkling Charles Williams made mutual indwelling, a mutual partaking of one another's lives, being, and burdens, central to his theological vision. Williams's term for all of this, carefully drawn from the trinitarian theology where that vision is grounded, was *co-inherence*. But for Williams co-inherence was not just a technical term for the way the Son is in the Father and the Father in the Son, and the way the Spirit proceeds from both and is himself the loving exchange of their being; it was also a way of talking about society, about our mutual indwelling with one another and with God, about what it means to be made in, and to bear God's image. Williams can be prolix and his prose, though exciting, sometimes revels in obscurity, but he put this all pretty pithily in a great passage in his essay "The Way of Exchange":

> The mystery of the Christian religion is a doctrine of coinherence and substitution. The Divine word co-inheres in God the Father (as the Father in Him and the Spirit in Both), but also He has substituted His Manhood for ours in the secrets of the Incarnation and Atonement. . . . He lives in us and we in Him, and we coinhere. . . . To love God and to love one's neighbor are but two movements of the same principle.[10]

Co-inherence, substitution, and exchange are the three pillars of Williams's theology and they are all forms of mutual partaking. Indeed, if Barfield suggests that partaking is about taking part, rather than taking *a*part, then Williams suggests that partaking also means taking someone else's part, choosing to stand in their place and carry their burdens for them. This is what Christ does for us and what we are called to do for

---

9. Barfield, *The Rediscovery of Meaning*, 19–20.
10. Williams, "The Way of Exchange," 129.

one another in Christ. As Williams goes on to remark in that essay: "Our natural life begins by being born in another; our mothers have to carry us. . . . The Christian Church demands that we shall carry out that principle everywhere by our will—with our friends and with our neighbours, whether we like our neighbours or not."[11]

There has been a particular poignancy in reflecting on the importance of the word "partake" in the midst of the coronavirus pandemic. The spread of the virus has made it abundantly clear that we all do partake in and mutually indwell one another. We are all utterly connected, for the chain of infection from one person in Wuhan to so many all over the world is a chain of unbroken physical connection and mutuality. The irony is that we have chosen to organize the world in a way that denies and sometimes desecrates that mutuality, and so we were unprepared for this shadow cast by the mutual partaking that we had denied.

For many people the immediate consequence of this demonstration that we are not islands, that we are in Donne's words "involved in mankind," was, again ironically, an experience of islanded isolation in lockdown. For many of us it also meant the loss of Communion, the very sacrament that most proclaimed the meaning of our mutual partaking and called us to partake, through that sacrament of a new vision of the world and one another. Indeed Williams, in the conclusion of the essay we have been citing, says: "The great Rite of this (as of much else) within the Christian Church is the Eucharist, where the co-inherence is fully in action: 'He in us and we in Him.'"[12]

Perhaps as lockdown eventually eases, we will have learned to value and acknowledge our mutuality, to partake of the goods of this world with and for and through one another, and to acknowledge one another again as "partakers of the heavenly kingdom," partakers whose part has been taken by the King of Heaven himself.

Bibliography

Avis, Paul. *God and the Creative Imagination*. London: Routledge, 1999.

Barfield, Owen. "The Rediscovery of Meaning." In *The Rediscovery of Meaning and Other Essays*, 11–21. San Rafael, CA: Barfield, 1977.

Coleridge, Samuel Taylor. *Aids To Reflection*. Edited by John Beer. London: Dent, 1993.

11. Williams, "The Way of Exchange," 129.

12. Williams, "The Way of Exchange," 131.

————. *Notebooks, 1819-1826*. Edited by Merton Christensen and Kathleen Coburn. London: Routledge, 1989.

Guite, Malcolm. *Faith Hope and Poetry: Theology and the Poetic Imagination*. Farnham, UK: Ashgate, 2010.

————. *The Singing Bowl*. London: Canterbury, 2013.

Midgely, Mary. *Science and Poetry*. London: Routledge, 2001.

Williams, Charles. *Selected Writings*. Edited by Anne Ridler. Oxford: Oxford University Press, 1961.

15

Peace

John Kiess

As in many cities following the death of George Floyd, thousands took to the streets of Baltimore in the early summer of 2020 to protest police brutality and demand racial justice. Standing at the intersection of Roland Avenue and Northern Parkway, my seven-year-old son Austin and I were among them. Austin's elementary school had forwarded an email about a protest being organized nearby, and I asked him if he wanted to go. He said he did. So we pulled out some poster board, a box of markers, and got to work on our signs.

We talked about George as we made them. I told Austin about the circumstances of his death, and he asked the kind of direct questions that children are adept at asking. Why was a police officer kneeling on his neck? Aren't police officers supposed to protect us? Why did he die? Why George?

We talked about how George was not the only one. That this has been going on for a long time, and that this kind of unfair treatment extends far beyond the police. Austin drew a stop sign and put "injustice" under it.

He asked what we were going to do at the protest. I said we were going to hold our signs, say some things about how we felt about this, kneel for a while, and then march.

"We are going to kneel?"

"Yes."

"Why?"

"To honor George."

"For how long?"

"Well, for as long as the officer was kneeling on him."

I hesitated to tell him how long exactly; a parent knows when to be ambiguous. But this didn't seem like the time. "About nine minutes."

"That's a long time." He was already protesting.

Soon after we arrived, we positioned ourselves about six feet away from those beside us and waited for the protest to start. Waving his sign, Austin delighted in getting passing drivers to honk their horns, especially the trucks. "Did you hear that big rig?" "I got the dump truck, Dad!"

Soon some chants started.

"What are they saying, Dad?"

"No justice, no peace."

"What does that mean?

"Well, it means you can't have peace without justice."

There wasn't much time to expand, although I would have liked to. The chant has always intrigued me for its multiple layers of meaning: a declaration that if justice is not done, the peace will not be kept; a descriptive claim about what real peace requires; among others. The biblical resonance of the chant speaks to me too, recalling the words of Isaiah: "the work of justice will be peace" (32:17), and Pope Paul VI's famous reformulation, "If you want peace, work for justice." The chant especially channels the outrage with which the Hebrew prophets greeted calls for peace that elide deeper cycles of injustice. "As a well keeps its water fresh," Jeremiah says, "so she keeps fresh her wickedness. . . . They have treated the wound of my people carelessly, saying, 'Peace, peace,' when there is no peace" (Jer 6:7, 14). In Ezekiel's telling imagery, the misuse of peace language is one of the marks of the false prophet; instead of going to the breaches and repairing the walls, they smear whitewash on them. "When the wall falls," Ezekiel asks, "will it not be said to you, 'Where is the whitewash you smeared on it?'" (Ezek 13:12).

For a volume focused on the way words lose their meaning, and how certain meanings might be preserved, rediscovered, or even reimagined, my mind returns to this chant, "no justice, no peace," and my time with Austin on that intersection. I think of the specific role that protests such as these—and the larger mass movements of which they are a part— play in safeguarding words, and in facilitating concrete judgments about which meanings represent misuses (peace without justice), and which do not (peace with justice). I think of the close relationship between words and bodies in such spaces: of the specific role the body plays in aligning itself with the meaning of words—on a sign, through the mouth, or as we know, on the receiving end of a baton or rubber bullet—and what credibility bodies lend to words in such spaces. As a parent, it was hard for me not also to take note of the formative role of such spaces in instructing the young about the meaning of words: that *peace* is not a word Austin can understand apart from justice.

Christians have long come to such spaces with an investment in how the words spoken there relate to their own theological understanding of them, and an appreciation that this is one important theater of theological witness. Martin Luther King, Jr. recalls an occasion early in the Civil Rights Movement when a white man in Montgomery approached him to register his discontent with the movement's tactics, saying they disturbed the peace. King responded that he did not believe the South ever had true peace. It may have had a "negative peace," which King described as "merely the absence of tension . . . in which the Negro patiently accepted his situation and his plight," but it did not have "positive peace," which is "the presence of a positive force, . . . the presence of justice and brotherhood."[1] The movement was indeed a revolt against negative peace, King said, but not positive peace, and it was this peace that they were trying to build. He put the point in theological terms:

> I think this is what Jesus meant when he said, "I come not to bring peace but a sword." Now Jesus didn't mean he came to start war, to bring a physical sword, and he didn't mean, I come not to bring positive peace. But I think what Jesus was saying in substance was this, that I come not to bring an old negative peace, which makes for stagnant passivity and deadening complacency, I come to bring something different, and whenever I come, a conflict is precipitated, between the old and the new, whenever I come, a struggle takes place between justice and injustice, between the forces of light and the forces of darkness. I come not to bring a negative peace, but a positive peace, which is brotherhood, which is justice, which is the Kingdom of God.[2]

Here King embraces the Gospel passage most difficult to reconcile with a peace agenda and uses it to show how expansive peace truly is. A peace that includes brotherhood and justice cannot but conflict with a

1. King, "Love, Law, and Civil Disobedience," 50–51.
2. King, "Love, Law, and Civil Disobedience," 51.

vision of peace that attempts to wring harmony out of segregation and brutality. For King, to march in the streets and stage boycotts, sit-ins, and other acts of civil disobedience was to be part of nothing less than the kingdom of God. The conflict that these actions precipitated was a sign that another vision of peace had broken into the world, and the inter-racial, inter-faith, ecumenical, cross-community character of the move-ment modeled the peace towards which it strode. Notably, theological meaning here—peace as the justice and brotherhood of the kingdom of God—is tied to practices that take Christians beyond the church and into coalitional fellowship with others. The integrity of theological meaning hinges upon worldly solidarity.

There is a longstanding tradition of Christian thinkers and activists who have drawn upon a broader theological horizon to distinguish dif-ferent kinds of peace and promote the building of a more just society. Let me highlight just a few.

Augustine's famous discussion of the two cities in the *City of God* pivots on a basic distinction between two kinds of peace. The earthly city pursues an earthly peace, limited to "a kind of compromise between hu-man wills about the things relevant to mortal life,"[3] while the heavenly city looks ahead to "a perfectly ordered and perfectly harmonious fellowship in the enjoyment of God."[4] This latter peace is "so perfect and so great as to admit of neither improvement nor increase."[5] Augustine makes much of the contrast between these cities: one is animated by self-love and the lust to dominate, the other is fueled by a love of God and neighbor; one broadens its frontiers through violence and conquest, the other through sacrifice and martyrdom. Still, while members of the heavenly city are on pilgrimage on earth, they are subject to the same necessities as members of the earthly city, so peace in the penultimate, earthly sense emerges as something of a shared pursuit between them. The difference consists in how they pursue this peace.

Rather than see earthly peace as its own end, offering its own ad-vantages, the pilgrims of the heavenly city make use of earthly peace as a support, "like a pilgrim in a foreign land," awaiting "the blessings which are promised as eternal in the future."[6] In this way, Augustine marries

3. Augustine, *City of God* 19.17.
4. Augustine, *City of God* 19.13.
5. Augustine, *City of God* 19.10.
6. Augustine, *City of God* 19.17.

Jeremiah's call to the exiles in Babylon to seek the peace of the city ("in her peace is your peace") with Isaiah's anticipation of an age when swords will be beaten into plowshares and humans will study war no more. "Here in this world we are called blessed, it is true, when we enjoy peace, however little may be the peace—the peace of a good life—which can be enjoyed here," Augustine writes. "And yet such blessedness as this life affords proves to be utter misery when compared with that final bliss."[7]

Elsewhere in his discussion, Augustine defines peace as *tranquillitas ordinis*, or the tranquility of order, and the expansiveness of his understanding of peace becomes clear when one considers how many spheres it encompasses. From the inner peace of well-ordered inclinations and desires, Augustine moves to the peace of body and soul, the household, human society, the fellowship between humanity and God, and finally, the peace of the universe.[8] Given this, one can understand why Augustine understands peace to be "the final fulfillment of all our goods,"[9] indeed, the "Supreme Good," to which even justice is finally ordered.[10] One can also understand why he believes peace in this ultimate sense eludes us in this life, because we are never fully free of conflict, either within ourselves or with others.

Peace on this account is a vast, holistic enterprise, and its moral demands fill Augustine, like the prophets before him, with a kind of holy restlessness, a sense of personal offense at uses that attempt to reduce peace to something less radical, hence his critique of the *pax Romana* as a peace in name only, masking all manner of injustice. At the same time, the fact that Augustine bothers with social critique at all reaffirms his underlying assumption that earthly peace *is* possible, that it always admits degrees of improvement, and that the pilgrim must never cease striving to foster a more just peace with one's neighbors.

Building upon Augustine, Aquinas offers his characteristic nuance, providing a number of further distinctions. He distinguishes peace from concord, true from apparent peace, and perfect from imperfect peace.[11]

Noting that even a band of robbers can enjoy concord, Aquinas argues that peace must add something else, namely, the ordering of inner

---

7. Augustine, *City of God* 19.10.

8. Augustine, *City of God* 19.13.

9. Augustine, *City of God* 19.11

10. Augustine, *City of God* 19.27.

11. Aquinas, *Summa Theologica* II–II 29.

appetites that enables one to join with others in a *well-ordered* concord.[12] This link between peace and desire, one of many debts to Augustine, is important and far-reaching, as it suggests "whoever desires anything desires peace, in so far as he who desires anything, desires to attain, with tranquility and without hindrance, to that which he desires."[13] To say all people desire peace, though, is to risk making peace so universal an aspiration as to drain it of all meaning,[14] so Aquinas finds it important to distinguish true from apparent peace. True peace is "where the appetite is directed to what is truly good," which alone can bring rest to our souls; apparent peace, on the other hand, is where the appetite is directed to something that "may appear good in a way, so as to calm the appetite in some respect," but which has "many defects, which cause the appetite to remain restless and disturbed."[15] While the band of robbers may appear to enjoy peace, the vice that unites them will eventually prove their undoing. Likewise, when Jeremiah and Ezekiel call out false prophets for crying "peace, peace," when there is no peace, it is the seductiveness of apparent peace they are warning about.

As for true peace, it may be had imperfectly or perfectly. Imperfect peace, which is possible in this world, is directed towards goods that are in fact true, but still disturbed by "certain things within and without."[16] Perfect peace, on the other hand, is "the perfect enjoyment of the sovereign good," Augustine's heavenly peace, which awaits us as our last end.[17]

Notably for Aquinas, peace is only properly understood as an effect, not a cause. It may surprise some readers to learn that Aquinas does not regard peace as a virtue; this is because he believes it flows from two other virtues: justice and charity.[18] Peace is an effect of justice indirectly, to the extent that justice lifts the obstacles that stand in the way of the realization of peace (Aquinas refers to none other than Isaiah: "the work of justice is peace").[19] It is a direct effect of charity to the extent that charity is a unitive force, uniting us to that which we seek. While peace will

12. Aquinas, *Summa Theologica* II–II 29.1.

13. Aquinas, *Summa Theologica* II–II 29.2.

14. On this point, see Coady and Ross, "St. Augustine and the Ideal of Peace," esp. 154–55.

15. Aquinas, *Summa Theologica* II–II 29.2 ad 3.

16. Aquinas, *Summa Theologica* II–II 29.2 ad 4.

17. Aquinas, *Summa Theologica* II–II ad 4.

18. Aquinas, *Summa Theologica* II–II 29.3–4.

19. Aquinas, *Summa Theologica* II–II 29.3 ad 3.

always be imperfect this side of the eschaton, the imperfect peace that is possible is only such because some element of justice and charity has gone before it. Peace here is no mere neutral starting point to which one adds justice, but peace follows from justice. No justice, no peace indeed. And no charity, no peace as well.

Coming back to the American context, there have been several memorable voices who, at other crossroads of national reckoning on race, challenged their listeners to discern the signs of the times and distinguish true from apparent peace. Long before the Civil War was over, Frederick Douglass was already warning about the shape of the coming peace, knowing that it would determine the shape of American society for generations to come. As he saw it, the war presented the opportunity for national regeneration, a full and sweeping righting of America's racial wrongs. But Douglass noted with dismay how war fatigue, combined with ambivalent Northern support for abolition, created the conditions for a peace that would obstruct one of the war's most important outcomes. Indeed, Douglass warned of a "slaveholding peace," brokered by North and South together, which, while formally abolishing slavery, would leave its racial foundations in place. When "the major part of anti-slavery profession is based upon devotion to the Union rather than hostility to Slavery," he said, when northern presses fire "the nation's heart with hatred for Negroes and Abolitionists," and when "a respectable colored man or woman can be kicked out of the commonest street car in New York where any white ruffian may ride unquestioned . . . we are in danger of a slaveholding peace."[20] Douglass's fears were borne out soon after the war, when the promise of Reconstruction was aborted, the rights of black Americans were denied, and orators and preachers began relativizing the war's causes, preferring, in the name of peace, to celebrate valor on both sides and bless memorials to Confederate and Union soldier alike.[21] "The livery of peace is a beautiful livery," Douglass said, "but in this case it is a stolen livery and sits badly on the wearer."[22]

Douglass held aloft another vision of peace, which he called "abolition peace," which entailed nothing less than "a new order of social and political relations among the whole people."[23] Abolition peace would

20. Douglass, "The Mission of the War," 565.

21. For an account of how the Civil War was remembered in the fifty-year period following the war, see Blight, *Race and Reunion*.

22. Douglass, "The Mission of the War," 559.

23. Douglass, "The Mission of the War," 560.

abolish not only slavery, but also all other forms of racial discrimination and inequality. It would "invest the black man everywhere with the right to vote and to be voted for, and remove all discriminations against his rights on account of his color, whether as a citizen or as a soldier."[24] It would deliver on the full scope of the war's verdict, passing not only the 13th, 14th, and 15th amendments, but enforcing them. It would create opportunities to address historic and seismic gaps in labor, education, and access to land. It would not shy away from declaring a right and wrong side in the war, and memorialize it as such. "Yes, let us have peace," Douglass declared, "but let us have liberty, law, and justice first."[25] "When the supreme law of the land is systematically set at naught," he continued, "when humanity is insulted and the rights of the weak are trampled in the dust by a lawless power; when society is divided into two classes, as oppressed and oppressor, there is no power, and there can be no power, while the instincts of manhood remain as they are, which can provide solid peace."[26]

While Douglass praised many churches for their early support of abolition, he assailed them for retreating from its platform when its goals were within reach.[27] The "Christianity of Christ," he famously said, should not to be confused with the "slaveholding religion of this land," whose church bells chime in time with the slave auctioneer's bell.[28] In truth, the whole heart of the church should "beat in unison with the heart of the Son of God," who at "the very outset of his mission among the children of men" was "careful to range himself on the side of the poor, the enslaved, and heart-broken victims of oppression."[29] Strikingly, it is the abolitionist, not the preacher, Douglass says, who has connected this "sublime declaration" to the plight of the enslaved; yet when the abolitionist appears at the doors of the church, pleading for entry on behalf of this "captured, bruised, maimed, and heart-broken people," she is turned away "with iron bolts."[30] The implication is clear: only a slaveholding religion could deduce slaveholding peace from the gospel; the Christianity

24. Douglass, "The Mission of the War," 560.

25. Douglass, "There Was a Right Side in the Late War," 629.

26. Douglass, "There Was a Right Side in the Late War," 629.

27. See Douglass, "The Anti-Slavery Movement," 311–31.

28. Douglass, *Narrative of the Life of Frederick Douglass, An American Slave*, 97–98.

29. Douglass, "The Anti-Slavery Movement," 320.

30. Douglass, "The Anti-Slavery Movement," 320–21.

of Christ impels Christians to join with their fellow countrymen and become abolition peacemakers.

Abolition peace, of course, was not accomplished, and it fell to subsequent generations of black activists and intellectual leaders—Ida B. Wells, Reverdy Ransom, W. E. B. Du Bois, Howard Thurman, among many others—to hold the nation's feet to the fire of its demands.[31] One hundred years after Douglass put two paths of peace before a divided nation, the options King drew for his audience were broadly the same: the negative peace of a racial caste system and the positive peace of justice and brotherhood. Indeed, his vision of beloved community, like Douglass's abolition peace, can be seen as a soaring imagination of all that a true, imperfect peace can entail, especially when one sees King in his later years turn his attention to persistent and widening racial disparities in employment, housing, health, and other areas. In his appeals to the soul-force of love, and his abiding investment in strategies that aim to transform the mindset of the movement's most hostile enemies, we see King deepening and expanding the core wisdom of predecessors who saw love and justice as the foundation of peace.

King had the moral vision to see that a century removed from the Civil War, America was still a post-war society, a society still awaiting the "just and lasting peace" that was promised but not achieved. He framed the civil rights struggle as a peace movement not only because of the tactics it employed, but also because it was invested in bringing about this long-delayed post-war settlement. It is a framing that remains deeply suggestive for our current moment.

All around us we see the enduring signs of what America's sectional reunion never resolved: the inter-generational disparities and inequities ushered in with slavery; the racialized terms of national memory and public memorialization; the racial roots of policing and their long after-life; state and local resistance to the enforcement of federal policy; among others. Many of these dynamics have worsened with time, compounded not only by neglect, but also by further injustices, from Jim Crow segregation to redlining, housing covenants, mass incarceration, and environmental racism.

But as we look around the world, we should also be encouraged by a countervailing trend: countries emerging from violent conflict have established truth and reconciliation commissions, authorized war crimes

---

31. See Gary Dorrien's magisterial two-volume history of black social gospel activism, *The New Abolition*.

tribunals, made apologies, constructed memorials to victims, granted reparations, orchestrated expansive plans of economic reconstruction, promoted community revitalization, and offered trauma and other public health services. Recent decades have witnessed an astonishing hunger to address the legacy of the past in deeply divided societies. Where these mechanisms have been implemented, they have mostly addressed injustices committed in the recent past, typically human rights abuses occurring in the context of armed conflict. The question that our moment now raises is whether they can be applied to contexts where the legacy of injustice is much longer, where the costs have accrued not simply over decades, but over centuries.

We do not have to speculate on the answer. There have already been numerous morally imaginative attempts to engage our racial past in ways that draw inspiration from these mechanisms. The 2004–6 Greensboro Truth and Reconciliation Commission, for example, held public hearings and gathered over one hundred statements on a November 1979 massacre that left five anti-Ku Klux Klan activists dead. Its report and recommendations provide a model for engaging events that crystallize America's deepest racial wounds.[32] The National Memorial for Peace and Justice in Montgomery, Alabama, dedicated to the memory of victims of lynching, was conceived by the Equal Justice Initiative with "the hope of creating a sober, meaningful site where people can gather and reflect on America's history of racial inequality" and ultimately participate in a new "era of restorative truth-telling and justice that changes the consciousness of our nation."[33] Among many notable features, it challenges communities to research, discuss, and erect historical markers of lynching in their own locales. H.R.40, a bill that proposes the creation of a commission to study and develop reparation proposals for slavery and other forms of anti-black discrimination, has long sat in the Judiciary Committee of the House of Representatives, but a diverse collection of individuals, from Ta-Nehisi Coates to the conservative commentator David Brooks, now support the idea.[34] Moreover, a number of institutions of higher educa-

32. The final report of the Greensboro Truth and Reconciliation Commission is available at https://greensborotrc.org/. For a helpful introduction to the work of this commission, see McIvor, *Mourning in America*, ch. 1.

33. "The National Memorial for Peace and Justice," Legacy Museum and National Memorial for Peace and Justice, https://museumandmemorial.eji.org/memorial.

34. See Coates, "The Case for Reparations," 54–71, and Brooks, "The Case for Reparations."

tion, including Georgetown University and Virginia Theological Seminary, have recently established reparations programs for their own role in slavery.[35] The list of institutions continues to grow.

In the wake of the death of George Floyd, many are now calling for a national effort that would scale these initiatives to a full, public accounting of America's racial injustices, bringing official acknowledgment and societal ownership to issues that have been disavowed, underplayed, or deferred for too long. This is the direction we see other countries heading as they wrestle with the implications of the Black Lives Matter movement for their own long-term legacies of injustice.[36] The world now looks to America for how it will do the same. As King said, justice delayed is justice denied. If peace is the work of justice, then justice delayed is peace delayed and peace denied too.

Back on the intersection with Austin, it came time to kneel. On sidewalks, medians, and parts of the street, young and old took to one knee, and except for the occasional passing of a car and helicopter overhead, the intersection was quiet. Austin didn't have any trouble kneeling, but my adult knees had to shift now and then. In that silence, down on our knees, it seemed appropriate to pray. Maybe it was a way to reclaim kneeling as a posture of humility and submission, rather than subjection and death. Or maybe it was a way for a father to take stock of the moment with his son. Sometimes when you're on your knees, you just pray. So I put my arm around Austin and we said a short prayer. We thanked God for bringing us there. We prayed for justice and consolation for George Floyd's family. We prayed for societal change that is sweeping and sustained, and our part to play in it. And we prayed for peace: for true peace, for positive peace, for abolition peace.

Then we got up, gathered our signs, and marched with the crowd down a wide-open avenue, Austin relishing the fact that we could walk straight through multiple red traffic lights. The protest finished and the crowd dispersed. On the ride home, Austin told his younger brothers all about the experience. When we got back, we made macaroni and cheese for dinner and played with Tonka trucks in the front yard until it got

35. See "Georgetown Offering Aid to Families of 272 Slaves"; "Seminary Creates $1.7 Million Fund to Pay Slavery Reparations."

36. The Belgian Parliament, for example, has approved a truth commission to examine the legacy of colonialism, especially in Congo under King Leopold II. See https://www.brusselstimes.com/news/belgium-all-news/117289/parliament-approves-commission-on-belgiums-colonial-past/.

dark. Before bed, Austin propped up the sign that he had made and said, "We're going to keep it, right?"

"Yes," I said. "We are."

Bibliography

Aquinas, St. Thomas. *The Summa Theologica*. 5 vols. Translated by the Fathers of the English Dominican Province. New York: Benziger Brothers, 1948.

Augustine. *City of God*. London: Penguin, 2003.

Blight, David. *Race and Reunion: The Civil War in American Memory*. Cambridge: Harvard University Press, 2001.

Brooks, David. "The Case for Reparations: A Slow Convert to the Cause." *New York Times*, Op-Ed, March 7, 2019.

Coady, C. A. J., and Jeff Ross. "St. Augustine and the Ideal of Peace." *American Catholic Philosophical Quarterly* 74.1 (2000) 153–61.

Coates, Ta-Nehisi. "The Case for Reparations." *Atlantic Monthly*, June 2014, 54–71.

Dorrien, Gary. *The New Abolition: W. E. B. Du Bois and the Black Social Gospel*. New Haven, CT: Yale University Press, 2015.

———. *Breaking White Supremacy: Martin Luther King, Jr. and the Black Social Gospel*. New Haven, CT: Yale University Press, 2018.

Douglass, Frederick. *Narrative of the Life of Frederick Douglass, An American Slave*. In *Douglass: Autobiographies*, edited by Henry Louis Gates, Jr., 4–41. New York: Library of America, 1994.

Foner, Philip S., ed. *Frederick Douglass: Selected Speeches and Writings*. Chicago: Lawrence Hill, 1999.

King, Martin Luther, Jr., "Love, Law, and Civil Disobedience." In *A Testament of Hope: The Essential Writings and Speeches of Martin Luther King, Jr.*, edited by James M. Washington, 43–53. New York: Harper Collins, 1986.

McIvor, David W. *Mourning in America: Race and the Politics of Loss*. Ithaca, NY: Cornell University Press, 2016.

New York Times. "Georgetown Offering Aid to Families of 272 Slaves," A21, October 31, 2019.

———. "Seminary Creates $1.7 Million Fund to Pay Slavery Reparations, A16, September 13, 2019.

16

The Priesthood of All the Baptized

Joseph S. Pagano

IN MY OLD OFFICE, there hung a rather large certificate in a gilded frame that read in part,

> BE IT KNOWN unto you by these Presents, that We, Stephen Andrew Miller by Divine Providence Bishop of Milwaukee, conferring Holy Orders under the Protection of ALMIGHTY GOD, in St. Paul's Episcopal Church in Milwaukee, Wisconsin, on the eighth day of December in the year of Our LORD two thousand four, did then and there, rightly and canonically, and according to the form prescribed in The Book of Common Prayer of The Episcopal Church, Ordain as a Priest in the ONE, HOLY, CATHOLIC, AND APOSTOLIC CHURCH, our beloved brother in Christ, Joseph Samuel Pagano of whose godly, sober and honest life and conduct, competent learning, knowledge of the Holy Scriptures, and soundness in the Faith, we are well assured.

That's quite a mouthful, and I must admit I am not overly fond of the language. I'm not a fan of the self-conscious archaisms, even as I recognize the proclamatory nature of the document. It is a public, not a private declaration. It is about the universal church, not a sect. But honestly, "BE IT KNOWN unto you by these Presents, that We . . . ." Elevated language is one thing. High flown, another.

My main concern with the certificate, however, is not its language, but its claim that on December 8, 2004 in Milwaukee, "then and there,"

I was ordained a priest. On the face of it, this is straightforwardly true. On that date, in that place, the bishop of Milwaukee and a good number of presbyters laid hands upon me and I was ordained a priest in Christ's church. But, deep down, I'm not too sure. If I had to choose a date, a "then and there," when I was made a priest I would say February 14, 1965, when as a six-week-old baby I was baptized in St. Francis de Sales Church in Riverside, California.

Don't get me wrong. My ordination was a powerful, Spirit-filled event. I consider it a sacramental rite: an outward and visible sign of an inward and spiritual grace. The grace in this case, as the Catechism says, is "the grace of the Holy Spirit" to those being "made" priests "through prayer and the laying on of hands by bishops." On that day, I knelt before my bishop and felt the full weight of the priestly scrum pressing me forward. The bishop laid hands on me and the gathered people of God sang *Veni Sancte Spiritus*. And the Spirit did. I felt the presence of the Holy Spirit at my ordination and I have relied upon the grace of the Holy Spirit throughout my ordained ministry.

Still I don't think I was made a priest at ordination. I believe I was made a priest when I was baptized.

It is strange, I realize, to consider baptism to be one of the most, if not the most, important events in my life when I have no memory of it. I was only six weeks old. The custom at the time was to baptize newborns before traveling. My first trip outside the home was to the local Catholic church. My mother is pretty sure I slept through the whole thing.

It was a private baptism. The priest, my mother and father, my two-and-a-half-year-old brother, two family friends, and I were present. My parents don't remember any details about the rite. To be fair, I was just born and my older brother was—let's just say—an energetic little boy. The only thing I am certain of—because how could it have been otherwise— is that water was involved and I was baptized in the name of the Father and of the Son and of the Holy Spirit.

I don't have a certificate for my baptism. It must have been lost during one of our family moves. My baptism is recorded in the parish registry, but that's about it. How different from my ordination. No framed certificate proclaiming, "BE IT KNOWN unto you." No mention of my "godly, sober and honest life." Just the bare fact that my nine-pound hunk of flesh was brought to the font of St. Francis de Sales Church, splashed with some water, and baptized in the name of the Triune God.

And yet, as sure as I am of anything in this world, I believe in baptism that I was united with Christ in his death and resurrection, forgiven my sins, adopted as God's child, made a member of Christ's body, the church, and an heir to the promises of the kingdom.

I also believe I was made a priest on that day.

Martin Luther claimed we are all ordained priests in baptism. These were fighting words.

Against calls for reform, the church, according to Luther, erected three walls. The first buttressed the church's claim that spiritual authorities were greater than secular authorities, the second, that only the pope can finally interpret the Bible, and the third, that the pope was superior to councils of the church. To knock down these walls Luther used baptism as a battering ram.

In the late medieval period, calls for the reform of the church came from many quarters. Mendicant orders (think Franciscans and Dominicans) took the gospel outside the monastery and into the streets. Humanists (think Erasmus of Rotterdam) criticized the pomp and worldliness of the hierarchy, the superstitions of popular piety, the logic-chopping of scholastic theology and called for a return to the simple religion of Christ. There were long lists of "Grievances of the German Nation" (*Gravamina nationis Germanicae*) dating from the early fifteenth century written by the secular estates against the abuses of the Roman Church. Nicholas of Cusa even appealed to the Holy Roman Emperor to take responsibility for the reform of the church. Luther's calls for reform were nothing new.

What was new, and indeed revolutionary, was Luther's theological argument for reform. In the "Address to the Nobility of the German Nation," Luther criticized the traditional distinction between the "temporal" and "spiritual" estates; that is, between the laity and the clergy. All people who belong to Christ through faith, the gospel, and baptism share in the priesthood of Jesus Christ and belong "truly to the spiritual estate." As Luther says, "For whoever comes out of the water of baptism can boast that he is already a consecrated priest, bishop, and pope."[1]

Luther holds up a newly baptized infant, a "priest, bishop, and pope," and the walls between the spiritual and the temporal estates come tumbling down. And when the walls come down, the Christian nobility had not only the right but also the responsibility to reform both church

1. Luther, *Luther's Works* 44, 129.

and society. That the territorial estates would increasingly take over areas of common life that used to belong to the church (e.g., education, care for the poor) was probably inevitable by Luther's time. That the electors would do so not simply because of their office as rulers, but because they were baptized as babies was a stroke of genius.

It should be noted that Luther didn't take "the priesthood of all the baptized" to mean what later Protestantism referred to as "the priesthood of all believers." As far as I know, Luther never used the phrase. He didn't understand the priesthood of all the baptized to be only about the individual's freedom to stand in direct relationship to God without the mediation of clergy. Ideas about each soul's direct access to God are far too individualistic for Luther. As Paul Althaus says,

> Luther never understands the priesthood of all believers merely in the "Protestant" sense of the Christian's freedom to stand in a direct relationship to God without a human mediator. Rather he constantly emphasizes the Christian's evangelical authority to come before God on behalf of the brethren and also of the world. The universal priesthood expresses not religious individualism but its exact opposite, the reality of the congregation as a community.[2]

The priesthood of all the baptized, therefore, is not about the Christian soul being free to say, "I am my own priest." Rather, the priesthood of all the baptized is about the church. In the body of Christ, we have all been freed to be priests for one another. We stand before God so that we can intercede for one another. We sacrifice ourselves to God so that we can serve one another. We proclaim God's word so that we can assure one another of the forgiveness of sin. As a priestly community we celebrate God's presence among us in word and sacrament, praise and fellowship. Our priestly ministry, however, does not limit itself to Christian community. Rather, it compels the church to pour itself out in service and witness to the world.

Luther bases his understanding of the priesthood of all the baptized on scripture. In the New Testament the priesthood that matters most is Christ's. In Hebrews, Jesus is called our great high priest (4:14–16). He bears our burdens by making sacrifice for us and by being a sacrifice for us. He intercedes for us so that we may approach the throne of God with confidence. He establishes a new covenant that promises eternal

2. Althaus, *The Theology of Luther*, 314.

salvation. Although it is only in Hebrews that Jesus is explicitly called a priest, other New Testament passages use priestly imagery to describe his ministry. Mark speaks of the Son of Man coming to "give his life as a ransom for many" (10:45) and Paul speaks of Christ's death as a sacrifice for us (Rom 3:25; 5:8; 1 Cor 15:3; Eph 5:2). For Luther, the church is founded on Christ's priesthood.

The priesthood of all the baptized flows from Christ's priesthood. Luther refers to two New Testament texts that speak about the priesthood of all the baptized. First Peter calls the church a "holy priesthood, offering spiritual sacrifices acceptable to God through Jesus Christ," (2:5) and "a chosen people, a royal priesthood, a holy nation, God's special possession, that you may declare the praises of him who called you out of darkness into his wonderful light" (2:9). Revelation speaks of Christ, who has "freed us from our sins by his blood," making the church a "kingdom, priests to his God and Father" (1:5–6). It is the whole church that has been brought to God through Christ's priestly ministry and the whole church that has the priestly calling of service and witness to the world.

The New Testament does not use the terms "priest" or "priesthood" (*hiereus, hierateuma*) for any office holders in the church. They are applied only to Christ and to the whole New Testament people of God. Various ministers in the church are called apostles, deacons, elders, overseers, teachers, evangelists, pastors, and prophets. But no priests. Perhaps this was to avoid confusion with Jewish priests who offered sacrifices in the temple. More likely, it was because the uniqueness of Christ's priesthood and sacrifice would not allow other priests beside him. Because of Christ's sacrifice "once offered," the idea of a priestly office within the church whose function is to offer regular sacrifice has been overcome. As J. B. Lightfoot says in regard to Hebrews, "Now this apostolic writer teaches that all sacrifices had been consummated in the one Sacrifice, all priesthoods absorbed in the one Priest. The offering had been made once for all; and, as there were no more victims, there could be no more priests."[3]

To make this point about the priesthood of Christ and the church, Luther used the term *sacerdotium* to refer to the universal priesthood of the baptized and the term *ministerium* to refer to the ordained ministry. All the baptized share in the eternal priesthood of Christ. Some of the baptized are called to the ordained ministry. Luther maintained

---

3. Lightfoot, *Dissertations on the Apostolic Age*, 233.

throughout his life that the office of proclaiming the word and administering the sacraments was instituted by Christ himself. He just didn't think that called and ordained ministers should be referred to as priests.

Anglican churches, unlike Protestant churches, retained the word "priest" for an ordained minister of word and sacrament. This has caused no little confusion because the English word "priest" has been used to translate both *presbyteros*, meaning an "elder or leader of a congregation," and *hiereus*, which we might think of as a "priest who offers sacrifices." That the English word "priest" came to be used for *presbyteros* seems almost happenstance. In Old English, *presbyter* became *proest*, in Middle English *proest* became *preest*, and in Modern English *preest* became *priest*. You can see how confusion can follow. The same English word "priest" can mean two quite different types of ministry.

Richard Hooker preferred the word "presbyter" to "priest." At first, Hooker says, rather diplomatically, let people use whatever language they choose: "call it a Priesthood, a Presbytership, or a Ministry it skilleth not." Hooker continues, however, more frankly: "In truth the word *Presbyter* doth seem more fit, and in propriety of speech more agreeable than *Priest* with the drift of the whole Gospel of Jesus Christ."[4] One meaning of the word "priest" seems to follow the drift of the "whole Gospel of Jesus Christ" and the other seems to be at crosscurrents with it. I would also add that one meaning of "priest" also seems to be at crosscurrents with the priesthood of all the baptized.

The ambiguity in the word "priest," however, has led some Anglicans to try to find ways presbyters can also appropriately be called priests. These attempts usually boil down to saying that they may be called priests because they somehow represent or signify the priestly calling of the whole people of God. R. C. Moberly argues that presbyters may properly be called priests because they embody "with an eminent distinctiveness" the "concentrated meaning" of the church's priesthood.[5] In the church, all priesthood flows from Christ's priesthood, his eternal self-offering before the throne of God. The priesthood of the church is a participation in the priesthood of Christ. Its whole life is one of loving self-offering to God and to the world, as Christ's own life was and continues to be. Ordained ministers, who are authorized to "represent, and act for, and wield ministerially" the powers of the whole church may be called priests

---

4. Hooker, *Of the Laws of Ecclesiastical Polity* 5.78.iii.

5. Moberly, *Ministerial Priesthood*, 260, 262.

because they personify the priesthood of the church.[6] Priests are not su-
per-spiritual people who offer vicarious sacrifices on behalf of a less holy
laity. Rather, priests are representatives who enable the priestly ministry
of the whole church. As Moberly says, "They are Priests because they
are personally consecrated to be representatives and active organs of the
priesthood of the Church."[7]

Moberly's argument helpfully emphasizes the corporate priesthood
of all the baptized. Revelation speaks of the church as kingdom of priests.
But when the author of 1 Peter refers to the church as a "royal priesthood," he uses the collective singular noun *hierateuma*. Not a plurality of
priests, but a body of priests. All the baptized are priests, a kingdom of
priests. But there is also a corporate priesthood of the church that is distinct from the priesthood of each of its members. Just like there is a guild
of artisans (*techniteuma*), a group of senators (*bouleuma*), and a body of
citizens (*politeuma*), so there is a priesthood of the baptized.[8] A corporate
dimension of the priesthood of all the baptized means that every member
of the church is viewed not only as a priest, but also as forming a collective priesthood from whom comes "the aroma of perpetual offering
towards God," and whose "arms are spread out perpetually to succor and
intercede for those who need the sacrifice of love."[9]

Moberly's, and indeed Anglicanism's, balanced approach to both the
personal dimension of the priesthood of all the baptized and the corporate priesthood of the whole church helps us to see the individualism
still lurking in Luther. As I have said, it is unfair to tag Luther with the
individualism of later Protestant formulations of the priesthood of all believers. And yet, when Luther speaks of the priesthood of all the baptized,
he emphasizes the activity of individuals for the sake of the community.
There is little talk of the corporate priesthood of the church. It's better,
I think, to say we need both: the personal priestly ministries of all the
baptized and the corporate priesthood of all the baptized.

I am Anglican enough not to mind calling those ordained to the
ministry of word and sacrament "priests." I am also fine with the ambiguity in the meaning of the word "priest." If it helps the church to be the
church, good by me. If calling clergy "priests" helps them to proclaim

6. Moberly, *Ministerial Priesthood*, 258.

7. Moberly, *Ministerial Priesthood*, 259.

8. For the examples I am indebted to Jean-Pierre Torrell, *A Priestly People*, 2.

9. Moberly, *Ministerial Priesthood*, 255–56.

God's word, rightly administer the sacraments, and build up the faithful, then call them "priests." It skilleth not. I am concerned, however, that what Boone Porter refers to as the "omnivorous priesthood," is causing us to lose a sense of the priesthood of all the baptized.[10]

The canons of The Episcopal Church speak of the "ministry of all baptized persons." Language about and around the ministry of all baptized persons is heard frequently in the church today, and, for the most part, this is quite a good thing. The canons state that "all baptized persons are called to ministry in Christ's name." Good. The canons also call on the church to help individuals identify their gifts so that they can "serve Christ's mission at all times and in all places." Good. The Catechism in the Book of Common Prayer states that the church "carries out its mission through the ministry of all its members." All good.

But, despite its best intentions, the language about the ministry of all baptized persons ends up in practice to be rather individualistic. All baptized persons are called to ministry in Christ's name, but they have all been given different gifts for ministry. The task of discernment then is for baptized persons, with the help of the church, to discern their distinctive gifts for ministry. Has God given me gifts for teaching? Gifts for caring for the physical environment? Gifts for serving with the poor and vulnerable? Gifts for preaching? Once I identify my gifts, I can, with the help of the church, carry out *my* ministry in church and in the world.

I fear that with talk about the *ministry* of all baptized persons we are losing a sense of the *priesthood* of all baptized persons. By identifying priesthood with the ordained ministry of certain individuals, we are losing sight of the priesthood of the whole church. In fact, "priest" often means one option among many when Christians try to discern their ministries. Am I called to be a doctor? A nurse? A priest? A deacon? A plumber? The fact that we have all been made priests in our baptisms is lost in the language of ministries. There is a certain irony that Luther's understanding of the priesthood as the common calling of all the baptized and the ministry as the specific calling of some of the baptized has been inverted in the ministry of all baptized persons.

The service of Holy Baptism in the Book of Common Prayer speaks of the priesthood of all the baptized. At the consecration of the chrism that is used in the sealing of the baptized the bishop prays, "Eternal Father, whose blessed Son was anointed by the Holy Spirit to be the Savior

10. Porter, "A Traditional Reflection on Diaconate in relation to 'Omnivorous Priesthood.'"

and servant of all, we pray you to consecrate this oil, that those who are sealed with it may share in the royal priesthood of Jesus Christ." And at the end of the service the celebrant and people welcome the newly baptized with these words, "We receive you into the household of God. Confess the faith of Christ crucified, proclaim his resurrection, and share with us in his eternal priesthood."

Priesthood is a ministry that we all share in Christ's church. It is not mine and it is not yours. It is based upon the priestly ministry of Jesus Christ who sacrificed himself for us and who intercedes for us. The whole church is called to embody this priestly ministry. As 1 Peter says, we are "a chosen people, a royal priesthood, a holy nation, God's special possession, that you may declare the praises of him who called you out of darkness into his wonderful light." That's the work of the whole church. We have all been made priests to each other by virtue of baptism. In the communion of saints, we are freed to stand before God and intercede for one another. We proclaim God's word and assure one another of God's forgiveness. We celebrate God's presence among us in worship, praise, and fellowship and we go out into the world in witness to God's love.

I cradle Hank in my left arm and bend my knees a bit so I can take a scoop of water from the font with my right hand. The head of the altar guild catches my eye as I straighten up, water spilling from my palm. She shoots me a look that says, "Don't make a mess."

Last time there was so much water on the floor that she threw down a bunch of towels to soak it up. When she bent to pick up the sopping towels she knocked heads with the ox carved on the side of the font causing an angry welt.

"But," I silently protest, "it's supposed to be living water. It's drowning water." My mind starts to drift and I correct myself, "No, better to say it's 'drowning water' then 'living water.' Death then resurrection. 'In it we are buried with Christ in his death. By it we share in his resurrection.'" The watery symbols swim, my mind floats.

Hank squirms in my arms as if to say, "Let's get on with it already."

I compromise. More than a sprinkle, but not so much as to require an emergency meeting of the altar guild. "Hank, I baptize you in the Name of the Father (swoosh) . . . and of the Son (swoosh) . . . and of the Holy Spirit (swoosh)." I try to keep the water flowing throughout the naming of the Triune God.

It's one of the many priestly negotiations I make every Sunday. I know all too well that it's not my ministry that makes things happen. Before the service, women in the sacristy expertly judge the temperature of the water in the ewer so that when it comes time for the baptism it is neither too hot nor too cold. A gentle touch from an usher prompts parents and godparent to say in unison, "I present Hank to receive the Sacrament of Baptism." A young acolyte holds open the water-damaged pages of the baptismal rite so that I'm not trying to juggle baby and prayer book.

Another acolyte magically appears at my side holding up a container of chrism. I plunge my thumb into the oil. I want Hank to smell the fragrance of balsam as I make the sign of the cross on his forehead while I say, "you are sealed by the Holy Spirit in baptism and marked as Christ's own forever." The acolyte silently recedes.

It's the church's work to baptize. I've got my part to play, but it's probably wise not to make a watery, oily spectacle of myself. Get out of the way and let people do their work. Get out of the way and let the sacrament speak. Get out of the way and let Christ act. We are at best servants and witnesses to the word attached to this watery sign.

I have come to think that Luther was right about infant baptism. Children have a faith that is properly their own. It's not the faith of the church or the faith of the godparents somehow standing in for them until they grow up. Rather the word spoken in baptism pulses in children's ears quickening a trust in them by which they cling to the promises of Christ. After all, didn't John the Baptist leap in Elizabeth's womb when a pregnant Mary came to visit?

I rearrange Hank in my arms so we can welcome the newly baptized and his tiny hand grasps one of my fingers. I take a moment to silently acknowledge the gift of receiving one of Hank's first priestly acts. Strengthened by his blessing, I face the congregation and we say, "Hank, we receive you into the household of God. Confess the faith of Christ crucified, proclaim his resurrection, and share with us in his eternal priesthood."

Bibliography

Althaus, Paul. *The Theology of Luther.* Philadelphia: Fortress, 1966.

Hooker, Richard. *Of the Laws of Ecclesiastical Polity. A Critical Edition with Modern Spelling.* Edited by Arthur Stephen McGrade. 3 vols. Oxford: Oxford University Press, 2013.

Lightfoot, Joseph Barber. *Dissertations on the Apostolic Age.* Reprint, Eugene, OR: Wipf & Stock, 2008.

Luther, Martin. *Luther's Works.* Edited by Jaroslav Pelikan et al. 55 vols. St. Louis: Concordia, 1955–86.

Moberly, Robert Campbell. *Ministerial Priesthood: Chapters (Preliminary to a Study of the Ordinal) on the Rationale of Ministry and the Meaning of Christian Priesthood.* 2nd ed. Reprint, London: SPCK, 1969.

Porter, Harry Boone. "A Traditional Reflection on Diaconate in relation to 'Omnivorous Priesthood.'" *Living Worship* 12.9, November 1976.

Torrell, Jean-Pierre. *A Priestly People: Baptismal Priesthood and Priestly Ministry.* New York: Paulist, 2013.

17

Providence

A Circumlocution

John Milbank

Providence is the wild side of religion that we no longer wish to know about. Ethics is the tame, respectable side, that allows us to put a slightly sacred gloss upon contemporary pieties about human behavior. But there is no real religion without invoking the perpetual providential whirlwind. And morality turns out to be dubious without it: not so much a mild comforting breeze as a lulling into complacency about the current human condition and the impossibility of pursuing any real good within its existing terms.

Ethics are the tablets of the law when we forget the terror and the mountain. Providence is located more directly in those narratives that mention God only obliquely: the story of Queen Esther, of the tumult of monarchic succession, of the corrupted kings David and Solomon, whose doings and destiny in Jerusalem were yet to foreshadow the subsumption of that other divinely appointed city of doubtful repute, namely Rome, into the very enterprise of the final salvation of the human race itself.

Providence is Donald Crowhurst drawn by a series of incremental mistakes and an overrating of his own capacities into a lone voyage during which he mysteriously caught a vision of the divine mercy.[1] It is the way in which the rancor of a gossiping neighbor can force someone to confront her real destiny to live with her true love in another country, whereas the genuine charity of friends and old loves seduce her into self-deception, as in the film *Brooklyn*, based upon the novel by Colm Toibin. It is the poetic combining of accidental synchronous events into a pattern, on the assumption that this reflects a fated reality beyond efficient causation, as for the traditional Chinese consciousness, pondered by Lawrence Osborne in his novel *The Ballad of a Small Player*. It is the realization that there is indeed no such thing at the mechanical level as chance: the fall of the dice is determined by invisible microscopic circumstances; the accidental synchronic conjunctures radiate outwards, more secret and ancient linkages of wider combinations. But it is also our sense of the imponderable fated guiding even of spontaneities, including our own freedom.

Providence is never remote, but always most immediate, just because it is the direct presence of God himself. But it is as much the presence of the enigmatic as of the consoling. If there is mercy here, it may not be immediately apparent, or if so can appear later to be disillusioning. The very people we are most drawn to for their beauty of character may lure us into a complicity in their own hidden vices until it is too late to withdraw. Only an easy moralism supposes that we could have recognized the bad signs if we had followed more exigently some rule book or been truly attentive. Such moralism does not want to face up to the real meaning of post-Edenic corruption. For this does not mean merely that the best is somewhat tainted, but that it is so radically distorted as to be impossible, without grace, to recognize. We cannot of ourselves and naturally untangle the enigmas of virtue, and grace operates only slowly, itself enigmatically and secretly. Why otherwise, as Augustine taught, would it be shown and given to us via the medium of strange cryptograms and obscure sacraments? As the rabbis know, the path to virtue lies through long reading of the signs, both in scripture and in nature, including the political nature of humanity. We begin to comprehend just why the Bible, far more than the Qur'an, contains just so many tortuous, if absorbing narrations.

---

1. Donald Crowhurst entered the Sunday Times Golden Globe Race in 1968, a competition to be the first person to sail solo, nonstop, around the world. His boat and abilities were no match for his competitors or the sea.

Nothing is more shocking than to discover that all of our daily good behavior is only inculcated so as to secure the solidarity of a war-band. From the respectable middle classes, this truth is always concealed, or by them hypocritically ignored. Of course, the workers, with their greater exposure to the elements, always suspect it. But the leaders of nations and of corporations directly know it, with whatever degree of avid complacency or sleepless unease. For at the margins of the city or nation it turns out that morality was largely a pretense: it was merely the necessary honor amongst thieves after all. At the margins, sheer narcissism and self-interest returns conglomerated and can only be eased by the relative nobility of imperial and world-religious projects, which must themselves still pay a price of ambiguous coercion and subjugation of ancient cults and localities.

Yet the Hebrew Bible/Old Testament does not shun this level: it knows that unless the prophets address kings, besides Moses addressing the individual, there can be no real arrival of justice. Christ adds that without the political extension of the private exercise of care and mercy there can still be no justice, which depends upon all creatures finding continuously their proper places in harmonious peace with others. Just in this way, the search for the good outreaches our sad intentions, which may serve merely to augment the power of the immensely violent, even while they appear to protect us from the depredations of the villain round the corner.

From this perspective, our most genuine ethical actions have to be seen as more like hermeneutic and poetic interventions: they require to be symbolic performances which seek to decipher the entrapment of the regularly good within the irregularly evil. They need speculatively to outreach their own fond and narrowly conventional intentions, which may be distorted into bad ones by the way they are later taken by others, and seek to proffer new spaces of genuine virtue and community that others may inhabit. The mark of the truly good action is the way in which it somehow anticipates and forestalls its own proneness to eventual distortion: like a true work of art, or the curious works of religious founders, its symbolic richness renders it always a source of newly creative extensions that can correct any misappropriations. Such actions must always diagonalize out of the peaceful set whose borders are after all defined by violence.

For we all live within compromised enclaves. This is, if you like, the political dimension of original sin. Every nation tracks back to conquest and usurpation. Every fortune to some past act of unjust seizure. To concentrate here merely upon the ongoing profits from slavery and so forth is insightful and yet does not take genealogical suspicion far enough. Focussed on obsessively it becomes a moralistic distraction from temporary ills; taken to the end it should be an impulse for all of us together to try to craft something new out of the inherent wreckage of the past. Not to ignore its violently sheltered benefits (which may include even the hierarchical and the paternalistic) but to rescue them from compromised containment—to release them into the continuum of the endlessly relational infinite.

Similarly, every family legacy is at another family's expense; every story of personal success conceals that moment when you humiliated another, less confident and fortunate child of hidden ability, egged on by your teachers. And that is to say nothing of the instances when so many of us bent the rules and walked through the gap that we deemed others too priggish to enter. Not that we were entirely wrong: so often indeed they were merely seeking the security of a trapped virtue and deluding themselves that their cowardice was upright probity. In the reckonings of providence, the weak fare no better than the strong—to go beyond Nietzsche but with him, in the spirit of Paul and Augustine.

Thus everywhere crime sediments into law and sin settles into patterns of everyday custom. Soon we do not notice that both are compromised at their core, that evil is not an exception but entirely pervades and corrupts the most general and universal. It was just this insight that propelled Augustine and others, in the wake of earlier philosophers, to found alternative communities, directly related to the realm of the cosmic intelligences, now more than ever understood as a spiritual community, or polis. Yet this very endeavor of rebirth seems but partial if it finds no place to reform natural birth and has to bypass sexual difference and human erotic relationships. Another mode of subtle and fallen idolatry intrudes to let us suppose that in general (even if some need to be called to celibacy) there is a choice to be made between sex and God or between finite and infinite loves, which cannot really be in a zero-sum competition. Then, inevitably, to include God within the finite game of either/or will be to substitute for God a human idol which will generally be male. For Augustine, despite his unique insights, which we can never ignore, this turns too easily into the unworthy thesis that beautiful women especially are not to trusted: that they lure men by their shallow surface away from the eternal source of true beauty, such that they and indeed all their sisters must be in time subordinated and can be abandoned without qualm for a life of fraternal seclusion.

We are now surely past the time for all that. Monasticism remains important and yet it still too much tended to leave the laity behind. We require, more than ever, more inclusive and everyday modes (the Shaker way will not do either), extending to the ambiguities of human loves and passionate conflicts (as Augustine rightly recognized) of liturgical and salvific community. We can never succeed, as Augustine also saw, in being good all by ourselves.

But naturally, this does not mean that we can simply be rescued from the vagaries of our own private biographies. Monasticism came nearer to that, but even that path could not achieve this. It is instead the case that community offers a certain salve through the practices of mercy, forgiveness, care, and reconciliation. Specifically liturgical community offers a symbolic language in which these mysteries can ever anew be recognized and come to pass. Above all, we see providence at work here. And yet not merely there. The cosmic church is never immediately apparent, even in the widest human dimensions. Something individual always escapes, such that autobiography is in one dimension more than collective history, and more than intermittent spatial gathering for various human censuses in various human forums of various definitions of citizenship.

Each of us must, to some degree privately, come to terms with our own past, and of course that is an ongoing task. Like Augustine, we must confess our false selves and embrace our true, divinely given self in combined worship with spiritual others, temporal and eternal. Yet perhaps for us today this self-reckoning is still more complicated. Just what is it that we have done wrong? It can appear almost impossible to sift our own malevolent contributions from our bad moral luck or the promptings of deceptive circumstance. Above all, past election of an apparent good turns out later to have been too often the election of a half-good that was also a half-evil, to the neglect of other and perhaps better half-goods that were also beckoning, had we been attentive. How to distinguish wisdom calling from the house-tops from the siren on the rocks or the woman on the street corner? The very imagery of the wisdom literature seems to suggest implied esoteric echoes that it exoterically denies.

Once we are complicit in a shared wrong choice or tainted conspiracy, can we with true honor extract ourselves all on our own? Is it always clearly and obviously just to betray our partners in crime, or can that sometimes smack of a suspiciously belated arrival of self-righteousness.

To have encouraged others in a compromised path and then to leave them alone upon it or exposed to a public demand for their own confession for which they are psychologically unprepared or constitutionally incapable—can that not on occasion be but a further and compounding lapse of responsibility? Does not one have to exercise here the patience of waiting for the possibility of a repentance that can only be collective in order to be authentic? One can see how this refusal of moral priggishness is often required at a social and political level and how its apparent exceptionality in our personal lives is actually normative for our collective existence.

There are existential dilemmas here that even Christians have usually ignored, with the rare exception of tortured spirits like that of the Scottish Episcopal theologian Donald Mackinnon. And Augustine is of help here only if we press to the end his most drastic metaphysics: the good lies in the referral of all goods, which are every one of them partial and fallen, to the ultimate, unlimited good of perfect harmony of soul, body, and community. From this perspective every wrong turn was also potentially a right one and all roads have the same destiny when trod in the right spirit. The wrongness of any choice consists not in its specific instance but in its deficiency, its privation. Such deficiency is not merely a matter of lack of purity of intention and honesty (here Augustine was insufficiently aware of their difficulty) but of that, plus the back luck of circumstance and of false advising. If evil indeed consists, as Augustine thought, in delusions of grandeur and failures of self-recognition, then part of that inadequacy is a failure to realize the sheer degree to which it has never been just "up to us alone," even at a finite level. Sometimes a shared guilt and a shared deficient course of action must continue to be borne until the right moment for repentance and reversal is providentially offered to us.

Of course there are actions and consistent habits and stances of which we know we must just outright repent. But those can be embedded within wider and stranger patterns of space and time that bear more the character of an enigmatic fate. Just why have certain unfortunate as well as fortunate things again and again occurred to us in slightly different ways? Why do we seem to be trapped in certain repetitions? The answers of psychoanalysis seem too often inadequate: something "occult" appears to escape such a mode of investigation, as Freud at times almost suspected. Since we have no reason to suppose that the psyche is something inward, private and "buffered" (if it is real at all, as consciousness attests) then we have every reason to imagine that it is open to the influence of hidden spiritual beings and that the interactive resonances between human spiritual beings, both in half-manifest and in hidden ways (such as shared dreams) are entirely real. After all, our culture is unusual in not allowing this and unsurprisingly (although implausibly) mostly fails to believe in the reality of soul or mind at all.

All this complicates the business of repentance. But again, the answers lie with a radicalized Augustine. Ultimately in his lineage, Eckhart declared, with his deliberate hyperbole, that it was impious to repent of anything. For the religious moralist our pasts, individual and collective, are catalogues of good deeds and bad, to be filed in separate columns. But not only is this archiving in hock to the ethical fashions of the day, it also seems impious in the register of providence. God, via the secondary causality of our freedom, has fully determined all that we have done: he has only not determined it insofar as it is evil, which is deficient, a lack of occurrence altogether. But that means that all we have actually done, since it is positive and so in some degree good, is not only good, but also part of the specific good that God has willed and understood since all eternity.

Another (if in other ways aberrant) Augustinian, Nicolas Malebranche, following the same inexorable logic of privation, pointed out that anyone who claims to regret any experienced pleasure is manifestly a liar. For by definition enjoyment is incompatible with regret, which is immediately pain and suffering. Our reflective thinking is only an extension of our sympathetic "common sensing," as the "Scotch metaphysics" understood, from Frances Hutcheson (after Shaftesbury and the Cambridge Platonists) through David Hume and Thomas Reid to James Ferrier, and in contrast to the reason/sense dualism of Kant. Reflection cannot, therefore, cancel out the verdict of our common sensing, whose feeling is immediate and ineluctable: it can only mutate and temper it. So all that one can honestly be contrite for is not having enjoyed life more—which means of course to enjoy the things of this world in due measure and proportion and with proper symbolic reference to the infinite. But this is the very opposite of wishing one had had "more of a good time," because it is instead wishing that one had suffered time more musically as a constant passing away and pointing of itself to the eternal that alone composes an earthly (because unearthly) beauty.

Instead of regretting our past and its pleasures, we need to cleave with loyalty to all that has happened to us, because it is God's will for us, it is who we are. This means realizing that in the very circumstances of the commission of a wrong, or in our falling into it, lie the seeds of its remedy. Every fault, as partially good, includes its own cure and offers thereby a new good not otherwise given to us. Each *culpa* is *felix*, not because it turned out to be for the calculable best, but because it is redeemed by a new upsurge of moral creativity, revelatory of the inexhaustible divine plenitude. For us the good arrives always as the unexpectedly reparative, and not that which conforms to our own prescribed rules. And yet just as such a reactive restoration it discloses to view once again the good as spontaneous fountain of generosity, which preceded the need for law as correction.

It follows that the usual ethical is only our fantasized good and that it is illusory. Our suppression of our passions always turns out to be a fascistic inhibiting of pleasure by force, which is of course perverse pleasure. We must instead seek the grace of immediate divine presence through the Son's sustained incarnation which will convert all of our desires into a seeking of the only genuine and shared pleasure whose name is the Bride, Jerusalem. And this grace is of course the continuous operation of providence. The pure good beyond our alternative of "good and evil" because it once preceded and later succeeds to the delusion of evil, which is ultimately nothing.

Thus true enlightenment dawns for us on the day that we realize that whenever we think to ourselves "that turned out to be providential," we are of course always right, simply because everything that occurs is ineluctably fated as providential.

The dark side of this dawning is that our suspicions that we are being punished by God for our failings is always also correct. However Nordically grotesque and superstitious, the musing of the Swedish botanist Linnaeus on this score, his core insight in this regard, remains true. This "punishment" is of course a metaphor: in reality, as Eriugena taught, God never punishes and we only suffer, redemptively, the painful undoing of our own wrongs. Yet because these wrongs have an unknown penumbra of influence and we cannot rule out their esoteric resonances with other wrongs beyond our ken, the ills that we suffer in part as the result of our misdeeds can truly take on an uncanny aspect, which the writers of fiction have best explored.

For the same reason, we are never wrong to suspect that a more general evil, either natural or social, in part afflicts everyone because of our own particular guilt. We are all, by tropical typology, Jonahs, and always to blame for the fate of Nineveh. Not to see this is to fail to realize that God lies beyond the contrast of the general and the particular. He is as close to the specific as to the totality and he perceives and operates a skein of causality and inter-linkage for which the universal has no priority over the individual. Ecological thinking is beginning to intimate some of this: we now know that the flapping of a butterfly's wing can cause a hurricane. There is no overriding totality "including" the entire set of created actors. The only inclusion is by God, who is infinitely in excess of totality.

It is on this account that we sometimes have to trust, as Kierkegaard saw, that only God, besides ourselves, can see the justice of a stance or course of action that we cannot bring into the light of day without being publicly condemned, because our insight into its exceptionality depends upon our unique and irreplaceable vantage-point, which includes our unique subjective orientation to circumstance. For evil is not the private positive following of a generally forbidden course. Rather, evil is nothing, insofar as it is the attempt to capture and control inscrutable divine prudence, which is providence, by our limited human prudence, which is but a sanctimonious and impossible attempt at self-capture. By the same token, ethics is not the autonomy of law, as Kant thought, but rather the heteronomy of mind ruling body and other spirits ruling the spiritual combination of mind and body in our persons, and God himself ruling the entire spiritual and material creation.

All finite prudence seeks to orient the actions of a thing to a single finite end. But God orients the actions of all things to the end that is himself. He is the trump card that is never alien to any card within the deck or to the whole deck itself. As the final end of all things he is not really in the category of mere end at all. He is also beginning and middle indissociably. In this sense, while all finite prudence is somewhat, if not reductively instrumental, divine prudence abolishes instrumentality altogether. Everything in the end carries equal weight and importance, albeit in its own degree.

This is why, for Boethius and Aquinas, providence is not at all the external action of God upon things. Providence is not the divine government or the divine economy, as far too many theologians suppose. It is rather the "type," Platonic form, or divine idea of all things insofar as they are focused upon an end. Of course, in terms of the divine simplicity this means that God's providence is nothing "in addition" to his origination of things in being in the first place. Metaphysically, there is only origination, even though this is itself for Aquinas *creatio continua*.

The name of the divine government, as opposed to his "reserved" sovereignty, is rather "fate." But fate is, on the other hand, not really distinct, as regards God, from the "type" that is providence. Instead, it is just the outworking or "explication" of "complicated" providence in the course of created time, as Thierry of Chartres had said in the wake of Boethius before Aquinas, and Nicholas of Cusa will repeat long afterwards.

Fate is the mediation of the immediate itself, just as what creation participates in is the imparticipable. This could make it seem that mediators—like angels, good daemons, Wisdom, and Jerusalem—are superfluous. But Aquinas explains that angelic mediators exist just because God shares his nonetheless entirely omnipotent power to rule. God is distant from nothing; he is the most proximate and intimate, as for both Proclus and Augustine, such that Maimonides, says Aquinas, was wrong to think that God less providentially guides non-spiritual creatures. Therefore, one can say that what God shares is inevitably his own divine power. Not just angels, one could validly conclude, but all creatures are of their very nature mediators in various serried ranks and modes of inter-connection.

Aquinas is clear that God just as fully determines contingent and spontaneous events, including free and rational processes, as he does efficiently determined ones. For Boethius all of that was economic "fate." Yet Aquinas seems to reserve the term "fate" for the mechanically ineluctable. This opens the way for him, in the wake of Augustine, inconsistently to suggest that God arbitrarily withholds from the unjust certain dangers and means of succor, while withholding possible traps from the just. He thereby recognizes the complex interconnection of temptation and circumstance, of moral and physical evil, of sin and death, and yet his persisting Augustinian theological dualism causes him to forget that the providential type is at one with the creating type, in turn at one with the internally emanating Logos, and therefore never wills for anything, anything other than the completest good. Thus, it would seem that in the case of the predestined unjust and their own wicked actions, Aquinas after all thinks in terms of a distinct willed "decision" involving less than the entire good for some creatures. The language of God's inscrutable justice, etc., cannot cover up this metaphysical lapse of taste and judgment. If the prudential divine willing of spiritual creatures does not lie fully within "fate" then this is because it involves some sort of voluntaristic surplus (according to the divine *potentia absoluta*) over the *explicatio* of eternal providence that is fully and entirely at one with it.

A similar dubiety hovers over Augustine and Aquinas's prepared-
ness to say that there can be imperfections in parts of the creation in
the interests of the perfection of the whole. For is not this mode of com-
placent aestheticism still after all too pagan? If God is perfect, how can
there be any imperfection, which means a deficiency even in any single
part of his production, especially in view of the point that creation is
really a continuous monadic series, for Augustine's deeper outlook, and
only a "whole" as bounded by God? Is there not after all some sort of
residue of the pagan recalcitrance of chaotic matter still at work here in
the conceptual depths?

Rather, we must say, providence is more complete than this, along
with fate as its economic and governmental outworking. In the line more
of Origen, the Cappadocians, Maximus, and Eriugena, we must instead
say that apparently necessary imperfections of the parts are only true of
a cosmos fallen away from its originally spiritual mode of embodiment
and materiality. For now, yes, the lion must eat the lamb, but one day he
will lie down with her.

Outside this eschatological, providential vision, outside faith in and
hope for Jerusalem, perfect cosmic charity and peace, it turns out that
our conventional ethics and piety is all a terrible sham. Contemporary
moralized religion, forgetful of the doctrine of particular providence, is
idolatrous and not encouraging of any genuine good. Such religion, like
the ignorant words of Job, smears God's design with darkness even as it
sheens commonplace pieties. We need to hear the voice from the perpetual providential whirlwind, not only to be comforted like Job that we
are dust, but also to hope in his inexhaustible reparative generosity.

18

Sacrifice

Bulrushes

Katie Karnehm-Esh

The woman conceived and bore a son, and when she saw that he was a fine child, she hid him three months. When she could hide him no longer, she took for him a basket made of bulrushes and daubed it with bitumen and pitch. She put the child in it and placed it among the reeds by the river bank.
(Exod 2:1–3 ESV)

During Holy Week 2017, I flew to Uganda on a research grant from my university. Several times a day I sat in the open-air concrete classrooms, taking notes. The shutters opened to the humid air outside where Ugandan students in bright clothes walked to class. In my room, lizards ran back and forth under my door while a cat mewed at me from the window. In the morning, a herd of monkeys galloped down the hill as the sun rose. If it weren't for the mosquito net hanging like a thick cloud over my bed, the idyll would be complete.

At the end of the week, I sat, clammy and long-skirted, in a class of American students debriefing their trip to northern Uganda. This was the part of the country Joseph Kony had ransacked years before, abducting women and recruiting child soldiers. It was horrible, and far away. In the midst of talking about the NGOs working to provide jobs and therapeutic services for women abused by Kony, I missed the conversational transition back to Mokono, the city we were in. A student mentioned a child sacrifice that had happened the week before. I was taking notes as fast as I could, but paused. "Excuse me for interrupting," I said. "Did you say sacrifice?"

The girls nodded.

"Like . . . an actual child?"

"Sometimes," they said, "the witch doctors would ask for a child sacrifice in exchange for a really big ask. Like crops, the success of a business, elections," one of them said. The idea is the bigger the sacrifice, the better the reward. Sometimes the person would sacrifice their own child, but usually they would find someone else's.

Uganda seemed to be full of other people's children. I'd visited two orphanage schools. One was for "bad" kids, one for blind kids. In the one orphanage, a vine slithered through a crack in the window and grew around the edges of the windows and ceiling, like a snake. Children ran and walked and tumbled everywhere on the grounds of the schools and orphanages and into the roads and dirt paths.

In January, I sit in my church's sanctuary listening to the occasional notes of the choir float up from the basement. My husband is downstairs rehearsing, and I am praying no one bothers me for the next thirty minutes. I don't know that we're three months pre-pandemic, four months pre-foster child, and my days inside a church building are limited. All I know is this is the moment when I can write today. My skin projects a defense shield; my jaw clenches when a voice approaches the sanctuary. But nobody walks in today, except for Jesus, falling for the third time at the stations of the cross nearest my pew. A white Mary looks down on her altar of votive candles, and I am scrolling through definitions of the word "sacrifice" on my phone.

I expect metaphors but what I get instead from Merriam-Webster are literal burnt offerings: "an act of slaughtering an animal or person or surrendering a possession as an offering to God or to a deity or supernatural figure. Noun. To offer or kill as a religious sacrifice. An act of giving up something valued for the sake of something else regarded as wise, important, or worthy." I read the definitions with the same morbid wonder as an Old Testament story of Abraham and Isaac, or Jephthah's daughter. To sacrifice means you must destroy or surrender a precious item for a higher purpose. You elect to give up or lose an item or person because something else, like your crops, or your devotion, is more important.

All the *somethings* indicate the nebulous nature of sacrifice. While religions and cultures might dictate what sacrifice looks like, for the dictionary's purposes, any valuable item qualifies, so long as it is given up willingly, for the purpose of gaining something else. Some cultures might require a dove as a sacrifice; somewhere else it might be a lamb or goat; in ancient—and modern—culture the sacrifice in question might be a human being.

In one of the oldest photos of my brother and me, we're standing on the rails of the wooden fence by our house. He's five, I'm seven, and we're watching the cows in the pasture below. Our mother is somewhere behind us with the camera. We can roam the entire farm as children, as long as we could hear our mother whistle for us. In the sun-filtered memories of my childhood, she's standing on the hill outside our yellow house in the noonday sun, her eyes scrunched up and sweeping across the pasture. Then she brings her thumb and index finger to her mouth in an O, breathes in, and whistles. We can hear her half a mile away; we and our dogs and our friends know to immediately start running. Who could ignore a call like that?

Mom was the queen of our world. She taught us to read, do long division, and make Jell-O. She orchestrated chores, piano lessons, ballet lessons, homeschooling, and five children's needs. We were always a little terrified of her, in an awestruck way, until around 6:00 or 7:00 p.m. when our awe turned to anxiety. Dad's gray car would blow dust up the driveway and she would retreat into making dinner. If we were excited for our father to come home, we also felt the creeping of her anxiety as she ceded her space. Her tone got sharper. When we had particularly exhausted her, or my father was late again, she might exclaim, "I haven't had a *shower* today! My friends play tennis! I can't play tennis! Did you get the clothes off the line? No, it's fine. *I'll do it.*" I hated when she martyred herself over dinner and the laundry; I was never brave enough to say I wished she would play tennis. I hated most how well I internalized the lesson.

Four months ago, on the Thursday before Easter, our social worker texted me to say they had a teenage boy, a refugee from Central Africa, who needed immediate placement. We had just received a license to be foster parents after a year of classes, paperwork, and vetting. Our plan had been to adopt a kid out of foster care, not do short-term foster care as service.

But it was the pandemic; all our plans were canceled, we were teaching from home, and we had a spare bedroom. Still, my old white fears flared up as I thought about a black teenage boy. I kept trying to find out if he was violent; if he would abuse animals; if he would try to run away; if I should hide our cooking knives; if we should lock all the animals and our most prized possessions in the room with us at night. "Flight risk," our social worker said. When the social workers tried to take the kids into protective care the previous day, the mother screamed *run* and this boy ran away for the night.

Eventually we stopped trying to predict what would happen, and said yes. He showed up two hours later. His backpack was torn and his hoodie had a yellow stain on the back. His barely five-foot body hunched like he was trying to disappear. The social worker walked him inside and clapped him on the back. "You have a powerful name, son," he said, and left. We showed him his room. He flinched when the dogs came out to meet him; the only words he said to us that night were "Wi-Fi?" We gave him the password and he retreated. All night I listened through the wall for sounds of him escaping. In the morning, I paused at his door, then sighed when I heard him roll over.

After we set our child up in his room, we watched the diocese's Maundy Thursday service on YouTube (and briefly smiled when former presidential candidate Pete Buttigieg had a cameo reading a scripture). As the sun set and the service of mourning continued, I could not shake how dark the world seemed, and how dark it stayed. I woke up early on Easter, wanting to feel excited to break my Lenten fast, but the stone that rolled away from the tomb landed on my chest. Through our wall, I heard our foster son crying. The resurrection light was cold and gray. The women at the tomb wept and so did I.

By mid-afternoon on Easter our foster son had barely left his room, drunk any water, or eaten. "I need to call the social worker," he said. "I feel sick." After he hung up the phone, he let me put my hand on his forehead. "You need to drink more water and take a break from your computer," I said. He nodded, asked my husband for a lemon, and went back to bed. I went to Walmart to buy him a soccer ball (I accidentally bought him a basketball) and some Gatorade. When I went into his room, he didn't move. I put two bottles on his nightstand, and resisted the urge to tuck him in.

I internalized a long time ago that being a woman, particularly a woman who became a wife and a mother, meant sacrifice and suffering. I went to therapy to unlearn that, but I have barely learned to curb this behavior—and this resentment—in my second marriage. And here I was on Easter, miserable in part because a small person living under my roof did not care how much I did for him. I looked at him sleeping. None of my Easter lunch had mattered to him. I could suffer for him, or I could be happy; my chances of him loving us back would be about the same.

On the campus where I stayed in Uganda, red flowers bloomed and monkeys called each other from the trees. Sunrises were a sudden rush, turning the gray light to pink. Promptly afterwards the monkey ran down the path to the campus. Every evening as the sun began to set, they raced back up the hill. *I could live here*, I thought, then realized I had to add the phrase *if I were white*. Behind me was a bathroom with running water. My meals were prepared in the hotel. I never had to go so far that the water-troughed roads were a problem. But when I did leave campus, I saw the women walking with yellow water cans on their heads, because most neighborhoods did not have running water. They balanced bushel baskets too, then cooked food over a fire as they watched their children and sold drinks from tiny shops.

I drifted from class, to interviews, to the open-air chapel on campus, to visits to orphanages and schools. I saw the women everywhere I went: thin figures with enormous burdens on their heads, carrying yellow jerry-cans of water. When I ate dinner with a host family, I and the American students were the only women at the table. The wife and sisters stayed in the outdoor kitchen except to serve us food. Because I was white, and a guest, I could sit at a table with the men. Because I was white, and a guest, I stayed in a guesthouse with running water and electricity and I did not have to walk miles to a school or a well. The only way I could live with my running water and the women's yellow water jugs was if I used some magical thinking. I would have to invent a fiction—*the women like it this way. This is their culture. Who am I to argue with someone else's culture?*—and invent more crippling fictions to make the story work. But I live in an Indiana town that publicly lynched two black men in 1930. I know how dangerous fictions of inequality and suffering can be.

In my church's sanctuary, I wait for the bodies to trickle in—mothers, college students, children, the occasional man off the street with a

torn army jacket, the man with schizophrenia who sometimes tells wom-
en at church he loves them and announces Long John Silver's is running a
special on tacos. If I sit up front, I usually don't have these visitors sit next
to me. I can be mostly alone in my pew as I stand, sit, genuflect, without
bumping into the person in front of me. If I sit in the back by the stained-
glass window of Noah's Ark, the door might open halfway through and a
man or woman might waft in, body odor and cigarettes with them. They
might jangle coins. They might ask me for money, walk out, or come up
for healing prayer.

At our church, the service revolves around the Eucharist. This sacrament involves the closeness of bodies. We kneel next to each other at
the rail of the altar. We drink from the chalice after each other. I believe
church should be for everyone; I also often feel a little superior that our
church did not flee to the suburbs in the 1970s. When I am sharing my
pew and nasal space with people who have less access to everything
than me, however, "everyone" begins to feel a little exhausting. Christ's
blood and body is for all of us, but sometimes those bodies are terribly
distracting.

I walk up to the altar anyway. The person in front of me might be a
college student kneeling awkwardly in a too-short skirt, a homeless man
in saggy dirt-creased jeans; a child swinging her body down the aisle. My
knees sink into the carpet, my elbows prop me up on the rail, and I cup
my hands like I'm waiting for God to part the ceiling and alight in my
hands, like raindrops, or a butterfly passing as a wafer.

We first began to use the word "sacrifice" in the thirteenth century,
from the Latin *sacrificium,* from *sacer* (holy) and *facere* (to make): to
make holy. The word we use to describe a bunt in baseball, a move in
chess, a bid in bridge, and most aphorisms about marriage and parenting
was originally a word that denoted creating holiness. When I looked up
the word in January, the dictionary said the highest usage of the word
was right after the Dow dropped in 2009. When I look it up this summer,
the dictionary includes example after example of pandemic sacrifices,
like sacrificing old people to reopen, or sacrificing children and school
teachers to have schools. The entry includes the sacrificed wedding or
graduation, or even a mention of a hiker sacrificing his hikes on trails
that have become too crowded.

Like sacrifice, the Latin origin of sacrament comes from *sacer* (sacred)
becoming *sacramentum* (holy oath). In Christian Latin, *sacramentum*

was used as a translation for the Greek *mysterion,* or mystery. When I first glance at the chart of word origins, I put *sacre* and *mysterion* together to get "sacred mystery," a definition that does not actually exist in this dictionary but applies to my faith anyway. Episcopalians allow the sacrament of Eucharist to fall in the category of a mystery; for me, I don't know quite how it works, but I believe it does. I have taken Eucharist once since March. A constant topic we come back to in church leadership Zoom meetings is whether we can make a plan to reopen church without Eucharist. My evangelical self still believes God is present despite the absence of this sacrament. Logically for me, the only choice is to continue to sacrifice this holy mystery right now. But tonight, on my fifth day of a pandemic-induced panic attack, I wish I were holding a wafer in my hand instead of just my orange antidepressant, and hearing *the body of Christ, broken for you,* not just the echo of crickets outside.

After the white mob in our town lynched two black men in 1930, someone cut down the tree where the men were lynched. No one was ever charged even though thousands of souvenir photographs were sold of the white mob there that night. For as long as I have lived here, some residents have called for a memorial while others refuse to consider it.

A few nights ago, at the courthouse, we came close to a version of church. Residents of our town stood single file, waiting for a turn to scoop some dirt into a bucket. After two years of waiting to get permission to take soil from the ground, we're sending the soil to the Equal Justice Initiative memorial in Montgomery, Alabama. Our memorial in Marion might be a long time coming but as one of the pastors said, the act of memorial has already begun. "Throughout scripture," he says, "we see God telling people to set up altars in particular places where only that particular event happened in that place." The altars, I realized, were not just for sacrifice, but for memory.

Sacrifice is a sharp but necessary knife, ready for surgical removal of tumors, excess. When I chose in January to write about sacrifice, I was thinking of the word *suffering:* a rusty edge, an overloaded backpack, shoes that don't fit, a marriage that feels like broken glass. For years, I interchanged these words until I believed that if I was suffering in my marriage, it was part of my sacrifice. I had heard enough women say that "Marriage is supposed to make us holy, not happy" to both hate it and internalize it. Woman, wife, mother seemed loaded with their jagged edges and burdens. Choosing to get married meant hitching myself to a wagon I'd always have to pull. I decided when I was twelve, and realized that women did not automatically grow up and marry men and shoot out babies, that I'd never do that. Then, of course, I did.

I try not to think about my first marriage, but when I do, I remember my dominant emotions being equal parts anger and resignation. When my former husband told me to give away the dog I was fostering because he decided that she hated him, I balked, but eventually did. When he increasingly kept me away from my family and friends, I stopped arguing. When I found myself having sex against my will, I eventually just dissociated instead of resisting. On good days, my unhappiness meant I could see pain other people were going through. On bad ones, my default response was to compare my misery to theirs. I knew, vaguely, marriage was a sacrament but if you had asked me at twenty-five what that meant, I would have thrown up my hands and said *this, I guess.*

God, apparently didn't ask us to suffer and to sacrifice all the time. The author of Hebrews 10:8 writes, "Sacrifices and offerings, burnt offerings and sin offerings you did not desire, nor were you pleased with them." Jesus, in Matthew 9:13, references multiple Old Testament passages when he says, "But go and learn what this means: 'I desire mercy, not sacrifice.'" I am constantly relearning that God would really prefer a life of mercy to a life of suffering. Our bodies were not called to be funeral pyres.

In late April, I take my foster son to Indianapolis for his first family visit. The drive takes an hour and fifteen minutes. After we wait about ten minutes, the visit supervisor says the parents aren't coming—a misunderstanding, another appointment perhaps. Our boy FaceTimes with them instead. I am grateful I have to wear a mask because it can cover the hard, angry line where my mouth used to be. After he finishes the call, we talk about two of the issues at hand—my foster son is scared of our dogs, and he isn't eating because we don't make African food. We solved one of those problems by going to the international grocery together. This could have been disaster—he walks slowly, the aisles are narrow and crowded, we both forget our masks in the car, and he's mumbling when I point to food and ask, "Do you like this? Potatoes? Cassava? Chicken?" Then he begins to pick up grapes, pineapple, chicken. In the frozen aisle he recognizes Chinese buns that he likes; in the cookie aisle he picks out cookies and a loaf of white bread his mom used to buy. We spend a long time in the toiletries aisle trying to tell the difference between hair dye and hair gel.

He talks to me the rest of the way home—about his sister that he's upset with, his memories of Africa, his languages. I barely need to say a word. When we get home, he helps me bring in the groceries. He unpacks the yellow pound cake he picked out and the spicy chips and says, "you can have some too."

This day is a small miracle. We still have some complicated days—he doesn't eat the taro root I make because I didn't make it like his mom does. We eventually learn that he is happier if I just make him hot dogs or chicken nuggets. Our family visits for a long time start an hour late, or happen with little notice. In the 2020 pandemic, the two of us have at least three Zoom meetings a week for his services, if not more. The day that his family visit starts three hours late, I text my husband complaining. He sends back a photo of water bottles full of urine under the boy's bed. When we ask him about it, he shrugs and says he's afraid of the dogs. A baby gate goes up in the hallway to keep the dogs from his room, but one of the dogs whines for an hour until I bring him into the room with us. We aren't raising an infant, to be sure, but sleep never quite feels complete.

Our son's father speaks some English. He actively dislikes us at first, then begins to warm up a little, waving goodbye and saying thank you at the end of visits. His mother seldom speaks unless she comes to a visit alone. My foster son says his mother doesn't know how to read, and attended little school. She doesn't speak much English, and mostly communicates by what she brings—packages of ramen noodles and juice boxes and her native language.

One night after his visit, his mother meets my eyes before we leave. "We love him," I say, my voice catching. She smiles a little and tugs at a tiny curl behind his ear; he fake scowls and jumps away. "You have a good son," I add. She nods, maybe understanding the intent behind the English if not all the words. She wears headscarves and African dresses when she meets us in the park, and smiles like it hurts.

In my guesthouse on the hill in Uganda, the world was quiet except for the monkeys and the birds and the cat calling under my door. I remember watching both the sunrise and the sunset from my doorway, even though that's directionally impossible. The mornings were a rush of pink to yellow and orange and then daylight. The evenings were just as sudden, but colored in reverse. Sometimes when I would walk farther up the hill, I'd pass a woman walking to or from one of the big houses at the top where she helped care for one of the white families.

I saw few children on campus, but I saw them everywhere outside the campus gates. Hundreds of them ran around in yellow uniforms at the school. Many more walked alone or in pairs on the dirt road leading to the main road, crowded with motorbikes and vans.

My foster son told me that once, when he lived close to Uganda, someone gave him a gun and tried to make him use it. "I was so afraid, I thought I would die," he said. "I hid for a long time, then ran home."

When I think of Africa, I think of him superimposed on those paths and busy roads. I also think of Egypt, specifically the beginning of Exodus when Pharaoh starts putting to death the male baby boys, so Moses's mother puts him in a reed basket in the water because he'd be safer there than on land. I wonder if Emmett Till's mother thought the same thing; if Trayvon Martin's mother did too. At some point in the reunification process, our foster son's mother mentions to the visit supervisor that she thinks the courts will let the children come home sooner if she doesn't see them at visits. I can somewhat follow this logic—*look, I am playing by the rules. I am suffering. Is it enough yet?* My foster son tells me they left their country because they couldn't find enough food; America was supposed to make their lives better. At some point it has—he goes to school and has enough to eat now—but he's also living with two white strangers instead of his family. I watch her hand cartons of juice to her children, hold her baby girl, and wipe her eyes at the end of a visit.

It is the fifth of August, almost five months since quarantine started, almost four months since our son reluctantly came to live with us. On Monday, the social worker calls to say our foster son is going home the next day. We have been planning for him to go home before school starts, so this isn't completely a surprise, but I'm crying by the time I hang up the phone.

A little while later, I knock on his door.

"Yes?" When he first came, his *yes* was clipped, tense. Now he gives his *yes* a sing-song lilt.

"Guess what?" I say.

"What?" He doesn't look away from his computer screen.

"You're going home tomorrow."

He freezes, then his face scrunches into a giant grin. "I'm so happy," he says. "Tomorrow?" Then he adds, "but what about my haircut?"

His parents' approach to haircuts with seven children was a pair of clippers, no guard. I'd promised him a haircut—he wanted a temple fade—before he went home. An hour later we are in a barbershop, surrounded by high school boys getting their back-to-school cuts. "How you doing little man?" the owner says. "You starting school? What music do you like? What are we doing with your hair today?" My son shows him a photo on my phone. "We can do that." I watch the barber trim, buzz, shape and style his hair. I feel like I've put him into the bulrushes for a test run, and someone has fetched him out safely.

Still, on Tuesday morning I send him in for his last therapy appointment, then sit in my car and feel the sadness well up again. I feel like I'm alone in a boat, a long way out to sea. Maybe Jesus on the cross has never moved me quite as much as Jesus in the boat, helping Peter back in.

Once, his therapist asked him if he was happy with us and he said, "Yes, but not forever." It was never supposed to be forever, of course. This was a child we were always going to return. On the way to meet the social worker who will take him home, I tell him we can be his white auntie and uncle; this makes him laugh. After we load his bags into the social worker's car, we make him take a selfie with us, and then hug him goodbye. "Ah come on!" he laughs, trying to dodge our arms, the camera. We hang around to watch the kids pile in the car and head towards home.

My husband calls the pandemic our exile. We haven't seen our own families since January or our students since March. We have no temple worship, no Eucharist—just church via YouTube and coffee hour via Zoom. What we have are huge civil rights upheavals, and daily death tolls. When the pandemic ends we will find altars and holy places everywhere. I can't see them right now; the anxiety in our jaws and arms and bellies is too thick. All I can do is listen for hints of the world made holy.

Foster parenting requires you to spend weeks, maybe months or years, trying to get a kid to trust you, and then one day they go home and you are suddenly just another adult they used to know. Evenings are quieter now that he isn't listening to K-pop in his room, or cussing in Spanish and Swahili as he plays a video game with my husband. We haven't used the air fryer in two days; I almost forget the daily smell of chicken nuggets and fries, or the pumpkin spice body spray he spritzed liberally.

We keep the door to his room open now, to air it out and let light into the hallway, but also to honor the empty space in some way. If the door were closed I would forget he was gone and find myself standing there again, listening for his breathing, or tears, or laughter.

I did not have a choice to send him home, but I did have a choice to let him in. Maybe this is the actual sacrifice of parenthood, and love: the moment you decide to welcome a person whom you will ultimately spend the rest of your life losing. If my mother could have foretold her future, would she have still have had five children with a man who would leave her? What would my foster son's mother have done if she'd known that in order to feed her children she'd have to immigrate, and her new country would take them away?

If I'd known in April that I'd grieve a kid who ignored me, disliked my food, and peed in water bottles in his room at night, would I have let him in?

Would Mary, had she known what was coming with Jesus?

I think of what may go wrong, now that he's home. I think of Moses's mother, setting his basket in the river. I think of Pharaoh's daughter giving him back again. I think of Moses only wanting to go home; of God whispering, "I do not want your sacrifices, but a holy life," and me wondering what the difference is. I part the bulrushes, wondering if Jesus died on the cross to save us or just to teach us to love better, to love at a loss, to love when your joys are outbursts of laughter and flashes of sunrise in a pandemic.

Bibliography

Armstrong, Karen. *The Lost Art of Reading Scripture*. New York: Knopf, 2019.

Cone, James H. *The Cross and the Lynching Tree*. New York: Orbis, 2013.

Dickey, James. "The Sheep Child." Poetry Foundation. https://www.poetryfoundation. org/articles/68914/james-dickey-the-sheep-child.

Douglas, Kelly Brown. *Stand Your Ground: Black Bodies and the Justice of God*. New York: Orbis, 2015.

Hummel, Maria. "James Dickey: 'The Sheep Child.'" Poetry Foundation. August 27, 2007. https://www.poetryfoundation.org/articles/68914/james-dickey-the-sheep-child.

Le Guin, Ursula K. "The Ones Who Walk Away from Omelas." Asia SocietyOrg. February 2, 2011. https://sites.asiasociety.org/asia21summit/wp-content/uploads/2011/02/3.-Le-Guin-Ursula-The-Ones-Who-Walk-Away-From-Omelas.pdf.

Magonet, Jonathan. "Did Jephthah Actually Kill His Daughter?" *TheTorah.com*. 2015. https://thetorah.com/article/did-jephthah-actually-kill-his-daughter.

"Sacrifice." *Merriam-Webster.com Dictionary.* https://www.merriam-webster.com/dictionary/sacrifice.

Tanner, Kathryn. "Incarnation, Cross, and Sacrifice: A Feminist-Inspired Reappraisal." *Anglican Theological Review* 86.1 (2004) 35–56.

The Bible. English Standard Version. Wheaton, IL: Crossway, 2001.

Watters, Kelsi. "Solidarity and Suffering: Liberation Christology from Black and Womanist Perspectives." *Obsculta* 12 (2019) 78–107. https://digitalcommons.csbsju./edu/obsculta/vol12/iss1/8.

19

Testimony

Robert S. Heaney

"What is the Lord doing in your life this month?"

On the odd occasion when the rector could not be present for the midweek parish Bible study, my grandmother, by popular acclaim, would become chairperson. In normal circumstances the meeting would take a familiar shape. Welcome and opening prayer would be followed by hymn singing and Bible reading. The rector, or other local luminary, would spend at least thirty minutes expositing and applying the text for the incoming week. The meeting would end with some more hymns or praise songs and a time of extemporary prayer. In abnormal circumstances, and in the absence of scripted scriptural exposition, my grandmother would often call the congregation to *testimony*. She would call us to witness in words to the presence and work of God in our lives. On one particular night of testimonies she looked straight to the back row and in my direction.

There was something about my grandmother's impulse toward witnessing words (testimony) that drew from deep wells of Christian history. Various testimonies of conversion and of deepened faith have become important in Christian tradition. It would be difficult to think of a more famous testimony than that chronicled by Saint Augustine in book eight of his *Confessions*. Not only does Augustine's account testify to his conversion but it also bears witness to the importance of testimony. For his testimony itself is, in part, a story of other testimonies that spoke to him and that the Holy Spirit used to bring him to faith.

. . . You, Lord, while [Ponticianus] was speaking, turned me back towards myself. . . . And suddenly I heard a voice from some nearby house, a boy's voice or a girl's voice, I do not know: but it was a sort of sing-song, repeated again and again. "Take and read, take and read." . . . Damming back the flood of tears I arose, interpreting the incident as quite certainly a divine command to open my book of Scripture and read the passage at which I should open. . . . I snatched it up, opened it and in silence read the passage upon which my eyes first fell: *Not in rioting and drunkenness, not in chambering and impurities, not in contention and envy, but put ye on the Lord Jesus Christ.* . . . I had no wish to read further, and no need: For in that instant, with the very ending of the sentence, it was as though a light of utter confidence shone in all my heart, and all the darkness of uncertainty vanished away. . . . Then we went in to my mother and told her, to her great joy; . . . she was filled with triumphant exultation, and praised You who are mighty beyond what we ask or conceive: for she saw what You had given her more than with all her pitiful weeping she had ever asked. For You had converted me to Yourself. . . . Thus you changed her mourning into joy. . . . Let my heart and my tongue praise Thee, and *let all my bones say, O Lord, who is like to Thee?*[1]

The testimony at work in Augustine's story is multi-dimensional. There is *God's own testimony* to Augustine, turning Augustine around to face the depths of his own sin and the riches of divine grace. God directs him to *scripture* and Romans 13 becomes a vital testimony in his conversion to Christ. Friends and guests in *dialogue* with Augustine, and particularly the testimony of Ponticianus, become crucial. Finally, he and his mother turn back to God in the testimony of *worship*.

Christian theology and witness begin as a response to *God's own testimony* to God's self and God's work. In word and deed, and in words that are deeds, God speaks. God speaks and creation breathes. Life exists because of the testimony of God across the unlit waters of chaos (Gen 1:1–3). We are alive in relationship because of the life-creating word of the creator (Gen 2:18–25). As part of creation, and set within creation, there was the possibility that humans would love creation more than the creator (Gen 3:1–7). This proved to be the case. We cut down the grandeur of creation, formed from God's witness and formed as God's witness

1. Augustine, *Confessions*, 8.VII, XII, 138–39, 146–47; 9.I, 151.

(Ps 19:1), making it into idols that block our view of God's beckoning love (Isa 44:12–28). This fundamental ecological sin did not prevent God's creative witness from continuing. God would not, and will not, give us up to the chaos of our own making. God spoke in dreams and visions calling a people to God's self (Gen 15:1). God redeemed and liberated the people of God (Exod 3:4–22). Generation after generation, God testified to God's nature of love and mercy ever calling the people away from chaotic idolatry and toward the deep relationality of eternal life. Again and again God called God's people back to their first love and their covenant commitments through prophetic testimony. Then, in these final days, God's Word came to us in Christ as divine testimony spoke re-creation (John 1; Heb 1:1–4).

The Irish Anglicanism I grew up in was serious about scripture, the Prayer Book, and proper submission to the rubrics. It was also deeply influenced by revivalism. Though embarrassing, when my grandmother invited me to step up to the front of the parochial hall and address the congregation and her question, it was not out of character for her or for the tradition. "Giving a word of testimony" was the least that any Christian could do. Saint Augustine would have been at home in my grandmother's meetings. Given the *Confessions*, he would have had a rip-roaring testimony to share at our midweek Bible study. As with Augustine, in my home parish there was a living expectation that lives were changed by God and that believers could put words to that change. Jesus was really alive and the Spirit of God was really at work in the world. At the heart of what it meant to be a Christian was an encounter with the risen Lord. That encounter and the conviction that Jesus Christ was central to Christian identity and formation framed every testimony I heard growing up.

At the center of a Christian understanding of God's own testimony to God's self is the person of Jesus Christ. Here is not an inanimate idol that would block our way to relationship with God. Christ is the icon (Col 1:15) that makes manifest the definitive revelation of God's testimony. The creator God who made us meets us in creation. God meets us in the flesh. God's transcendence as creator remains but this holy transcendence is not an abstraction. God comes to us in God's own terms and calls us to a life renewed in encounter with divine grace and mercy.[2] Christ is not an idea or set of ideas that we can simply capture and comprehend. Rather, Christ is God's testimony, calling us to learn, to discover, and to discern.

2. Janz, *God, the Mind's Desire*, 192–221.

God's incarnate testimony creates a community of learning (disciples). That community is to be a community of testimony. God's testimony is life-giving and calls a people to testify to that life. Through God's creative, re-creative, and incarnate Word, God is renewing a people that embodies and bespeaks an inbreaking renewal of all creation. This renewing testimony is the golden thread running through the stories of God's people in history and in scripture.

The very text of *scripture* itself is testimony and depends upon testimony. Yet, if I had a dollar for every time someone has said to me, "preach the gospel and if necessary use words" my retirement would be more secure than it looks today. For some, the idea of testimony as witnessing words fills them with dread. It associates them with a stream of faith they shun as little else but talk or they worry that testimony displaces the primacy of action. Preach the gospel, yes. But, "whatever you say, say nothing."[3] This impulse and the words to preach but not speak are attributed to Saint Francis. There is a noble impulse in the appeal to pseudo-Francis that wants to prioritize action over talk. However, as with my grandmother and Augustine, testimony as witnessing words is not talk independent of lived reality. On the contrary, it is testimony arising from lives changed by the work and witness of God. Scripture, at the very least, is a library of such testimonies from across the generations. The biblical text that we have today, like an age-long process of chain-letter writing, is linked together by a commitment to testimony and the importance of testimony.[4]

Walter Brueggemann sums up the theological significance of the Hebrew scriptures as testimony.[5] All of creation, the psalmist reminds us, testifies to the glory of God (Ps 19:1–4). The commandments and the wider law are a testimony of God (Exod 31:18). The Davidic dynasty is a testimony to God's love (Isa 55:3–5). The people of God are a witness to God's saving power in history (Isa 43:10–13). In suffering, too, testimony can arise on the hard way of faith and the hiddenness of God (Job 16:6–22; Isa 52:13—53:12). Scripture is not simply God's testimony or a collection of testimonies to God's being and action. Within the pages of the Bible there are multiple voices, narratives, claims and counter-claims. There

---

3. Heaney, *New Selected Poems*, 78.

4. Brueggemann, "Theology of the Old Testament," 33. Bauckham, *Jesus and the Eyewitnesses*.

5. Brueggemann, "Theology of the Old Testament," 28–38 at 32.

is testimony, counter-testimony, and contestation.[6] For Brueggemann, scripture is like a courtroom where testimony and counter-testimony are heard regarding the claims of Israel and Israel's God.[7] Yes, God is "sovereign and steadfast."[8] But, too often, the people of God face circumstances that cause real experiences of injustice, ambiguity, and abandonment.

Reflecting its courtroom sense, testimony in the New Testament includes the witness to truth based on personal knowledge or experience (John 1:6–8; 15:27; Acts 7:58; 10:39). Testimony is eyewitnesses recounting what they saw and what they heard from Jesus (John 1:19; 15:27; Acts 22:18). Most importantly, Christian testimony is the apostolic witness to the resurrection of Jesus (Acts 1:21–22; 1 Cor 15:3–8).[9] It is act and it is content (John 19:35). Testimony sounds forth in counterpoint to the life of Christ and the life received from Christ. Suffering for the sake of Christ is a form of testimony or can create an opportunity to testify to the gospel of Christ (Matt 10:18; Luke 21:12–15). Testimony sounds forth even in the discordance of a life cut short and given up as witness to Christ (Acts 22:20; Rev 2:13; 20:4). The most radical testimony and witness (*martys*) is martyrdom. In the face of imperialist powers that would seek a totality of power and sovereignty that belong only to the creator, martyrs down the ages laid down their lives as testimony that it is Christ, and not Caesar, who is Lord.

Neither the Old nor New Testament silences or smooths over the cries of anguish, anger, doubt, and lament. At the heart of the gospel is a faithful child crying out, under the deadly weight of empire, "my God, my God, why have you forsaken me?" (Matt 27:45–46). This too is testimony. It is the cry of the faithful in praise and in pain. Testimony is not an endless or mindless cascading of words about the greatness of God. It is also the testing of the claims of faith in the dialogue of life.

Testimony is *dialogue*. The most fervent witness to the Christian faith understands that to communicate well, bridges must be built toward the language and lived realities of people's lives. Cultural, philosophical, linguistic, and emotional learning and inter-change are part of testimony. Testimony is always a conversation between witness and world. However, the bridges that testimony builds are two-way. Testimony is about

6. See Brueggemann, *Theology of the Old Testament*, 117–44, 317–58.

7. Brueggemann, *Theology of the Old Testament*, xv–xvii.

8. Brueggemann, *Theology of the Old Testament*, 313.

9. Bauckham, *Jesus and the Eyewitnesses*, 5–11.

a to'ing and fro'ing between minister and ministered. In the to'ing and fro'ing witnesses discover that the boundaries of evangelized and evangelist themselves are made problematic and porous. Theological claims are not simply clarified in public conversation. The public calls Christian witnesses to account for the claims they make about divine love, justice, and community. Public witness is stepping into a deeply pluralist zone of interaction where claims to truth and religious identities are challenged, problematized, and destabilized.[10] Such testifying, however, does not take such disputatious shape simply by social necessity. God's own witness challenges, problematizes, and destabilizes easy assumptions and settled identities.

Imagine yourself in Jerusalem on that Pentecost day. Rushing wind and fiery tongues disrupt well-rehearsed festivities. You, amidst a crowd of pilgrims from every corner of the world (Acts 2:5), are left wondering, "what does this mean?" (Acts 2:12). You stand in a public space of inquiry that was blown open by the Spirit of God. In that space, Peter testifies to a resurrected Messiah. Some question, some doubt, some sneer, and some believe (Acts 2:12–42). God's own witness opens up space for testimony that, in turn, opens up space for consternation, contestation, and discernment. What does this mean? Again and again the Jesus movement and the wider gentile world would be drawn into dialogue precisely on the nature and significance of the Nazarene. Most famously, this Jewish messianic movement would have to face radical change to long-held theological convictions as it faced the reality that this same Spirit of Pentecost was at work in the lives of gentiles. The so-called Jerusalem council (Acts 15) becomes the turning point in the Acts of the Apostles and in Jewish-Christian history. Gentiles do not need to become Jews to follow the Jewish Messiah. God's own witness makes categories of identity unstable and transgresses community boundaries (Eph 2:11–22).[11] A new kind of community and identity, opened up by the prophetic Spirit of God, became possible. Testimony is more, then, than dialogue. It is *prophetic* dialogue. Testimony unveils the bold claim made for Jesus as fulfilment of age old promises (Acts 2:36).[12]

Christian testimony witnesses to the implications of saying, "Jesus is Lord." Followers of God have found themselves testifying to the saving

10. See Heaney, "Public Theology and Public Missiology," 201–12.

11. Heaney, "Public Theology," 204–12.

12. Bevans and Schroeder, *Prophetic Dialogue*.

activity of God in times of peace when they possess relative power. But they have also found themselves testifying to the grace of God in circumstances of threat, unrest, and uncertainty where they possessed little power and influence. Dialogue, then, must not be imagined simply as dispassionate leisurely colloquia. It may be a constant exercise for one's very survival as a person of faith in the face of injustice. Prophetic testimony is a commitment to the poor (Rom 16:24–28; 1 Cor 16:1; Gal 2:10) that foreshadows the possibility of a just world.[13] It is speech of a church that speaks as the poor and for the poor, all the while recognizing the deep resources for change that already exist with the church.

Prophetic testimony does not simply aim at lifting up the downtrodden. It also aims at bringing down the powerful (Luke 1:46–55). To declare the lordship of Jesus Christ, as each Christian does, is to dethrone every other power that would make a competing claim. Jesus is Lord. Caesar is not Lord. Nation, whiteness, wealth, technology, capitalism, military might, the human individual—none of these is Lord. Testimony to the lordship of Jesus, however, is not self-evident. There are those who, consciously or unconsciously, submit to the lordship of patriotism, racism, capitalism, militarism, and individualism. To testify prophetically to the lordship of Christ is to disrupt such idolatry and bring down such idols. It is to hope and resist on the way to becoming a beloved community that will be a sign and foretaste of God's inbreaking reign as it gathers around word and sacrament fed by God's provision for the renewal of the world.[14]

Testimony is public. Christian testimony is public because the work of God is public. The life, ministry, death, and resurrection of Jesus took place in public. The testimony of God in Christ was encountered in public. The response of the community of Jesus as it submits, in faith, to baptism is public. Christian testimony is public because it is response to the witness of God in the context of God's call to relationship and community. The response to God's own testimony, as experienced in human lives and as recorded in biblical texts, takes place in public and, crucially, in public worship. Therefore, testimony is *worship*.

Worship turns the church, always, towards the world. Testimony precludes any temptation to make the church a private endeavor or private society. The public testimony of the gospel is that God's regard is

13. Bevans and Schroeder, *Prophetic Dialogue*, 60–61. Bevans, *Constants in Context*, 369–73.

14. Hill, *Prophetic Rage*, 82–113.

on the least of the world and that the proud must be humbled to receive the grace they need for salvation. In baptism and in Eucharist, deep solidarities, overflowing from God's loving initiative, create a strong countercurrent to a world that would construct identities and communions of like-minded people alone.[15] A renewed way, a renewed people, and the inbreaking of God's reconciling kingdom are experienced in these acts of public worship and witness.

When Christians gather around the table of the Lord it is the aforementioned inbreaking reign and reconciled community that they get a glimpse of in the liturgy. A community of testimony is gathered by the risen Christ to listen, give, praise, receive, and go out into the neighborhood and nations in testimony that demonstrates and discerns God's reign. Our words and actions come into sync, even if but for a moment, with the eternal testimony of God's reign. Our voices join with the voice of heaven to testify to the ultimate victory of God's mission in bringing healing to all of creation. The end breaks in and the future is poured out before our very eyes. The local assembly joins with the heavenly assembly in a unity of heaven and earth and in a unity of the now and the not yet. This unity is the risen Jesus Christ ascendant and present to his church. The assembly is transformed in public as God's grace comes to us in hands empty of any claim to self-satisfaction or self-justification. At the Lord's table we "receive one another with Christ and Christ with one another; we at once receive Christ and the church in which we receive him."[16] Our testimony is not birthed by human agreement, affinity, or agenda. It is all gift. It is all God's grace.

The testimony of worship is grace and it is judgment. Often the church fails to enact the vision of unity and grace that has been opened to it in the paschal mystery. False testimony is always a possibility. Lies "in the heart of the witness" can cause worshippers to bear false witness and subvert the purpose of the worship of the church.[17] The liturgy anticipates such unfaithfulness and ever calls the church to penitence and repentance. Rowan Williams reminds us that gathering at the altar puts us at the table of the risen Christ but it also puts us in the place of the unfaithful disciples (Luke 22:14–34).[18] The liturgy evokes humility and it

---

15. Williams, *On Christian Theology*, 212–13.

16. Jenson, *Systematic Theology: Volume 2*, 222.

17. Ricoeur, "The Hermeneutics of Testimony," 443.

18. Williams, *On Christian Theology*, 204.

evokes testimony always in a penitential key.[19] Testifying to the church's pilgrimage toward God's promised end of reconciliation is to simultaneously testify to the ongoing deep need for reformation. God's own testimony invites us to open our hearts, lives, and institutions to recognize how they are complicit in sin. This is a call to the renewing gift of holiness that comes in processes where Christians, across differences, open themselves to correction and discipline. Lest we confuse our work with the work of God it is important to recognize that holiness is not the church's achievement. Holiness is the gift of God. What makes the church holy is God's presence in her midst continually reconciling her to God's self. The church's holiness is found in its continual turning towards the grace of God amidst the histories of life-giving testimony and death-dealing deeds. Testimony, formed by worship, is public thanksgiving and it is public penitence as the church awaits the fuller revelation of God's reign.

Despite my best efforts to slouch out of sight my grandmother had caught my eye. There was no avoiding an answer to her question. "What is the Lord doing in your life?" I have absolutely no recollection of how I answered her question on that wet and windy fall evening. I have confidence that it was, at worst, incoherent and, at best, inchoate. I do not now remember that invitation to testimony with resentment. Her invitation remains with me. It animates my ongoing commitment to theology that is storied and to processes of formation that shape leaders who can give voice to the hope that is within them (1 Pet 3:15).[20]

God calls the church to testimony in light of God's own testimony and the testimonies of the saints throughout the ages. God calls the church, formed by scripture and worship, to a bold humility in the public square. God knows, we need an articulate church and a people of God with a testimony that can overcome the powers of evil (Rev 12:11). What, then, will be *your* testimony?

19. See Farwell, *The Liturgy Explained*, 32–33.

20. See Heaney, *Post-Colonial Theology*, 11–41; Heaney, "Missiology and Ministry," 279–91.

Bibliography

Augustine. *Augustine: Confessions, Books I–XIII*. Rev. ed. Translated by F. J. Sheed. Indianapolis: Hackett, 1993.

Bauckham, Richard. *Jesus and the Eyewitnesses: The Gospels as Eyewitness Testimony*. Grand Rapids: Eerdmans, 2006.

Bevans, Stephen B. *Constants in Context: A Theology of Mission for Today*. Maryknoll, NY: Orbis, 2004.

Bevans, Stephen B., and Roger P. Schroeder. *Prophetic Dialogue: Reflections on Christian Mission Today*. Maryknoll, NY: Orbis, 2011.

Brueggemann, Walter. *Theology of the Old Testament: Testimony, Dispute, Advocacy*. Minneapolis: Fortress, 1997.

———. "Theology of the Old Testament: Testimony, Dispute, Advocacy Revisited." *The Catholic Biblical Quarterly* 74 (2012) 28–38.

Farwell, James W. *The Liturgy Explained*. New ed. New York: Morehouse, 2013.

Heaney, Robert S. "Missiology and Ministry." In *The Study of Ministry: A Comprehensive Survey of Theory and Best Practice*, edited by Martyn Percy et al., 279–91. London: SPCK, 2019.

———. *Post-Colonial Theology: Finding God and Each Other amidst the Hate*. Eugene, OR: Cascade, 2019.

———. "Public Theology and Public Missiology." *Anglican Theological Review* 102 (2020) 201–12.

Heaney, Seamus. *New Selected Poems: 1966–1987*. London: Faber and Faber, 1990.

Hill, Johnny Bernard. *Prophetic Rage: A Postcolonial Theology of Liberation*. Grand Rapids: Eerdmans, 2013.

Janz, Paul. *God, the Mind's Desire: Reference, Reason and Christian Thinking*. Cambridge: Cambridge University Press, 2004.

Jenson, Robert W. *Systematic Theology. Vol. 2, The Works of God*. Oxford: Oxford University Press, 1999.

Ricoeur, Paul. "The Hermeneutics of Testimony." *Anglican Theological Review* 61 (1979) 435–61.

Williams, Rowan. *On Christian Theology*. Oxford: Blackwell, 2000.

20

For the Whole World

Amy Peterson

I WANT TO TELL you about the things I love, but I don't have words for them. What's the word for an overgrown bush that's hollow on the inside, like a cave? What's the word for live oak branches that perfectly form to your ten-year-old body, offering a shady seat in the sky? What adjective describes the sweetness of just-snapped sweet peas, or the feel of dirt that's soft and loose when you dig into it and find treasure, red potatoes? There ought to be a name for the patch of sky that appears between the tops of trees when you lay flat on your back and look up. Or for the particular kind of tired that comes from crawling through water for half an hour, the way it leaves you shaky and loose and warm, or for what the sun does, drying, freckling, burning, and replenishing, all at once.

Sometimes I wonder: if we had better language—stronger, truer language, more precise—would we care more? If I'd had names for those things I loved as a child, would my love have lasted longer?

Christian theology ought to have given me better language for all this, a better story about how I relate to the earth. And yet, little in my Christian education taught me to name, or to cherish, the things I loved in childhood—the snap peas, the hollow trees, the patch of sky between the leaves. I learned that immaterial human souls and the word of God had value; the rest of it, the end-times preachers said, the rest of created matter didn't really matter—we could use it however we pleased, we could abuse it for our short-term gain, because ultimately it would burn.

It's burning already. The twenty warmest years on record have happened in the last twenty-two years, putting more than a million species at risk. The size and strength of wildfires have increased, and so has the frequency of high intensity hurricanes. Air quality is worse, crop production is weaker, infectious diseases are stronger. By 2050, there will be more plastic in our oceans than fish.

Children protest, skipping school, inviting us adults to remember our love for the more-than-human creatures we live with—or, if not that, at least our love for our own children. I'm trying.

When my daughter was small, we lived on a dead-end road in the rural Midwest. To break up our long days at home together, we'd go for walks. I learned quickly that these "walks" would never raise my heart rate enough to count as exercise. We began at the edge of our driveway, where cement crumbled into fine rocks and dirt, and we stayed in this spot for the first half hour or so. Rosie would plant herself there, picking up handfuls of the dust and watching it move through her fingers, throwing it, trying a soft-shoe routine in it. Eventually we'd move, but still slowly: there was so much, after all, to see. Rosie's first word was "bird," spoken while a chubby finger smudged the front window. She was always looking.

Recently we've been trying to see that way again, and to learn the names of the things we see. My children are nine and eleven now, and this spring they used an app on my phone to identify all the plants growing in our backyard: scarlet bee balm and sacred bamboo and wisteria and English holly and Russian iris. We noted on a calendar the day that a cardinal laid eggs in her nest, and counted the days until the eggs hatched. We watched the babies, all knobby and pink and raw, all beak and wingbone, turn into puffballs and fall to the ground, then begin to fly.

In the winter, my friend Lauren invited me to join her on a guided tour learning to identify the winter silhouettes of deciduous trees. I told her that it's one of my life goals to know the names of the trees in my neighborhood, and at the end of the walk, she asked, sort of baffled, why. What use is it to know their names?

It's become common in our friendship that I only realize what I think about things when Lauren asks me questions like this, and so I only realized as I was answering that it's not utilitarian. It's about love. I want to know their names because I want to love them better. Because unless I know their names, I'm not really able to see them; they exist as wallpaper to my life, rather than as creatures with whom I share life.

Most Sundays for the past decade, I've followed Father Jim through the Holy Eucharist Rite II, and it has formed my view of the world around me. Now, it's not just the words, but his cadence and lilt that play in my mind every time I pray. Jim would always rest for a beat after the phrase "a perfect sacrifice"—a perfect sacrifice, he'd say, and then a pregnant moment of silence, drawing our attention to the weight of what was to come, spoken a full octave lower—*for the whole world.*

It wasn't until last year that I found myself asking questions of this bit of liturgy. Who and what is included in that line, I wondered. In what sense was Christ's sacrifice for the whole world?

I pause the liturgy and mentally rewind: this prayer has been all about humanity. God made us, we fell into sin, became subject to evil and death, and God sent Jesus to share our human nature, to live and die as one of us, to reconcile us to God. And then, only at the end, this mention of the whole world. What would happen if we read this phrase backwards into the whole prayer?

> Holy and gracious Father: In your infinite love you made us *and all creation, the plants, the animals, the ocean and dry land, the sun, moon, and stars,* for yourself; and, when we had fallen into sin and become subject to evil and death, *when we had fallen into sin and subjected all creation to its damages, when all creation began groaning, awaiting our redemption,* you, in your mercy, sent Jesus Christ, your only and eternal Son, to share our human nature, *to take on flesh, composed of stardust and water molecules, matter which cannot be created or destroyed, air we breathe, water we drink,* to live and die as one of us, to reconcile us—*all of us, luna moths and bumblebee bats, pufferfish and hooded seals, baobab and rosewood, prairie grass and orchids, red dwarfs and pulsars, archaea and protozoa, minke whales and meteors*—to you, the God and Father of all.

In the Eucharist, we celebrate our redemption with bread and wine; we find the real presence of Jesus in these gifts of wheat and grapes transformed by fire and microbial communities. Jesus was made of matter like this, and Jesus was the perfect sacrifice for matter like this, for microbes and green beans and geckos and sun motes and us.

Saint Athanasius tells us that Christ came to earth not only to save humans, but to "recreate the universe." For Christ to take on human flesh, composed as it is of matter recycled from the beginning of the world, means that he did not just redeem humans: he redeemed *all of creation*.

If God will make all this new, why try to save it? When I read the news, and it says we are careening toward the point of no return, the point at which rising temperatures do irreversible damage, part of me wants to shrug and sigh and say that it's too late, all we can do is hope in an eventual miraculous rescue.

But even when it's too late, love works. We don't abandon our dying parents or grandparents—we work to make sure they are comfortable, well-cared for, never alone. We ask them questions for as long as we have them, we memorize their stories. We hold hands until we can't any more. I want to do the same for the earth, and all her creatures.

Tucked in canyons and hidden in forests, forgotten orchards in the Pacific Northwest grow wild with apples nearly lost. Amateur botanists and retirees travel, often on foot, in search of the hidden treasure abandoned in these nooks and crannies of the earth.

The nonprofit The Lost Apple Project works methodically at this romantic task: they collect "old maps, county fair records, newspaper clippings and nursery sales ledgers" to determine which homesteaders bought which apples trees, and then they set out to see if any are still there. The Associated Press reports "The task is huge. North America once had 17,000 named varieties of domesticated apples, but only about 4,500 are known to exist today." When the apple detectives find an old orchard, they note it and return in the winter—"often on foot or on snowshoes in freezing temperatures and blinding snow"—to take cuttings. Among the apples they've revived are "the Sary Sinap, an ancient apple from Turkey, and the Streaked Pippin, which may have originated as early as 1744 in New York."[1] They scour out-of-print reference books for names and histories of the fruits they find.

Maybe I can be like those apple tree hunters, stalking the world for evidence of God's love, caring when even one manifestation of that love is lost, and finding it anew in every created being.

My friend Bob writes poems about the walks he takes every day, and about God. Once, I listened to him teach about the relationship between

---

1. Gillian Flaccus, "10 Pioneer-era Apple Types Found in US West." April 15, 2020. https://apnews.com/article/4b08b6e30cbe37697120466d56f294a5.

nature poetry and the spiritual life. The poet's task, he said, is the revelation of presence—an awakening to the astonishing fact that things are, though they need not be. The poet's task is to be willing to see, and to find words even where there are none—like Lewis and Clark, who added over 1,500 words to our language as they journaled their way across the continent. To witness the world, to tell about it, to practice astonishment.

This is the Christian's task, too—to look for what is, to call it by name, to recognize God's love in every crunch of apple and crash of wave, to proclaim that Jesus's incarnation and death and resurrection are indeed *for the whole world*, and to practice loving every scrap of it, even as it changes and dies.